KIDS LOVE ISRAEL
ISRAEL LOVES KIDS

A TRAVEL GUIDE FOR FAMILIES

A travel guide is necessarily selective. Entries in this book were chosen for their suitability for family travel. The decisions about what was included were made solely by the author and publishers. No organizations or commercial establishments paid for listings. All facts were carefully researched and checked as of the end of 1995. Nevertheless, bus routes, phone numbers, hours of operation, and admission charges change. Occasionally, sites are closed for renovation or repair. We recommend you call ahead to check all places you wish to visit.

Complaint? Contact the Control Division of the Ministry of Tourism, 24 King George Street, Jerusalem. PHONE: (02) 754-810, 754-820, or fill out a form at any Government Tourist Information Office. All issues are handled — unsatisfactory service and merchandise, rude behavior, broken commitments.

KIDS LOVE ISRAEL
ISRAEL LOVES KIDS

A TRAVEL GUIDE FOR FAMILIES

by Barbara Sofer

photos by Karen Benzian

KAR-BEN COPIES, INC.   ROCKVILLE, MD

To Yaakov, Avi, Josh, Hadas, Yael, and Hanna

IN MEMORIAM

We mourn the death of Prime Minister Yitzhak Rabin who led Israel through war and forward to peace. Just two months before his death he convened the Prime Minister's Conference on Peace Tourism and expressed his hope that tourism would play a prominent role in a new era in the Middle East. We dedicate ourselves to that mission.

Library of Congress Cataloging-in-Publication Data

Sofer, Barbara.
    Kids love Israel. Israel loves kids / by Barbara Sofer. — (Rev. ed.)
       p.   cm.
    Includes bibliographical references and index.
    ISBN 0-929371-89-5 (pbk)
    1. Israel — Guidebooks.   I. Title
DS103b.S64 1995   95-41562
915.69494'54—dc20   CIP

PREFACE

"What's new?" is the question I was asked most often while revising this book. In the seven years since *Kids Loves Israel* was first published:

• More tourist sites have been developed, and many have interactive programs designed for children, such as computers at archeological sites and treasure hunts at museums.

• The Israel Hiking Trail has been completed, and the phone system has vastly improved.

• More Israeli families have cars and two-day weekends. To accommodate them, there are more playlands and amusement parks, parrot and monkey farms, jeep trips and Bedouin experiences.

• Rustic accommodations, less formal than hotels, are available on kibbutzim and moshavim, and in Arab and Druze villages.

• Israelis who have traveled abroad have learned the importance of patience and courtesy. Travel industry workers are encouraged to take courses on improving customer service.

Some things haven't changed! Israelis are still crazy about children. Recently at a concert in Jerusalem, a mother sitting in the first row propped a baby bottle on the stage. The singer bent down, picked it up, paused, and filled it with his own mineral water. "Hot night!" he said. The principles of traveling with children haven't changed either. If you abandon the notion that "the right way is the adult way," you'll enjoy your trip more. Exploring Israel as a family can be a bonding experience. My fondest childhood memories are of traveling with my family, and I hope my children will feel the same way.

Kids Love Israel simply couldn't have been revised without the patience, dedication, and humor of editor/publisher Judye Groner. I thank her and Madeline Wikler for their devotion to this project. Photographer Karen Benzian played a role far beyond that of picture-taker. She was a full partner in this effort, whether dashing through a crater to catch camel-riders at sunset, or fighting seasickness to capture the Tel Aviv skyline. I couldn't have done it without her.

Never did we visit sites without bringing along our best critics—kids, my own and others. Cheerful even on long days when we checked out a new site every hour, they were discerning judges of the strengths and weaknesses of each activity. Many thanks.

This edition, like the first, should be a springboard for your own creative touring. Parents should remember that children are the best camouflage for having fun yourselves!!

JERUSALEM 3000

Not long ago I was touring David's City in Jerusalem. My guide pointed out that archeologists found signature seals here which bear the name of the scribe mentioned in the Biblical Book of Jeremiah. It brought to mind those old "George Washington Slept Here" jokes. But George Washington lived only 200 years ago. King David slept in Jerusalem 3000 years ago!

Odd as it sounds, that doesn't feel so long ago. Sheep crossing the street still hold up traffic in this town. Not far from the site of David's house, children and adults continue to study his complex personality as if he were a contemporary monarch. Every nursery school child has a repertoire of David songs, such as "David Melech Yisrael," David, the King of Israel lives forever.

On the tour we saw the water tunnel through which David's commander-in-chief, Yoav, probably led a commando unit to conquer the Yevusi, an ancient tribe that no longer exists. Today, 3000 years later, one of my sons is serving in a unit like Yoav's.

Some guides will tell you that David chose Jerusalem because it was a neutral zone, between the Northern and Southern Kingdoms. King Solomon claimed that God, not his father David, chose the city for the site of the Temple. And in Ezekiel we read, "Thus says the Lord: This is Jerusalem I've set in the midst of the nations."

Jerusalem has had a more complex history than most cities. Even in dark times, when it was a ruin of charred stones, the prophet Zechariah predicted a time when, "the streets of the city will be full of boys and girls playing."

They are now...in Jerusalem, in Tel Aviv, in Haifa, in the northern hills, in the desert caves. What better celebration of Jerusalem's 3000th birthday could there be?

ISRAEL

METULLA

Lebanon

Syria

SAFED

HAIFA
TIBERIAS

← KINNERET

BEIT SHEAN

THE NORTH
(Galilee)

TEL AVIV

Jordan

MEDITERRANEAN SEA

JERUSALEM

DEAD SEA

BEERSHEBA

MITZPEH RAMON

THE SOUTH
(Negev)

Egypt

EILAT

← GULF OF EILAT

CONTENTS

GENERAL INFORMATION

JERUSALEM

THE OLD CITY

THE NEW CITY

EILAT

APPENDIX

Thousands of teens visit Israel each year, with their families and more often with youth groups. We've highlighted sites that teens can visit on their own, particularly places where Israeli teens congregate. Look for the teen logo!

GENERAL INFORMATION

KIDS LOVE ISRAEL

Passengers often break out in spontaneous applause when their plane touches down in Israel. What is it about a country the size of New Jersey that inspires such emotion, even from first-time visitors?

A rich history, diversity of people, and variety of landscape make Israel a compelling destination for a short trip...or a year's sabbatical. If your family has a strong religious orientation, the country will have special meaning for you. But even if you are not "religious," you will appreciate Israel's spiritual importance in the history of the world.

Israel is a children's paradise...a land of history and adventure where a child's imagination can run free. Whether children are turning an olive press at the Maccabean village of Modi'in, or watching cows being milked in a computerized kibbutz cowshed, you'll feel their vistas expand as they take in the past, present, and future.

Israel is an easy country to tour with children. Kids thrive in the wonderful weather and the unparalleled freedom that Israel offers.

Distances are manageable. Within a few hours, families can be anywhere in the country, from a desert oasis to a snow-topped mountain. Public transportation is available, inexpensive, and safe.

You may have visited Israel before, without children. If you were on an organized tour or mission, you probably spent a lot of time visiting museums, historic landmarks, antiquities, and art galleries. Perhaps a friend or relative took you to one or two favorite sites off the beaten track.

This travel guide encourages you to discover Israel from a different perspective. It focuses on your children's interests, excitement, and pace. Instead of studying Roman artifacts in the Israel Museum, you might create a collage at the recycling center in the Museum's Youth Wing. Or explore the Billy Rose Art Garden, where children are allowed to climb the impressive sculpture. On this trip, you might pass up the artists colony in Ein Hod for the water slides at Atlit. Instead of the antiquities of Meggido, you may visit those at Sachne, conveniently located at the site of a magnificent natural pool and park.

Discover the child in yourself! Join your kids in walking Jerusalem's ancient ramparts and wading through its water tunnels. Experience the desert from the back of a camel, not the seat of a bus. "Feel" the source of the Jordan from an inner tube, and don't miss the animal safari, "magic road," or tank park.

ISRAEL LOVES KIDS

If there ever was a country that had a love affair with youth, it is Israel. Because Israelis have so many children themselves, they are understanding of children's foibles. In Israel you will see children on buses (often traveling alone), on field trips, in fancy restaurants, at weddings, in museums, even at recitals of the world's most celebrated artists.

Israelis love their own children, and they will love your children, too. Don't be surprised if a soldier with a machine gun offers your toddler a stick of gum. Or if a long-haired teenager hops off the bus to help you lift your stroller. Or if your 10 year-old is invited to a scout meeting by kids s/he meets at the pizza parlor.

Israelis are passionate tourists. They love to go on family expeditions to new archeological sites and nature reserves. They enjoy showing off their country and will be outgoing and hospitable to you and your family.

Kids Love Israel — Israel Loves Kids is geared to the young and the young at heart. Wonderful guidebooks are available for adults who want to visit Israel, but few take into consideration the interests and needs of children and families.

Tourism has developed rapidly in Israel, and with it, hundreds of new programs that will delight you and your children. Within these pages you will discover how easy it is to ride a jeep through the Judean desert, dig for ancient pottery, or begin a computer search for your genealogical roots.

Israel can be a difficult country for a child to grasp. Our superb tour guides are world famous for their in-depth historical explanations — easily lost on an action-loving 10 year-old. You may find the differences between a Herodian and a Hasmonean stone fascinating, but I guarantee that after five minutes, your 8 year-old will be shuffling his feet and looking for the nearest kiosk.

The rule with children is: **Do it, don't say it.** If a child can climb into a castle and pretend to be a guard, s/he will understand how that edifice was strategically important. Children like to touch, feel, smell, and taste, as well as see.

Be flexible. How long you spend at a site will depend on the ages and interests of your children. Children need to unwind, to eat and drink frequently, and to have fun. Don't plan day after day of intensive touring. Fortunately, there are wonderful recreation areas near all the major tourist sites, so you can combine touring with relaxation and adventure.

Kids Love Israel — Israel Loves Kids presents a potpourri of options to suit varied tastes. It is not a recipe book, rather a springboard for creative touring in a wonderful country.

BEFORE YOU COME

A successful trip to Israel begins well before you leave for the airport. Part of the fun of traveling is the planning and anticipation. Let your children take part.

Talk about everyone's expectations for the trip. If your children attend religious school or belong to a youth group, they have learned about Israel and may have definite ideas on places they wish to visit or friends they wish to see. It's fun to get in the mood:

- Read books about Israel (see *Bibliography),* and play Israeli music. Get a set of Israeli *Monopoly* and learn the roads and towns as you play.

- Start a folder of material about Israel. Contact the Israel Government Tourist Office. 350 Fifth Ave., 19th Floor, New York, NY 10118. **PHONE:** (800) 596-1199; (212) 560-0639; **FAX**: (212) 629-4368. Watch for updates in the travel section of your local newspaper.

- Write for **Isracoup**, a coupon book with discounts for hotels, restaurants, museums, and much more. 3 W. 16th St., New York, NY 10011.

- Subscribe to *Eretz Magazine*. It has articles on nature, geography and archeology in Israel. You become a member of the Eretz Travel Club and can get a faxed listing of events for the week you'll be in Israel and discounts on their family-friendly tours. It's $45 for six issues; SPNI members get a discount. POBox 565, Givatayim, 53104. **PHONE:** (03) 571-2681; **FAX:** 571-4184; **U.S.:** (800) 681-7727 (Toll-free)

- Call the American Society for the Protection of Nature, ASPNI, and request the brochure *Israel Nature Trails,* a listing of their family tours, from short hikes to week-long adventures (see *Specialized Tours*). **PHONE:** (800) 524-7726.

- To volunteer for an archeological dig, write Dept. of Antiquities, Ministry of Education and Culture, POBox 586, Jerusalem 91004. **PHONE:** (02) 287-602, 287-603

- Your children might like to establish contact with Israeli children. You can advertise for a pen-pal through the *Jerusalem Post,* Romema, Jerusalem, or via the Internet.

- If you are going to be in Israel for the summer or for Passover, and your children want to go to day or overnight camp, sign up in advance (see *Camps*).

- Post a map of Israel near your breakfast table, and point out where different cities are.

- Join an Israeli travel forum on the Internet and share questions and ideas with other travelers. The e-mail address for Jerusalem 3000 activities is http://wwwl.huji.ac.il/jeru

- Order your rental car well in advance, especially if you're going to be in Israel during the summer or holidays (see *Renting a Car*).

- Write your Israeli friends and cousins and tell them you're coming and hope they can join you for some fun.

- Plan to do a mitzvah or two. **Rabbanit Bracha Kapach** in Jerusalem runs a wedding dress loan service for brides who cannot afford their own. Ask around, and if you find someone willing to donate a gown, make room for it in your suitcase. **PHONE:** (02) 249-296. **Yad Sarah,** the loan service for medical supplies, appreciates donations of hearing aids, glucose testers, and other equipment to loan to handicapped people, including tourists. **PHONE:** (02) 244-242

If someone in your family is disabled, write to the **Society for the Advancement of Travel for the Handicapped**, 347 Fifth Ave. #610, New York, NY 10016. PHONE: (02) 447-7284. Ask for their Fact Sheet on Israel which lists accessible hotels and agencies for the disabled. The **Israeli Ministry of Tourism Infocenter** has information on wheelchair accessible sites. PHONE: (800) 596-1199 (Toll-free)

PLAN AHEAD

Remember, you're traveling with children! Begin your plans by abandoning your notions about the "right" way of traveling. Checking off tourist sites on itineraries and spending a lot of time at museums is not the only way to travel. It certainly is not the way to go with children.

Make a list of those sites you absolutely want to see no matter what, and work them into your plans. You may want to see some of these sites without your children.

Plan to get an early start each day, and to alternate active and passive activities. Some families like to tour in the morning and visit a recreation area in the afternoon. Read the history of the sites you will see, so you can give your children some of the highlights beforehand. Children are more interested in museums or historic sites if they know something about the artist's life or the battle fought.

You and your children will be spending more time together than usual. Although togetherness has a romantic charm, you can have too much of a good thing. Allow times and places when your child can be alone to think — on his/her own blanket at the beach, reading in the hotel, or climbing at a playground. Children need time to relax and absorb all their new experiences. You will need some time alone, too.

Chances are, you will know well in advance that you are coming to Israel. If you make reservations for certain popular spots and hotels, you will avoid disappointment later. I have noted those places which generally require reservations many months ahead.

If you are calling Israel to reserve hotels, tours, or camps, remember that the time difference between Israel and New York is usually 7 hours, except for a few weeks in spring and fall when the

U.S. and Israel are not both on Daylight Savings Time (called *Summer Clock* in Israel). Then the time difference is 6 hours.

Traveling with children you will see a different Israel from the one most tourists see. You will visit more recreation spots, be involved in more family activities, and probably meet more Israelis. If you are like me, you will enjoy this type of touring.

GROUP TOURS

Many tourists visit Israel in organized tours, with flights and land arrangements set out beforehand. While these tours may be excellent for adults, they are not always ideal for children. Even on tours that include the opportunity to become a Bar or Bat Mitzvah, the ceremony may become another event on an adult-oriented tour.

Several national and local organizations now offer tours geared more to family needs. They include the Ramah Programs in Israel, the Jewish Community Centers Association, UJA, JNF, B'nai B'rith, Emunah Women, and many local federations and Jewish centers (see *Appendix*). If you cannot find an organized tour that suits your family, you might do better to travel on your own, working out a personalized itinerary.

TRAVEL AGENTS

Shop around for a travel agent who knows a lot about Israel. In particular, look for special tour packages that are marketed outside of Israel only. For example, if you are planning to visit Eilat, ask your travel agent about special Eilat package deals which are often cheaper when booked abroad. You should be able to make just about all your reservations before you come.

GETTING THERE

The flight to Israel is long. You can take a direct flight (the non-stop flight from New York is approximately 10½ hours), or make a stop in Europe on the way. Take into consideration your budget and the needs of your family. Non-stop flights are most in demand, sometimes cost more, and are usually booked further in advance. Ask your travel agent about group flights. Charter flights are often cheaper, but may not offer as great a discount for children. If your children are flying alone, inform the airline ahead of time. Ground and flight crews will be helpful.

Some airlines offer Family Plans, but it may be cheaper to take advantage of promotional fares.

Many families and tour groups choose El Al, Israel's national airline, because of its excellent security, and because once you board the plane you're "already in Israel." But many carriers fly, including TWA, British Air (in conjunction with USAir), Swissair, World, Tower, Air Canada, Czech Air (through Prague), and Arkia (from Gatwick).

> You can get to Israel by boat as well. There are regular sailings from Europe to Haifa, and some Mediterranean cruises stop at Haifa or Ashdod.

Choosing Seats

Because you will need a block of seats, you should ask for them when you make your reservations. Try to get at least one window seat, so your children can follow the trip over land and water. Baby cots may be available in the middle section, but they are useful only for children under a year old. If you do need a cot, take one or two seats close to the aisle of the middle section, and ask for the window seats across the aisle. There are a few bulkhead seats with extra leg room, and the upstairs window seats on the 747-400 have extra space as well.

Meals

El Al and Tower Air serve only kosher food. On other carriers, you must reserve kosher meals in advance. Vegetarian and dairy meals are usually available on request, as are special children's meals. It's a good idea to confirm your order before departure. Although baby food is available on most flights, it's wise to bring your own. Flight attendants will warm your baby's bottle or food.

Security

Your bags will be carefully checked and you will be questioned about parcels you may be carrying for friends. Leave toy guns at home, and do not accept packages from strangers.

WHEN TO COME

Most tourists come to Israel in the summer, because children in the Northern Hemisphere are on vacation. Israeli children are also on vacation in July and the beginning of August, so summer camps and children's activities are plentiful. But keep in mind that tourist facilities will be crowded. The first three weeks of August are the busiest of all. Make reservations early. Trips during Passover, the High Holidays, and Sukkot also require advance reservations.

During the winter, hotel rates are lower and there are fewer tourists. You may be lucky and get beautiful sunny weather, or you may run into a week of rain or snow. Snow falls several times most winters in the mountain areas — Jerusalem, Safed, and the Hermon. Spring and fall provide ideal weather for touring, although there are fewer special activities for children.

WHAT TO BRING

Clothing: Take comfortable, easy-to-launder clothing. Israel is a casual country, and you won't need anything fancy. Women and girls must have a skirt, and a blouse with sleeves that reach the elbow, for visiting religious families and holy places of all religions. Men and boys may wear shorts most of the time, but they should have a pair of long pants (not jeans), a sport shirt, and a kippah (yarmulke) if they plan to go to synagogue, tour holy sites, or visit a religious family for Shabbat. If you're invited to a wedding or Bar/Bat Mitzvah, women should pack an afternoon dress or suit. Most men don't wear jackets and ties to synagogue, but they may to a festive reception.

If you are coming in the **summer**, leave your raincoats home. There is no rain in Israel in summer. Bring light, casual clothing and two bathing suits per person.

For a **winter** trip, plan to dress in layers. You may get warm, sunny days or rainy, cold periods. So bring a light shirt, a turtleneck jersey, a sweater, warm coat or jacket, and rain boots and hat. A raincoat with a zip-in lining is convenient. Corduroy is a versatile fabric for the winter. Don't forget a bathing suit; there are places to swim, even in winter.

In **spring** and **fall,** you won't need a coat, but include a jacket or sweater for evenings, and some light clothing in case it gets hot.

Knapsack: Each child should have his/her own backpack with crayons, a pad of paper, and a notebook or scrapbook for a trip journal. You might want to add a deck of cards, a paperback book or two, and pocket tissues.

> Most airlines require that you check in two hours prior to departure. Bring a game, book, or walkman to entertain your child while you're waiting to board. Kids get bored quickly wandering through duty-free shops, particularly when you won't buy them all the fancy toys and games they see!

Water canteens: The need to drink to prevent dehydration cannot be emphasized enough. It is expensive and not always convenient to buy soft drinks, and they are not as thirst-quenching as water. Use a canteen for tap water or a shoulder carrier for bottled water. My children prefer canteens that hook onto a belt. You can buy them in Israel. Each family member should have his/her own canteen.

> Israel's tap water is safe to drink. Sometimes on a kibbutz or roadside, you may find water taps that are not for drinking. These will be clearly marked. If you can't read Hebrew, ask.

Sunscreen is a must. Look for a waterproof lotion rated 15 or higher, and make sure you and your children use it daily. **Sun hats** are another necessity. The kind with a brim is best. If you want an Israeli hat, buy one as soon as you arrive. **Sunglasses** are a good idea. Make sure they have UV protection.

Cameras and film are available in Israel but it may be cheaper to bring them. Develop a roll of film before you come to make sure your camera is working. A lead bag will protect your film from repeated airport x-ray. Israel has one-hour discount developing centers. If you develop your pictures in Israel, you can use the time on the plane ride home to create an album. Disposable cameras are inexpensive in the U.S. You may want to get one for each of your children.

Portable tape recorders and players: If you will be taking long bus or car trips, a tape player and story or song cassettes will help children pass the time while traveling. Sometimes they even distract motion-sick children.

Insect Repellent is useful if you're going to hike or camp out.

Medicines: Pack basic items such as aspirin, an antihistamine, cold medicine, and something for motion sickness and diarrhea. If you or your children take prescription medicine, bring enough for your stay. You can't count on finding the drugs you need, but it helps to have a prescription for the generic equivalent. Bring an extra pair of **eyeglasses** — and a copy of your prescription.

Before you come, check with your health insurance agent to find out how to handle payment for health care or hospitalization if you need it. You might want to ask your physician and dentist for the names of colleagues in Israel.

Adapter plugs (2-pronged round plugs) for your appliances. Israel is on 220V current, so if your hair-dryer, shaver, or other appliances are not dual voltage, you'll also need a transformer.

Rubber sandals or old sneakers (not flip-flops) if you are planning to be at the rocky beaches of Eilat or the Kinneret.

Gifts: Each person over age 17 may bring in $125 in gifts duty free. Israeli kids enjoy the latest American fads, such as small electronic toys, novelty watches, tapes and CDs, and printed T-shirts. If you are bringing electrical appliances, check with a store that specializes in appliances for export.

ON THE PLANE

The trip to Israel may be the longest plane ride your children have taken. Come prepared. Your carry-on luggage should include:
• Story, sticker, and puzzle books
• Magic markers, crayons, and a writing pad
• Magnetic board games such as checkers and chess
• Gum and/or hard candy for take-off and landing
• Snacks. You usually can get soft drinks on the plane.

> El Al has a supply of toys and games for children of different ages. Ask the flight crew.

Use the time on the plane to go over a map of Israel with your children. It is fun if each child has his/her own map. Point out the main cities and the major sites you will visit. Play "I know a town that begins with 'A,' or 'Alef' if the child knows Hebrew. You can also review important Hebrew words (see *Dictionary*) and familiarize yourself with Israeli currency (see *Money*).

WHEN YOU LAND

For security, your plane may land mid-field at Ben Gurion Airport, and you will be taken to the terminal by bus. You will go through passport control, claim your luggage, and pass through customs. You can change money at the airport banks or get shekels in an ATM machine, but if you don't have time, taxi drivers will accept dollars.

Customs

No one will even look up when you walk through customs with an ordinary camera, but if you have a camcorder, you may be stopped by customs officials who will ask you to leave a deposit to be refunded at departure. This is to insure that you won't sell or give your equipment to an Israeli, who must pay duty on luxury items brought into the country. The same applies to all major appliances. You need to declare them or risk paying a heavy fine for illegally importing goods. You can bring in whatever you need for personal use and up to $125 in gifts.

FROM THE AIRPORT

You have a range of choices to get from the airport to major cities:

Buses are the cheapest. United Tours runs a bus between the airport and Tel Aviv daily (including Saturday) every half hour, except between midnight and 4 a.m. The bus stops at the northern railroad station and at the Promenade near Tel Aviv's hotels. Buses also run frequently from the airport to Jerusalem except Friday night and Saturday.

Sherut (group cab): This is the most popular means of leaving the airport. For a fixed fee, a 7-seat taxi or larger van will take you directly to your hotel or apartment. The price (under $10 per person) and service are good. The disadvantage is sometimes having to wait for the van to fill up, and/or having to circle the city to drop others off at their hotels.

Private taxis are easily available from the airport. They cost between $35-40 to Jerusalem (less to Tel Aviv), which may be reasonable if your group is more than three.

Tal Limousine Service runs vans which take up to 10 people. Current prices are $25 to anywhere in Tel Aviv and $47 for anywhere in Jerusalem. For a genuine limo the cost is about double. Tal has a Ticket Counter near Gate 9, but you should order ahead by FAX. The company is connected to Arkia Airlines and you may be able to reserve through your travel agent. **PHONE:** (03) 972-1701 **FAX:** 972-1705

DEPARTURE

Departure Flight Information: PHONE: (03) 973-1111 (Hebrew); 973-1122 (English). From Jerusalem, **Nesher Taxi** will pick you up at your hotel or apartment and take you to the airport for about $9 per person. Reserve one day before your flight. 21 King George St. **PHONE:** (02) 231-231

If you are flying El Al, you can check in the night before at the El Al Office in Jerusalem or Tel Aviv, or at the Tel Aviv Hilton. This will avoid long lines at the airport on your day of departure.

Each person must pay a departure tax when leaving the country. The tax may have been included in the purchase price of your ticket. Check with your travel agent.

> If you take a side trip to Jordan or the Sinai, you also must pay a departure tax. The amount depends upon your destination and the port of exit.

FIRST THINGS

Once you're settled, be sure to get **Maps** (at your hotel or a local tourist office), **Telephone Cards** (see *Telephones*), **Bus Passes** (see *Getting Around*), and **Israeli Money** (see *Money*).

Israel's official **languages** are Hebrew and Arabic, but many people speak some English. The official **day of rest** is Saturday (Shabbat). Offices, schools, and stores are open Sunday-Friday, though many close early on Friday, and some observe two-day weekends — Friday and Saturday.

The symbols for **restrooms** are OO and WC.

Israel is a **security-conscious** country. Your purse and parcels will be checked at museums, supermarkets, and government offices. Do not leave parcels unattended, and report any suspicious objects you see.

JET LAG

Don't be surprised if your children are either wired, lethargic, or both after you arrive. Kids get jet lag, too. Plan an easy schedule for the first few days. One theory is to get lots of sunshine to help your internal clock adjust to the new time zone.

MONEY

The main unit of currency is the Israeli **shekel.** It is divided into 100 **agorot**. Prices are marked **IS** or **NIS** to indicate shekels. If a price is marked in dollars, you can often pay the shekel equivalent. Check the newspaper for the daily exchange rate. At press time, December 1995, the rate was 3 shekels to the dollar.

Don't bother to get shekels before arriving. The exchange rate outside the country is invariably to your disadvantage, and there are banks and ATMs at all arrival points in Israel.

VAT or *mam*

This 17% value-added tax applies to all purchases and transactions, except hotel rooms, hostels, organized camping sites, car rental, tours, and hotel meals charged to your room. Purchases in Eilat also are VAT-exempt. Tourists who purchase goods with foreign currency (or a foreign credit card) are entitled to a refund of this tax on purchases above $50 made at a single store approved by the Ministry of Tourism. Keep your receipts, so that you can get your cash refund at the airport. Remember to allow extra time before your flight.

Credit Cards

You can use major credit cards at hotels, restaurants, and stores. VISA is accepted more often than Mastercard or Amex. If you lose your card, report it immediately:

American Express: PHONE: (03) 524-2211
VISA: PHONE: (03) 572-3573
Isracard/Eurocard: PHONE: (03) 576-4444

Banking

Changing foreign currency in a bank is a two-step process. You must go first to the teller assigned to such tasks, and then to the cashier. Have your passport with you. Lines are often long, so exchange what you might need for at least a few days.

Keep your bank receipts. If you want to change shekels back to dollars, you can do so only if you have receipts showing that you changed an equivalent amount into shekels. In general, it is a good idea to save all receipts in Israel.

Most banks open by 8:30 a.m., close at 12:30 p.m., and open again from 4-6 p.m. Branches in the bigger cities are open later in the evenings. Except in certain Christian and Muslim areas, banks are closed Friday afternoons and all day Saturday.

ATMs

The good news is that you can use foreign cash cards (Cirrus and Plus) and credit cards in many **Automatic Teller Machines (ATMs)** in the major cities and at tourist centers. If the instructions are in Hebrew, an Israeli will be glad to help you. Machines will allow you to withdraw shekels only, except for one at Ben Gurion airport that issues foreign currency such as dollars, deutschmarks, and francs.

> If you are planning to use ATM machines, make sure you know your PIN number!

Israel Bonds may be cashed at the main branches of Israeli banks. The service charge is between one-half and one percent.

TELEPHONES

Telephone service, which is organized into a semi-public company called Bezek, has vastly improved. Public phones are plentiful, rental cars have phones, and you'll often see Israelis chatting on cellular phones as they shop in the supermarket or walk down the street. Most token-operated phones have been replaced with phones that take magnetic phonecards, but a few — mostly in restaurants and at tourist sites—still accept tokens or shekel coins. Some phones at tourist areas also accept credit cards.

Telephone Cards

Phonecards can be purchased at post offices, shops, and kiosks. They come in denominations of 20, 50, 150, and 250 units. When you place the card in the phone, the window at the top will show messages units left. A local 3-minute call uses one unit. Long distance calls depend on the length of the call, distance, and time of day. When you call out of town, units get used up rapidly. When you hang up, the card should pop out and you'll hear a beep reminding you to take it. A phone card is an inexpensive way to place international calls, but make sure you have purchased one with many units.

Phone Numbers

As Israel's telephone system continues to grow and improve, phone numbers change. Currently, they are in the process of changing from six to seven-digit numbers. If the number you are dialing has changed, you should get a recording to that effect. If your party doesn't answer after you've tried a couple of times, check with the Information Operator (Dial 144). If s/he doesn't speak English, ask for a supervisor (*mifakahat*).

Telephone Directory

There is a new English language edition of the Jerusalem Yellow Pages. Other city phone books have small English sections. If you can't find the number you need, ask a hotel concierge or Israeli friend to look it up in the much larger Hebrew edition.

Important Access Numbers:

Overseas Operator: 188
Information: 144
Time: 155
AT & T: 177-100-2727
Sprint: 177-102-2727
MCI: 177-150-2727

UK BT: 177-440-2727
South Africa: 177-270-2727
Canada: 177-105-2727
Germany: 177-490-2727
Australia Testra: 177-610-2727
Australia Optus: 177-611-2727

Access to these numbers is free. You're charged only after you're connected to the number you've requested. The cheapest time to call the U.S. is usually between midnight-7a.m., but check with your long distance carrier.

POST OFFICE

The main post offices in Jerusalem, Tel Aviv, and Haifa are open Sunday-Thursday 8 a.m.-7 p.m.; Friday 7 a.m.-noon. Branch offices are usually open mornings 8 a.m.-noon, and afternoons 3:30-6 p.m. Post offices are closed Wednesday and Friday afternoons and Saturdays. For postal information, **PHONE:** 177-022-2121 (Toll-free). Yellow mail boxes on the street are for intra-city mail; red boxes are for all other mail.

LAUNDRY

Should you use your cousin's washing machine? Appliances, hot water, and electricity are expensive in Israel, so ask first. You can find self-serve laundromats in the main cities, but the prices are high. Another option is to rinse out your lightly-soiled clothes and send the rest to the laundry.

SHOPPING

Stores are generally open from 8:30 a.m.-1 p.m. and 4-7 p.m. Department stores and shops at the malls are open all day. Stores close early on Fridays and are closed Saturdays and holidays.

HEALTH CARE

Israel has good health care and hospitals. If you need a doctor, consult the hotel staff, or ask a friend. Expect to pay a fee similar to what you would pay in the U.S. Ask for a receipt in English and in dollars, so that you can be reimbursed by your health insurance company.

Blue Cross-Blue Shield participants are eligible for prepaid hospitalization at both Hadassah hospitals in Jerusalem. **PHONE:** (02) 776-040

The daily papers and **Magen David Adom** (Israel's Red Cross — **PHONE:** 101) have information about which hospitals are offering emergency care in various specialities (such as pediatrics, maternity, or internal medicine) on any given day or night.

If you are in Israel as a student or visiting professor, you may be able to take advantage of one of Israel's cooperative health plans, called *kupat holim.*

The **National Poison Control Center** at Rambam Hospital in Haifa runs a 24-hour hot line. **PHONE:** (04) 529-205

Services for Persons With Disabilities

You can borrow medical equipment, such as crutches or a wheelchair, from the **Yad Sarah** branch closest to you. This volunteer organization, which also provides disabled transport service, was founded in memory of a woman who died in the Holocaust. Most equipment is free, but you are required to show your passport and leave a deposit. **PHONE:** (02) 244-242

The following organizations offer information about handicapped access and services:

MILBAT — The Israeli Center for Technical Aids and Transportation. **PHONE:** (03) 530-3739

ILAN — The Israeli Foundation for Handicapped Children. **PHONE:** (03) 524-8241

Roof Association of Organizations of Persons With Disabilities 30 Ibn Gabirol Street, Tel Aviv **PHONE:** (03) 696-6212

GETTING AROUND

Walking

Walking is the best way to see Israel, but be careful crossing the street, and pay attention to crossing lights. Most drivers do not stop at crosswalks. Don't jay-walk. You may get a ticket!

Buses

Israel has a marvelous, inexpensive bus system that will take you almost anywhere in the country. You can even take the bus from Tel Aviv to Cairo every morning (except Saturday). Children enjoy the new double-decker buses that run frequently on the Jerusalem-Tel Aviv line.

Buses run from 5 a.m. to midnight in the big cities. They do not run from late Friday afternoon through Saturday after sunset, except in Haifa and East Jerusalem. Currently the fare is about $1. In Jerusalem you pay the same fare no matter how far you go.

In Haifa and Tel Aviv, the fare depends on the length of your ride. Single rides cost the same for adults and children over 5. You don't need exact change, but it speeds things up. Except for children under 5 who ride for free, everyone can save money with a variety of bus cards:

Cartisiya: These cards, which can be purchased from the bus driver, give you multiple rides within a city. Adults get a discount of about 10%. Children (up to age 18) and seniors (over age 65) get an even larger discount; their *cartisiyot* are half price. You can use a *cartisiya* to pay for more than one rider. Tell the driver to punch it *pa'amayim* (twice) or *shalosh pa'amim* (three times).

Hodshi Hofshi: These "month free" passes allow one person to ride as many times as s/he wishes within a city for a whole month. Two persons cannot share a *hodshi hofshi.*

Israbus Ticket: These can be purchased from Egged Tours (not the regular bus station), and allow unlimited travel on Egged buses all over Israel. You can ride from Eilat to Metulla and back. There are tickets good for a week or more. Remember that within Tel Aviv, there is a different bus company: Dan.

> Kids enjoy wearing their bus passes in special brightly-colored holders which you can buy at Steve's Packs (at the back of Rejwan Square, Jerusalem) as well as from street vendors.

The first few seats in the bus are reserved for the elderly, handi-capped, pregnant women, and those holding babies. If you are sitting there, and an elderly person comes on, you should relin-quish your seat unless you are in one of the above categories. Children older than six are expected to give up their seats.

Sherut

For traveling between the main cities, you may want to choose a *sherut*, a group taxi that runs a fixed route for a fixed fare. Often the depot is near the Central Bus Station.

Taxis

Taxi, monit, and *special* are the names used by private taxis. You can call one by phone, or hail one in the street. Taxis are required by law to operate their meters in urban areas Make sure the meter is running and that it is set for the correct rate (fares are higher at night). There is no charge for extra suitcases, and tipping taxi drivers is not customary. To go out of town in a taxi, fix a price before you get started. The driver is prohibited from smoking while you are in the cab. If a driver seems to be taking advantage of you, record his name and taxi number and report his behavior to the Ministry of Transport, Clal Bldg. 97 Jaffa Road, Jerusalem.

Trains

Israel's railroad will take you from Jerusalem to Tel Aviv, and from Tel Aviv up the coast to Nahariya. Riding the train is very inexpensive. Children under age 4 ride free, between 4-10 they pay half fare, and over 10 they pay the same modest fare their parents pay. At present, there is only one train a day from Jerusalem to Tel Aviv. It leaves at 4 p.m. weekdays, 11:30 a.m. Fridays and holiday eves. Frequent trains connect Tel Aviv and the North, and there is a train from Tel Aviv to Rehovot. Pick up a schedule at the nearest station for about ten cents.

Treat your children to a ride on the train. I like to ride the train north from Tel Aviv to Haifa or Nahariya; it's faster than by car. The Jerusalem-Tel Aviv ride is scenic but very long. Trains have snack bars, which children love to visit for a cold drink and pastry.

Jerusalem Railroad Station. PHONE: (02) 717-764

Tel Aviv Railroad Stations. PHONE: (03) 693-7515

If you know Hebrew and have access to a touch-tone phone, you can call for a recorded update on train departures and arrivals: **Tel Aviv** PHONE: (03) 565-2200; **Haifa** PHONE: (04) 303-133.

Hitchhiking

Those romantic days when one could hitchhike (*tremp*) all over Israel are gone. **Don't let your children hitchhike at all.** You also should be careful about whom you pick up. Our personal rule is to take only soldiers in uniform.

Bringing Your Car

A tourist who brings a car to Israel is exempt from Israel's heavy import tax if s/he agrees to take the car out of the country within six months. A tourist who buys a car in Israel must pay customs duty and VAT, but will have both refunded with interest when s/he leaves the country with the car.

AAA members can get travel and tour information and emergency road service from **MEMSI**, Israel's auto club. **Tel Aviv:**

20 Rakevet St. PHONE: (03) 564-1122; **Jerusalem.** 31 Ben Yehudah St. PHONE: (02) 259-711. **Emergency Road Service:** PHONE: (03) 564-1111 (Tel Aviv); (02) 250-661 (Jerusalem).

> **Seat belts:** All passengers—front and back—must wear seatbelts all the time. Children under age 14 must ride in the back seat.

Renting a Car

Car rental may be a good option for your family, because it gives you great flexibility. Family vans are available, but very costly. For touring, you might do just as well to hire a guide with a large car. **Hertz, Avis, Budget, Dollar**, and **National** have branches in Israel. You may wish to contact smaller, local companies, but read your contract carefully. Most rental cars have phones, but you must make sure the phone is activated. You will be charged only if you use it. If you need a car seat for your toddler, request one when you reserve your car.

Parking

Parking meters are new in Israel. In many areas, you still need to buy parking tickets available at banks, kiosks, and ticket agencies. You mark the hour, day, and date, and place the ticket in the driver's window so that it is clearly visible. Each ticket is good for an hour and you can use up to three at a time. If you park illegally, you may get a ticket and/or a "Denver Boot," with instructions on how to reclaim your car.

> Never leave valuable items in plain sight in your car, and try not to leave them at all when you park in big public lots or at tourist sites. Don't leave camera equipment for long periods in a hot trunk.

Planes

Ben Gurion Airport in Lod, between Jerusalem and Tel Aviv, is the biggest airport in Israel. Chances are, you will arrive here. The airport has clean restrooms, a post office, bank, synagogue, snacks bars and restaurants, and duty-free shopping.

Sde Dov is Tel Aviv's domestic airport, used for internal flights by Arkia and Shahaf airlines.

Atarot is Jerusalem's airport for domestic and international flights. Arkia Airlines provides transportation between the airport and the airline's Jaffa Road office.

Eilat has an airport for domestic and international flights. It will soon be getting a new airport to accommodate increasing traffic from international charters.

Other airports are located at **Mitzpe Ramon** in the Negev, and **Machanayim, Rosh Pina, and Haifa** in the Galilee.

Limo-Copter, a helicopter charter, is located at the Herzliya Airport. PHONE: (09) 504-095; FAX: (09) 508-708

FOOD

Hungry, thirsty children are terrible tourists. Always be prepared with snacks. Even if you are a "no-snacks-between-meals" person, consider altering your policy. Your children will be hiking and walking in a hot country and will need more food, and certainly more to drink than usual.

Meals

Many Israelis eat their main meal at midday and a light dairy meal in the evening. Children usually have a mid-morning snack called *aruhat eser* (10 o'clock meal) of a sandwich and drink. If your child goes to day camp, expect to pack him/her *aruhat eser* to take along. Families often enjoy cake and coffee in the afternoon, especially in summer. This is *aruhat arba*, the 4 o'clock meal.

Most children have little patience at the dinner table. *Felafel*, pizza, and other "fast food" are good, nutritious alternatives for many of your meals. Instead of three formal meals a day, stop at a roadside watermelon or ice cream stand, eat hot pita from a market vendor, buy *sabra* (cactus fruit) from a boy on the street, or watch a baker prepare *borekas* (turnovers) and then eat some. This is, after all, a vacation.

The Friendly *Makolet*

Street corner grocery stores (*makolet*) open as early as 7 a.m. They have fresh rolls and dairy products daily. Many storekeepers will slice cheese and/or cold cuts for you. They sell a variety of drinkable yogurts and chip-like snacks, such as *Bamba, Bisli,* and *Kefli.* You also can buy packs of fruit drink, called *Tropit* or *Templi*, which you drink with a straw. Chocolate milk comes in individual boxes with straws, and in small plastic bags.

If your children will not drink plain water, buy concentrate to add to the water in their canteens. The concentrate is often called *petel*, the Hebrew word for raspberry, but it comes in a dozen flavors. The real Hebrew word is *tarkiz*. *Petel* does not need to be refrigerated. You can keep it in your room and fill canteens each morning. Milk and juice also are available in boxes that do not require refrigeration.

> Major supermarkets, most hotels, and many restaurants are kosher. If you're not sure, ask to see the certification.

Supermarkets

A supermarket is an excellent source of carry-out meals. Not only can you get sliced meat or cheese and fresh bread, but many supermarkets sell prepared salads, condiments, fresh baked goods (including *borekas*), and even grilled chickens. Cornflakes, peanut butter, chocolate pudding, and other favorite kids' food are available. If you are renting an apartment and have a large order, remember that for a small charge, supermarkets will deliver. In some markets, you need a 5-shekel coin to use a shopping cart. When you return the cart, you get your coin back.

> Israeli kids' favorite sandwich is *mimrah shokolad*, chocolate spread on white bread. But try to keep this a secret from your kids. Chocolate spread is a hazard to young teeth!

Take-Out Food

Most cities have numerous take-out food stores which offer entire prepared meals, including meat dishes, vegetables, side-dishes, and salads. Some have home delivery.

EATING OUT

Thousands of restaurants compete to feed your family in Israel, from the humblest roadside sandwich shop to the most elegant kosher restaurants in the world.

Fast Food

Felafel: The cheapest whole meal is *felafel*. For about $2 you can eat nutritious fried chickpea balls, *tehina* (sesame sauce) and salad in a pita. For children, always ask for half a portion *(hetzi mana)*. It holds up better in small hands. If your child is still hungry, s/he can order another half at no loss in price. Be careful! One of the optional sauces for felafel is very, very spicy (*harif*). Most *felafel* stands and roadside kiosks are safe. But use your judgment. If the place looks dirty, or has no patrons, try another.

Borekas, turnovers filled with cheese, spinach, or potato, are sold in specialty stores, bakeries, and supermarkets. They're best when they're fresh and hot! Look for the new pizza *borekas*!

A ***baguette*** is a long French bread. You can order a mini-*baguette* sandwich with tuna, cheese, or other fillings.

Burgers and such: McDonalds, Burger King, Subway, Ben and Jerry's, Carvel and other fast food chains have opened all around the country.

Pizza parlors are very popular. Avoid "individual' pizzas, which are overpriced, in favor of pizza by the slice or an American-style family-size pizza. Most pizza parlors have home delivery.

Grill Restaurants

These restaurants offer Middle Eastern fare cooked on an open fire. Few have children's menus, but you can ask for an extra plate so that children can share. Our children love these restaurants. Some offer such large portions that we order one main course and extra french fries ("chips"). A bargain is *kubeh* soup, a rich broth with meat-stuffed dumplings and vegetables; it's a full meal for small children.

Main dishes include *shishlik* (grilled meat on a skewer), *kebab* (ground meat on a skewer), *shwarma* (grilled turkey or lamb thinly sliced and served in a pita) and *shnitzel* (breaded and fried chicken or turkey cutlets). Many grills offer steak, but children may find the local cuts too tough to chew. Certain grills will give you a smaller portion of meat and salad in a pita. Some serve a *mezza*, assorted Middle Eastern salads, such as *humus* (chickpea dip), *tehina* (sesame dip), *baba ganooj* (eggplant dip), stuffed grape leaves, and *kubeh* (meat-stuffed bulghur), as an appetizer or with the meal.

Some restaurants add a 10-15% service charge to the bill. Checkyour bill. If it says "service not included," leave a comparable tip.

FEELING AT HOME

The **Association of Americans and Canadians in Israel (AACI)** is your address for information about studying, working, and especially immigrating to Israel. Stop by one of the offices for a listing of family happenings. You might find picnics, speakers, potluck suppers, day trips, and sporting events, sometimes sponsored by Israelis hailing from your own hometown. The AACI **Little League** is a great place for your children to meet local, English-speaking children. If grandma and grandpa are along for the trip, they can choose from a broad selection of activities for senior citizens.

If you are considering a sabbatical in Israel or making *aliyah* (immigrating), an AACI counselor will be helpful.

Jerusalem Office: 6 Mane Street. PHONE: (02) 617-151
Tel Aviv Office: 22 Mazeh Street. PHONE: (03) 720-9799
Haifa Office: 8 Wedgewood Street. PHONE: (04) 384-319

Other Newcomer Organizations

British: PHONE: (02) 634-822
French: PHONE: (02) 630-987
South African: PHONE: (02) 630-801, 618-135
South American: PHONE: (02) 634-836

Community Centers (*Matnasim*)

Many neighborhoods and development towns have multi-purpose community centers. Youth activities include movies, arts and crafts, folk-dancing, and sports. For the center closest to you, contact the main office of the Israel Community Center Organization. PHONE: (02) 793-377.

Youth Movements

Israel's youth movements combine educational programs with hiking, games, and fun. Most children join in the 4th grade. The largest group is the *Tzofim* or Scouts. The largest religious youth movement is *B'nai Akiva*. Meetings are usually on Tuesday and Saturday afternoons. They are conducted in Hebrew, but most Israeli children know some English. If you are here for several months, your children may want to join a group. If you are on a short trip, they can attend as guests of Israeli friends.

LEARN HEBREW

If you want to learn to read, write, and speak Hebrew, you can enroll in an intensive language course called an *ulpan*. Some have morning classes so that afternoons are free for touring. Others are offered on kibbutzim. Children who will begin an Israeli school in the fall can attend an *ulpan* camp (see *Camps*).

Ulpan begins every month at **Beit Ha'Am**, 11 Rehov Bezalel in Jerusalem. PHONE: (02) 254-156, 254-257

Ulpan Akiva in Netanya offers residential *ulpan* programs which include Hebrew or Arabic lessons for families. Write POBox 6086 Netanya . PHONE: (09) 352-312

There are summer Hebrew classes at **Moadon Ha'oleh**, 9 Rehov Alkalai, Jerusalem. PHONE: (02) 633-718 and **Hebrew Union College,** King David Street, Jerusalem. PHONE: (02) 203-333.

If you are staying in Jerusalem for six months or more, check out *ulpan* classes at the **YM/YWHA** (*Beit Hanoar Haivri*) PHONE: (02) 789-441, and **Ulpan Etzion.** PHONE: (02) 732-568. Or contact the **Kibbutz Ulpan Information Department**, 17 Kaplan Street, Tel Aviv. PHONE: (03) 521-2222, or the **Israel Aliyah Program Center**, 110 E. 59th St., New York, NY 10022. PHONE: (212) 339-6060.

LEARN JUDAISM

Nishmat: The Advanced Jewish Study Center for Women offers summer and year-round study, with provisions for childcare. A recent program was "Parent and Child: An Exploration of Our Most Cherished Bonds Through Classical Jewish Sources." PHONE: (02) 421-010; FAX: 419-752

Discovery. PHONE: (02) 272-355 gives three days of intensive Judaism at the Old City **Aish HaTorah Center.** Probe your roots while you gaze out onto the kotel! For believers and skeptics alike, and for teens, young adults, and adults of all backgrounds.

WHAT'S HAPPENING

Publications

The Friday edition of Israel's English language newspaper, *The Jerusalem Post*, plus the local city supplement (*In Jerusalem* or *Tel Aviv Metro*) will help you plan your stay. The bi-weekly *Jerusalem Report* is also in English. If you read Hebrew, get the city papers like *Kol Ha-Ir* in Jerusalem and *Ha-Ir* in Tel Aviv.

Hello Israel, This Week in Israel, and *Your Jerusalem* are free in hotels. Published weekly, they include a calendar of events, maps, and discount coupons. Even if you're not staying in a hotel, stop in and pick up copies. A list of cultural events is given out at Tourist Offices, and billboards have up-to-date information.

Keeping in Touch

The Monday *Jerusalem Post* includes selections from the Sunday *New York Times* (including the crossword puzzle!). The *International Herald Tribune* and *The Wall Street Journal* (a day late) are sold at larger bookstores and newsstands. New issues of *Time* and *Newsweek* are available each Tuesday.

Radio

You can hear the news in English, French, Yiddish, Spanish, Hungarian, Russian, Ladino or easy Hebrew! Check the *Jerusalem Post* for current times. English broadcasts are generally at 7 a.m. and at 1 and 5 p.m. on Radio 1, 1458 AM in Jerusalem and Eilat; 576 AM in Rosh Hanikra and the north.

Television

Israel Broadcasting has two stations: Channel 1 with commercials, Channel 2 without. Channel 1 has English news Sunday-Thursday at 6:15 p.m., Friday at 4:30 p.m., and Saturday at 5p.m. Most hotels have in-house cable with children's programs and CNN. You may be able to catch episodes of your favorite sitcom in English.

Movies and Theater

Every city has movie theaters. Hebrew films generally have English, and sometimes French subtitles. Call ahead to find out. Most foreign films are shown in their original language with Hebrew subtitles. There are some plays, puppet shows, and story-telling hours in English. Sometimes you can get simultaneous English translation earphones for plays.

AFTER 8 FOR TEENS

The word "pub" is used rather loosely in Israel for restaurants in which young people gather in the evenings. Some of them are rather wholesome, although they serve beer, while others cross the line of good taste. In Jerusalem, the Ben Yehudah-Nahlat Shiva area, with its many outdoor eating places, is where you'll find Israeli teens in the summer. Sidewalk vendors sell earrings and braid hair. Nightlife breaks up just before the last buses of the evening. Teens also gather at the new malls, especially on Saturday night (*motzei Shabbat*). They love rock concerts, movies, and political demonstrations!

ORGANIZED TOURS

The three main tour companies in Israel are **Egged**, **Galilee**, and **United Tours**. They offer half-day, full-day, and week-long tours of the country. Their prices are fixed by the Ministry of Tourism and are almost identical. Children get a discount. Tours are guaranteed to take place. Galilee Tours leave from Jerusalem and Tel Aviv. You can book ahead in the U.S. PHONE: (800) 874-4445 (Toll-free); or in Israel: 177-022-2525 (also Toll-free). United Tours leave from Jerusalem, Tel Aviv, and Eilat. Children under 5 years old are not accepted. In the U.S., book through Gateway One. PHONE: (800) 682-3333 (Toll-free); in Israel: (03) 693-2310. Egged has tours from Jerusalem, Tel Aviv, Haifa, Tiberias, and Eilat. PHONE: (02) 304-422; FAX: 304-885

Small children rarely enjoy organized tours for more than a day, and I don't recommend them. Even on tours to Massada or the Stalactite Caves, children tend to get restless during the often lengthy lectures that guides give about the historical and cultural significance of sites. Likewise, a bus of adult tourists may not be happy about stopping for your child to get a drink or use the bathroom. You are probably better off seeing these places on your own, or with a private guide who can be flexible.

Whether or not you decide to take an organized tour, it's helpful to pick up brochures from tour companies, travel agents, and hotels.

SPECIALIZED TOURS

Neot Hakikar-Fox Travel: Children over 6 can take part in these jeep tours which range from a day in the Judean hills to a 3-day camel safari in the Sinai Desert. Children do not get a discount. Neot Hakikar also offers diving safaris from Eilat and the Sinai. Head Office, 78 Ben Yehudah Street Tel Aviv. PHONE: (03) 522-8161; FAX: (03) 522-1020. Jerusalem Office: 5 Shlomzion Hamalka St. PHONE: (02) 236-232

The **Israeli Youth Hostel Organization** offers several 8-day hiking tours, reasonably priced Eilat and Sinai trips, and one to Egypt. These trips are for ages 15 and up. The organization also has "Do It Yourself" package deals including accommodations, breakfast and dinner, an open Egged bus ticket, and park entrances. PHONE: (02) 252-706

Israel Cyclists and Touring Clubs exist in every city. For information about outings, races, and rental in Jerusalem. PHONE: (02) 619-416; in Tel Aviv, call Galgalei Etz. PHONE: (03) 571-1122

SPNI

Israel's nature society, the **Society for the Protection of Nature in Israel (SPNI)** is in a category of its own. In addition to being nature's watchdog in Israel, the Society is deeply involved in educating young Israelis towards an appreciation of nature, history, and the environment. The Society runs a network of Field Schools (see *Where to Stay*), tours, and camps. Most SPNI guides work regularly with children.

SPNI sponsors 1-15 day tours in English, including camel safaris in the Eilat mountains, bike rides around the Kinneret (Sea of Galilee), and jeep treks in the Sinai desert. There are day-long trips around Jerusalem and hikes in the Judean mountains emphasizing nature and the environment. Tours are rated as to level of difficulty, but children must be over age 10. SPNI also has a Hebrew-speaking summer camp for children in July and August.

You can join the **American SPNI** for a $36 tax-deductible contribution ($25 for youth and seniors), and receive periodic updates on tours, field schools, and special programs. This is a worthy organization to support. Write ASPNI, 28 Arrandale Avenue, Great Neck, NY 11024. PHONE: (800) 524-7726

SPNI offices and Field Schools are listed in each geographic section. The Jerusalem Office is at 13 Helena Hamalka Street. **PHONE:** (02) 244-605; **FAX:** 254-953. The Tel Aviv Head Office is at 3 Hashfela St. **PHONE:** (03) 638-8677; **FAX:** 383-940. Reservations made be made from abroad through Mosaic Tours Travel. **PHONE:** (800) 524-7726; **FAX:** (305) 672-0923

> Children, senior citizen, and SPNI and youth hostel members get discounts at many tourist sites.

STUDENT TRAVEL

ISSTA, the Israel Student Travel Association, specializes in youth travel and can help students up to age 26 make reservations in inexpensive hotels and dorms and for tours around the country. Their offices are:

Jerusalem: 31 Hanevi'im. **PHONE:** (02) 257-257
Tel Aviv: 109 Ben Yehuda. **PHONE:** (03) 527-0111
Haifa: 2 Balfour. **PHONE:** (04) 669-139

PRIVATE GUIDES

The most luxurious way to tour is to hire your own personal guide with an air-conditioned car to show you the country. This costs between $150-200 a day for 4-10 people. You can customize your tour with stops and starts whenever you want.

Make sure that you hire a guide certified by the Ministry of Tourism, and ask for someone who is particularly good with children. A certified guide should have the official badge provided by the Ministry. Guides can be arranged through most travel agencies and hotels. To hire an **SPNI** guide, contact their Division of Tourist Services in Jerusalem. PHONE: (02) 244-605. **Archaeological Seminars, Inc.** will arrange a jeep tour anywhere in the country with a private guide for about $250 per day. PHONE: (02) 273-515. A casual arrangement with a taxi driver is not recommended.

PARKS

Israel's 250,000 acres of forests are run by the Jewish National Fund (JNF), called *Keren Kayemet L'Yisrael;* the Israeli Parks Authority; and the Nature Reserves Authority. Parks range from roadside picnic spots with a few tables and a water tap, to large areas with trails, sports facilities, fishing, and swimming. During the holiday weeks of Sukkot, Hanukkah, and Pesach, most parks offer family activities including drama, music, arts and crafts. Small parks are noted by roadside signs. You can get a map of parks at the JNF office in the Jewish Agency building, King George Street, Jerusalem.

> Because of Israel's dry climate, fires start easily. Please take special care to put out your campfires. Despite all of JNF's work, fires destroy as many trees as are planted each year.

National Parks Ticket

For about $15 you can buy a pass to over 40 sites operated by the National Parks Authority. It's good for a month. This is a considerable savings for adults, but not necessarily for children, because children's admission is usually minimal. The ticket is sold at the National Parks Office, 4 Rav Aluf Street, Tel Aviv, as well as at Massada, Megiddo, Caesarea, Herodian, Tel Jericho, or Yad Mordechai. PHONE: (03) 695-2281

Natureland Pass

The Nature Reserves Authority sells a pass for 12.50 (half-price for kids), which is good at the 17 reserves around the country. It also gives you a discount on rental cars and film. You can buy it at any nature reserve or at the main office, 78 Yirmiahu St., Jerusalem. PHONE: (02) 371-257

BEACHES

Swimming in the Mediterranean is a treat you and your kids won't want to miss. From mid-April until the first rains in late October or November, the water is warm enough for swimming. Beaches with a breakwater are more appropriate for small children. If your toddler is afraid of the sea, try slow immersion. Play in the sand at the water's edge, and then go in slowly. Keep your child at shoulder level, and maintain eye contact while in the water, so s/he feels secure. Don't rely on the lifeguard, especially at crowded beaches. Be your child's personal lifeguard. And don't forget to put sunscreen on both of you.

Remember to check the flags on the beach:

Black Flag — Sea is stormy; no swimming

Red Flag — Moderate waves; swim with discretion

Blue and White Flag — Calm sea

Separate Swimming: To accommodate religious families, many of Israel's beaches have separate sections or hours designated for men and women. You can get the schedules from the tourist office, the local municipality, or the beach itself.

BABIES AND BEFORE

Pregnancy

Visitors frequently remark on the many pregnant women they see in Israel. In fact, Jerusalem has the highest Jewish birthrate in the world. If you are pregnant, you will feel right at home, and can be assured of good prenatal care.

Keep in mind as you plan your travels, that it is easier to find medical personnel with a Western orientation in the major cities. You can arrange for routine prenatal blood tests and examinations. Check with your health insurance provider at home to find out how to arrange for payment. Ask for a receipt in English (and in dollars) for medical care received.

The Israeli Childbirth Education Center, associated with the National Childbirth Trust in Great Britain, is an excellent resource for the following:

• Finding the right gynecologist/midwife
• Enrolling in a childbirth preparation class
• Locating a breast-feeding counselor
• Seeking information on women's or children's health problems

The Center has offices in Haifa. **PHONE:** (04) 376-820, Jerusalem. **PHONE:** (02) 653-6596, and Ra'anana. **PHONE:** (09) 774-6511. Pleasant, English-speaking women will provide prenatal, birth, and postnatal support.

> **Women's Lobby** has information on women's issues. **PHONE:** (02) 392-156, 439-966

Birth

If you want or need to deliver your baby in Israel, you will be more comfortable doing so in a major city medical center. Your baby will be delivered by a staff midwife unless you specifically pay for a private doctor to be present. Doctors are on call in all hospitals if they are needed. Only doctors associated with a hospital can deliver babies there.

If you have a problem or go into labor and cannot get in touch with a private doctor, go straight to the hospital emergency room on duty. A list appears daily in the newspaper, or call Magen David Adom, Israel's Red Cross. **PHONE:** 101.

Brit Milah and Baby Naming

If you give birth to a son in Israel, get a list of *mohelim* (ritual circumcisers) from the hospital. Most hospitals have a special room for the ceremony, but you can have a brit at home, in a synagogue, or at a rented hall. If you give birth to a daughter, most synagogues will be happy to assist in the baby-naming.

Babies

The only complaint you may have about traveling with a baby in Israel is that Israelis may try to be too helpful. Do not be insulted if someone suggests that you put a sweater or a hat on your baby, or offers you other advice. Israelis love babies, their own and everyone else's.

Disposable diapers, pacifiers, baby formula, and baby food are available at supermarkets and pharmacies. Special baby equipment stores in major cities also stock these items, as well as umbrella strollers and baby carriers.

Even if you never use a bottle for your baby at home, a supplementary water bottle is a good idea in Israel in the summer. Your child needs to drink more in a hot climate.

Use sunblock on babies and small children. Rub it into their hair as well, especially if they throw their hats off.

A front or back baby carrier is useful for touring in Israel, because many tourist sites involve rugged terrain. Practice at home, to build up the appropriate muscles for using a carrier. If you are bringing a stroller, make sure it is collapsible. A heavy carriage or stroller is difficult to get on and off buses. You also will have to pay additional fare for a carriage; collapsible strollers are free.

Babysitters are plentiful in Israel. Many women offer childcare, and teenagers babysit for pocket money. Babysitters usually get paid about $3 an hour. If you are staying in a hotel, ask at the desk for a referrral. If you are renting an apartment, ask a neighbor with children to recommend someone reliable.

Eating Out. Except for the fanciest, most restaurants are tolerant of babies, and many more are now supplying baby seats and boosters. Most will be happy to warm a bottle or a jar of baby food, though certain meat restuarants may not want you to feed a baby milk products in the restaurant. Breast-feeding babies in public is not generally accepted behavior. Be discreet; cover yourself with a shawl or towel.

BAR/BAT MITZVAH

You don't have to be religious, and you don't have to be 13 to celebrate your child's (or your own) Bar or Bat Mitzvah in Israel. Bar Mitzvah is the "coming of age" in Judaism, in which a child assumes the obligation to fulfill certain commandments, and has the privilege of being able to lead the prayer service. The minimum age for a boy is 13; for a girl it is 12. Older children and adults who have never been called to the Torah as a Bar/Bat Mitzvah are encouraged to do so.

Bar Mitzvah

The favorite setting for a Bar Mitzvah ceremony is the *Kotel,* the Western Wall in Jerusalem. The Ministry of Religious Affairs will arrange a traditional ceremony at the Kotel. The officiating rabbi will speak English and be familiar with Western customs. Write 237 Jaffa St., Jerusalem. PHONE: (02) 274-422. Even if you haven't planned ahead, you can, with two days' notice, arrange a Bar Mitzvah. You will be asked if you are bringing your own *minyan* (ten men) or if you want to join an existing prayer group.

The ceremony includes taking out a Torah scroll from inside the Kotel ark, putting on *tefillin*, and saying the blessings before and after the reading of the Torah. A boy can do more or less, depending on his skill and desire. Bar Mitzvah ceremonies usually take place on Mondays, Thursdays, and Rosh Chodesh (beginning of a new month) when the Torah is read.

You cannot bring refreshments to the Wall, but many families throw hard candies at the Bar Mitzvah boy. Do not be surprised to hear loud trilling, something like an Indian chant, the traditional sound of North African Jews celebrating.

Women and girls can watch from the other side of the *mehitzah* (divider). If you come early (before 7 a.m.), try to reserve the tables in the back, closest to the women's section, so the ladies can have a better view of the happenings.

Bat Mitzvah

Bat Mitzvah is less straightforward in Israel, because this ceremony is not celebrated by many Orthodox Jews. Options include a service in a Conservative, Reform, or Reconstructionist synagogue, or at an historic setting such as Massada.

Bar/Bat Mitzvah

To arrange a Bar or Bat Mitzvah, write at least a month ahead to the Ministry of Tourism-Bar Mitzvah Dept., Jerusalem 91000. You can choose the Kotel, Massada, or Neot Kedumim. They'll also give you a choice of rabbis to suit your level of observance and knowledge of Hebrew. The Bar/Bat Mitzvah will receive a certificate and gift. Call to confirm arrangements after you have arrived. **PHONE**: (02) 754-877; **FAX**: (02) 754-970

Many **hotels** in Jerusalem will help you plan a Bar/Bat Mitzvah if you hold a breakfast or luncheon there after the ceremony.

The **Reform Movement** will arrange a Bar/Bat Mitzvah. Write 13 King David St., Jerusalem. **PHONE:** (02) 203-448; **FAX:** 203-451

The **Conservative (Masorati) Movement** office will match you with an appropriate Israeli congregation. Call and tell them about your child and what kind of service you would like. **PHONE:** (02) 782-433; **FAX:** 782-441

Rabbi Naamah Kelman specializes in creative ceremonies for Bar/Bat Mitzvah. **PHONE:** (02) 619-761

Neot Kedumim, the Biblical Landscape Reserve, has a creative Bar/Bat Mitzvah program that includes a Biblical picnic breakfast or lunch, a Torah service in a shaded overlook, a mezuzah treasure

hunt, and a nature tour based on the child's haftarah. A Bat Mitzvah can lead hands-on activities to discover Biblical women role models in their natural setting. **PHONE:** (08) 233-840; **FAX:** 245-811.

The **Western Wall Heritage Foundation** will take a Bar Mitzvah boy and his family on a special tour of the tunnels under the Kotel. The program includes a chance to operate the interactive computer program on the history of Jerusalem and see an audio-visual show. **PHONE:** (02) 271-333

Several locations around the country will happily assist you in planning a creative Bar/Bat Mizvah program. Check their listings elsewhere in this guide:
- Camel Riders (north of Eilat)
- Alpaca Farm (Mitzpeh Ramon)
- Tel Hai (north)
- Donkey Farm (near Neveh Eitan)
- Beit Guvrin Caves (between Jerusalem and Tel Aviv)
- Tower of David
- Genesis Jerusalem (Old City)

Federations, synagogues, national Jewish organizations, and travel agencies in the U.S. and Canada often organize Bar/Bat Mitzvah tours. Check ads in your local Jewish newspaper, or call your synagogue or organization.

DAY CAMP

In Hebrew, day camp is called *kaytana,* and each session a *machzor.* Day trips are *tiyulim.* Most municipalities run day camps for the first three weeks of August. Some are general, with arts and crafts, swimming, and hiking. Others concentrate on specific subjects such as basketball or computers. Most camps are in sessions from Sunday through Friday. Check in May or June with the recreation departments in the city where you will be staying to get a listing of day camps.

Some schools, the SPNI, and the Jerusalem YMCA also run day camps with sleepover options during Sukkot, Hanukkah, and Passover.

Camp for Preschoolers

Up to age 5, most children attend camps run by nursery school teachers and their assistants, who are allowed to use school facilities to run private camps. You probably will need to know an Israeli to make inquiries about such camps in the neighborhood in which you will be living. These camps usually run the first three weeks in July. After that date, high school students organize informal, two-week, home-based day camps. Notices are posted in supermarkets or on telephone poles near nursery schools.

School-Age Children

New camps are opening every year, as this aspects of recreation increases in popularity. While the majority of camps are conducted in Hebrew, in most situations some children and counselors will be able to communicate in English and/or French, and non-Hebrew-speaking children will do fine. In the last few years. more English-speaking camps have opened designed to teach Israeli children to speak and play in English. Day camps cost up to $150 per week.

JERUSALEM

Jerusalem Municipal Summer Camps. Camps are run at schools and community centers. Generally they are morning camps open to children entering first through sixth grade and cost less than private camps. **PHONE:** (02) 257-181

Camp Ramah runs a special day camp for children from abroad at the Goldstein Youth Village in Jerusalem. Counselors speak English. The day, which goes from 8a.m.-2 p.m., begins with morning prayer and includes lots of hiking, crafts, nature, music, sightseeing, and daily swimming. A 3-week session costs $395. Ramah also runs camps for Israeli children from kindergarten through 8th grade in Jerusalem, Ashkelon, Beersheba, Hod Hasharon, Omer, and Arad. Write to Ramah Programs in Israel. POB 196, Jerusalem. **PHONE:** (02) 790-243

Horev Day Camp a religious camp, offers swimming and hiking in the mornings. Boys and girls are in separate groups. Horev Elementary School. Kovshei Katamon St. **PHONE:** (02) 635-274

Kiryat Noar Camp, called Boystown in English, runs sports and special interest camps (computers, electronic, carpentry) for first graders on up. There is a large swimming pool. 20 Rav Frank Street, Bayit Vegan. **PHONE:** (02) 441-211

Moshav Beit Zeit offers an extended day program in the Jerusalem Hills. **PHONE:** (02) 332-239

YMCA has two, three-week sessions for children ages 4 and up. There are Hebrew, English, Arabic, and mixed language groups according to your preference. You can choose a short or long day program including swimming, ecology, art, photography, music, martial arts, and drama. Camp does not meet Fridays and Saturdays. The fee is between $200-300 per session. 26 King David Street. **PHONE:** (02) 257-111, 253-433

ICCY Day Camp has two three-week sessions with an emphasis on art. 12A Emek Refaim Street. **PHONE:** (02) 664-144

SPNI's Summer Nature Program includes week-long camps and special tours for kids, including pre-schoolers. **PHONE:** (02) 244-605

Museum of Natural History Nature Camp. Dates change each year. 6 Mohilever St., German Colony. **PHONE:** (02) 631-116

Merchavim Summer Camps has separate camps for religious boys and girls focusing on computers and electronics, and a touring camp for non-religious children. **PHONE:** (02) 652-5179

King David Horseback Riding Camp. Held at Neve Ilan, about 15 minutes from Jerusalem, the program includes week-long day camp for ages 6 and up, plus a week-long sleep-away ranch experience for ages 12 and up. Children learn riding, care of horses, and use of a lasso. Time is allowed for swimming. **PHONE:** (02) 340-535

Ein Yael Living Museum. The camp focuses on hands-on arts and crafts methods used in ancient times. It is located in the Refayim Valley near Malcha on the site of an ancient farm, and includes the ruins of a Roman villa. There are daily workshops in pottery, weaving, mosaics, and agriculture, as well as a three-week camp. PHONE: (02) 413-257

Hemed Camp is a large Israeli day camp with swimming and traditional camp activities. PHONE: (02) 249-949, 231-016

Hassadna Music and Dance Camp, sponsored by the Jerusalem Conservatory of Music and Arts, holds afternoon classes in classical and modern dance, voice, art, and kung fu for children 4-18. 22 Emek Refaim Street. PHONE: (02) 632-763; FAX: 630-017

Bible Lands Museum Camp for children ages 6-12 focuses on a variety of interesting themes. PHONE: (02) 611-066

Israel Museum Summer Camp has two, two-week sessions concentrating on different art topics. PHONE: (02) 633-278

Gal Yardeni Sport and Nature Camp, located on a farm in the Jerusalem Forest, focuses on drama, music, art, and nature. Children as young as 3 can attend one of the camp's three sessions. PHONE: (02) 852-104

Neve Ilan Biking Camp features five days of mountain bike touring for ages 10 and up. PHONE: (02) 343-359, 339-380

TEL AVIV

Neve Nofesh is a source for information on camps in the Tel Aviv area. Kfar Hayarok. PHONE: (03) 647-9098; FAX: 647-9077

Tel Aviv Municipal Summer Day Camps. PHONE: (03) 521-8662

Tel Aviv University Day Camp. Three, three-week sessions for children ages 5-13 are held on campus. Activities include computers and chess. Lunch is served, and camp ends at 3 p.m. The cost is about $450 per session. PHONE: (03) 640-8909; FAX: 640-9674

Beit Hatfutzot Diaspora Museum has camp programs on museum themes for kids of all ages. PHONE: (03) 646-2020

Camp for Diabetic Children is sponsored by the Israel Organization for Childhood Diabetes. 5 Jabotinsky Street. PHONE: (03) 546-2717

Man and His World Natural History Museum in Ramat Gan has a summer camp program. **PHONE:** (03) 631-5010

Safari Summer Camp is held at the Safari Park. Call in the spring for program details. **PHONE:** (03) 631-2181

Kifak Camp in Ramat Gan is for children ages 3-13. There is a wide choice of arts and crafts and sports activities. 16 Einstein Street. **PHONE:** (03) 574-6555; **FAX:** 547-7722

CENTRAL

Ganim runs five different days camps for ages 4-12 in the Ashkelon, Ramle, Rehovot, and Rishon areas. Transportation is provided. Some camps have one three-week session, others two. 12 Hasadeh St., Rishon LeZion. **PHONE:** (03) 964-2250; **FAX:** 964-9191

Havat Hahavayot in Kfar Mones, north of Netanya, includes swimming, arts, and touring for children 4-14. There are two, three-week sessions. **PHONE:** (09) 622-623

Kef and Shashua, at Beit Yehoshua, near Netanya has an English-language section and a separate religious section. There is swimming and camp activities for children 6-14. Lunch is included. **PHONE:** (09) 627-444.

Computer Courses for Kids ages 6 and up take place in Netanya. Programming and computer tricks are taught. 60 Baari Street. **PHONE:** (09) 625-885.

HAIFA

Hod Hacarmel. PHONE: (04) 253-901

Kaytanah Kayit v'Gil. Children are picked up in Haifa and transported to several area kibbutzim for a camping/farming experience. There is one three-week session for children ages 4½-13. **PHONE:** (04) 257-618; **FAX:** 342-013.

SLEEP-AWAY CAMPS

Camp Ariel. Kfar Silver, Ashkelon. Orthodox, American-style sleep-away camp for boys and girls entering grades 4-11. The 3-week sessions include religious instruction, swimming, sports, arts, computers, and touring. **PHONE:** (02) 669-540; **FAX:** 665-113

Summer Adventure. Aloni Yitzhak Youth Village near Benyamina. English-speaking camp for boys and girls in grades 6-9. Two 12-day sessions with sports, arts and crafts, and total English language immersion. Field trips organized for kids from abroad. The food is kosher. **PHONE:** (06) 378-551, 378-707

Camp Metzad. Gush Etzion. Religious sleep-away camp for boys and girls 6-14. PHONE: (02) 993-2265

Camp Bnos Chofetz Chaim. Kibbutz Choftez Chaim. Girls ages 10-18 from America and Europe come to study Torah and participate in camp and farming activities. Religious program run in English. PHONE: (08) 593-708; U.S.: (718)-282-6350; FAX: (718) 282-6350

Camp N'vei Ashdod. Six-week English-speaking, religious girls camp for ages 10-17. Hiking, swimming, touring, and Torah study. PHONE: (02) 651-8517; U.S.: 141-24 71st Rd., Flushing, NY 11369; PHONE: (800) 2-ASHDOD (Toll-free)

Givat Hayeladim, Box 151. Even Yehudah. Three 12-day sessions for campers ages 5-14. Most of of the 120 campers are Israelis. Family-run, experienced camp. Kosher but not religious. PHONE: (09) 699-011; FAX: 686-107

Camp Tapuz. Kibbutz Regavim, near Caesarea. International summer camp for ages 6-18. Two sessions. PHONE: (06) 380-394; FAX: 380-395

Grand Slam Baseball Camp. Kibbutz Gezer. Certified coaches and US major league players are the instructors at this overnight camp for boys and girls 8-15. Swimming, crafts, and touring are included. Food is kosher. PHONE: (09) 950-239; (08) 270-690; FAX: (09) 774-4348

Camp Samson. Kibbutz Tzora between Jerusalem and Tel Aviv. Two-week sessions for English-speaking youth ages 11-15. Wide range of sports and arts and crafts activities and tours. Kashruth and Shabbat are not observed. PHONE: (02) 990-8222; FAX: 990-8565

UNIVERSITY CAMPS

Galil Center. Kiryat Shmoneh. New program for teen-agers from abroad. Includes touring. PHONE: (06) 953-500

Tel Aviv University. Two-week program for 10-12th graders. Sixty courses in science, philosophy, history, and law are taught in Hebrew. Courses in international relations and life sciences are taught in English. Courses meet 4 hours per day, five days a week. PHONE: (03) 640-8469; FAX: 640-8184

Weizmann Institute of Science. Summer residential science program for 80 gifted high school seniors world-wide. PHONE: (08) 343-958; FAX: 344-130; APPLICATION: 51 Madison Ave., #117, New York, NY 10010

Bar Ilan University. Day camp for 7-11th graders in Ramat Gan.. PHONE: (03) 531-8207.

Ben Gurion University. Residential camp for 7-11th graders in Beersheva. PHONE: (07) 461-086.

Atomic Energy Center. Program for outstanding 10-11th grade physics students. Taught in Hebrew. Youth and Science Dept., Nahal Sorek. PHONE: (08) 434-496.

Volcani Institute for Agricultural Research. Residential program for 11th graders. Youth and Science Department, Beit Dagan. PHONE: (03) 968-3650.

Technion International Science Camp. 4-week research program for students 16-17. PHONE: (04) 294-541; U.S. (212) 262-6200.

TEENS AND YOUNG ADULTS

The **American Zionist Youth Foundation** publishes *Guide to Israel Experience,* an anthology of dozens of programs for teens and young adults between 12-35. They include summer, vacation, semester, and year-long experiences in scouts, sports, creative arts, sci-tech, adventure, and learning. For a copy, write 110 E. 59 Street, 3rd Floor New York, NY 10022. PHONE: (212) 339-6916; (800) 27-ISRAEL

You should also contact your local Jewish Federation, Jewish Community Center, synagogue, and youth organization for information on their programs for children and families.

WHERE TO STAY

Choosing a Base

If you are staying longer than two weeks, it is helpful to think of one city as a base, and to plan day trips from there. I am prejudiced toward Jerusalem, because I find it the most fascinating city in the world, and because it offers so many interesting activities for children.

Think Ahead About Shabbat

In Jerusalem and Tel Aviv, there is no public transportation from an hour before sundown Friday until an hour after sundown on Saturday. In Haifa, buses run on Shabbat. Taxis are available in most places, but they charge higher fares on Saturday. In Jerusalem, certain areas, such as Meah Shearim and Har Nof, are closed to vehicles on Shabbat.

If you want to go to the Kotel (the Western Wall) on Friday night or Saturday morning, it is most convenient to be in a hotel or apartment within walking distance.

HOME EXCHANGE

If you are interested in swapping homes with Israelis wishing to visit your community, contact:

Vacation Exchange Club. POBox 650, Key West, FL 33041. **PHONE:** (800) 638-3841

Homelink Israel. 49 Sheshet Hayamin St., Jerusalem. **PHONE:** (02) 812-726; **FAX:** 811-178

HOTELS

There are over 300 hotels in Israel, from small simple inns to 5-star luxury hi-rises. In every section of this book, we have noted a few with facilities particularly suited to families. Consult your travel agent or a standard guidebook for a more complete listing.

Children in Your Room: Many hotels in Israel do not allow more than one child in their parents' room. Some permit up to two, but few will accept three or more. Crowded hotel rooms are not pleasant. In the end you are better off paying a little more for comfort. Most hotels can arrange adjoining rooms so your children are nearby, but not underfoot. Remember, this is your vacation, too.

Hotel Meal Plans: Most, but not all hotels include an "Israeli breakfast" in their base price. Expect a buffet with a variety of salads, cheeses, juices, yogurt, rolls, and sometimes eggs and smoked fish. Before you plan your day, find out when breakfast is served. You might want to go swimming first and come back for breakfast between 9-10 a.m. If this is your strategy, keep crackers and juice in your room for early morning snacks.

Some hotels require that you take "half-board" during your stay. This means that in addition to breakfast, you pay for either lunch or dinner at the hotel. There is usually a set menu that includes soup, meat, side dishes, and dessert. As small children rarely appreciate hotel cuisine, I try to avoid hotels that require half-board. Few things annoy me more than paying for a meal my children have barely touched. Lately more hotels are offering suitable children's menus.

Luxury Hotels: The category 5-star connotes luxury — in the quality of the room, the lavishness of the meals, and the diversity of recreational facilities. In my experience, small children do not appreciate the luxury, but teenagers do.

You will, of course, pay for this luxury. A double room in a 5-star hotel in high season can easily cost $150 or more a night. However, many 5-star hotels follow the International Family Plan which offers generous discounts for children. A child who sleeps in his/her parents' room is free. If you have two children, they sleep in a separate room, and you pay for two single rooms. Always do the total calculation before coming to conclusions about which hotel is the least expensive for your family.

Hotel Chains:

Israel Hotel Reservation Center. This center officially represents the Sheraton, Isrotel, and Kibbutz Hotel Chains, but can book other hotels, as well as find you an apartment or bed and breakfast in Jerusalem. **PHONE:** (800) 552-0141 (U.S.Toll-free); (800) 526-5343 (Canada Toll-free)

Now you can get a list of Israeli hotels, including addresses, phone and fax numbers, facilities, and prices on the Internet!

http://www.netmedia.co.il/info/hotelassoc/

Moriah Chain has a 9-day plan which includes their hotels in Tel Aviv, Jerusalem, Tiberias, Eilat, Haifa, and the Dead Sea. One child under 18 in parents' room is free. **PHONE:** (800) 221-0203 (U.S. Toll-free)

Best Western offers fly-and-drive package deals and a one-price hotel pass with a choice of accommodations at any of the dozen hotels in the chain. There are reduced rates for children in their parents' rooms. **PHONE: U.S.:** (800) 528-1234 (Toll-free); **BRITAIN :** 018-541-0033

Holiday Inn. Two children up to age 19 may stay in their parents' room for free. All hotels have children's clubs and provide gifts for visiting children. **PHONE: U.S.:** (800) 465-4329 (Toll-free)

Dan Chain has Superdan programs for seven nights at any of their hotels in Jerusalem, Tel Aviv, Haifa, Caesarea, and Eilat. **PHONE:** (800) 223-7773/4 (Toll-free); (212) 752-6120

KIBBUTZ GUEST HOUSES

An important industry in many *kibbutzim* and *moshavim* (Israel's cooperative farming communities) is running hotels for tourists. Set in the countryside, these accommodations can be truly lovely — spotless, air-conditioned rooms with patios, swimming pools, sports centers, petting zoos, and beautiful grounds. You can expect breakfast in a well-organized kosher dining room and full tourist services. Other meals often may be eaten inexpensively in the members' dining hall.

Children will like the grounds and the rural atmosphere, but a disadvantage is being far from city-based evening cultural activities. Guest houses with facilities that appeal to children are listed in the appropriate sections. Contact the **Kibbutz Inn and Guest House Association** for a listing, and ask about their 7-Day plan. A brochure is available: POB 3193, 61031 Tel Aviv. **PHONE:** (03) 524-6161; **FAX:** (03) 523-0527

> If you are traveling with children, you cannot volunteer on a kibbutz or moshav in exchange for accommodations.

RUSTIC LIVING

A wide variety of rooms are now available under the heading of rustic accommodations. In Israel, they're often referred to by the German word "tzimmerim." Some are regular B and B's, others are small apartments at kibbutzim, moshavim, or private homes. Most have small kitchens and an informal atmosphere, making them family-friendly. The only problem is that it's not easy to get an up-to-date listing. We've listed a few in the geographical sections, and suggest you check newspapers and regional tourist boards for a current list.

The **HOME** kibbutz chain represents 30 kibbutzim with three levels of accommodations from $25-50 per person per night including breakfast. There's a discount for children. Write for their brochure: DN Halutza, Kibbutz Mashabei Sadeh, 85510 Israel. **PHONE:** (07) 565-134; **FAX:** 565-145.

HOLIDAY VILLAGES

Some holiday villages feature luxury, beach-front cabins that rent for up to $250/person/day; others have back-to-nature huts with cooking facilities that sleep up to six in a room and cost only a few dollars. Many have children's activities.

APARTMENT HOTELS

Apartment hotels are excellent places for families. Most have one or two-bedroom apartments with linen service and a fully-equipped kitchenette. I like this style of hotel, because I can keep food on hand for kids who wake up hungry early in the morning. And if we are too tired from a day of touring to eat in a nice restaurant, we can make sandwiches "at home." Some apartment hotels have maid service, washers and dryers, baby-sitting service, and grocery delivery. Monthly and long-term rates can be negotiated. Apartment hotels are listed in the geographic sections.

RENTING AN APARTMENT

If you are coming for at least three weeks, you might want to rent a furnished apartment from an Israeli who is going abroad for the same period. Ask friends who may know neighbors willing to rent their homes. Then check the apartment ads in the classified section of the *Jerusalem Post International Edition.* If you can get a copy, the Friday *Israeli Jerusalem Post* runs a translation of classified ads from major Hebrew newspapers.

Real Estate agents also can find you an apartment. Anglo-Saxon is one firm that works all over Israel. Write a letter with all your requirements to 2 Hasoreg Street, Jerusalem. **PHONE:** (02) 251-161. There is a minimum fee of 10% of the rent, or a fixed annual sum. Israeli Apartment Rentals needs a month lead time to find you an apartment in the big cities, but only a few days if you want a rural location. Write Abraham Schachter, POB 7255, Haifa. **PHONE/ FAX:** (04) 340-821

BED AND BREAKFAST

If you want to rent a room in a private home, you can meet Israelis and save money. Rates run $30-60 per night, depending on the location, room size, whether or not you share a bath, and type of breakfast served. There is a limited choice of homes appropriate for families, but it's worth a call. Contact **Bed and Breakfast.** POB 24119, Jerusalem. **PHONE:** (02) 817-001; **Good Morning Jerusalem.** Binyanei Ha'uma. **PHONE:** (02) 511-270

HOSTELS

Israel's hostels have vastly improved in recent years. Many have family rooms, and unlike European hostels which are often self-catering, you usually get breakfast and can often get a low-priced hot lunch, dinner, or even full board. The food is kosher. You generally pay by the number of persons in a room. In 1995, one person in the Karei Deshe Youth Hostel on the Kinneret paid $30; a family of six paid $16.50 per person or $99 for bed and breakfast in a family room with bunk beds and two bathrooms.

There are 32 hostels within the framework of the **Israel Youth Hostels Association** which offers packages of 7-28 days including room, half board, unlimited bus travel on Egged, and free entrance to National Parks. The Association's travel bureau is happy to assist groups and individuals in planning their trips in Israel and to Egypt, the Sinai, and Jordan.

Members of the International Federation of Youth Hostels are entitled to a discount. Make arrangements well in advance for busy seasons in busy hostels: fall in Eilat, summer in Tel Aviv. Contact the Israel Youth Hostels Association, Dorot Rishonim Street, Jerusalem, **PHONE:** (02) 252-706; **FAX:** 250-676; 235-220

CHRISTIAN HOSPICES

Generally, the cities visited on a Christian pilgrimage have hospices, lodgings for travelers. Those with private rooms usually allow children. Those set up as hostels may not. Children's discounts vary. A disadvantage is that hospices generally have fixed meal times. You can get a list from the Christian Information Center or Government Tourist Office Pilgrimage Division in Jerusalem. **PHONE:** (02) 257-456

ISRAELI COUSINS

Most Israelis live in small apartments. If you don't mind crowding, and your cousins insist that you stay with them, please note the following:

Hot water is always limited. Even with a solar heater, the tank holds only 30 gallons. When you shower, do it quickly. The average Israeli uses only one-fourth the water of an American!

Out-of-town phone calls are expensive, and they are not listed separately on the phone bill. Calls are cheaper in the evenings.

Be considerate of Israel's siesta (between 2-4 p.m.), especially on Shabbat. If your kids want to play, take them to a park!

Say "thank you" by taking your cousins out for dinner.

CAMPING

Camping is one of the least expensive options for traveling with children. It offers an opportunity to mix with families from all parts of the world and to get close to nature. If you are coming for several weeks, you might want to stay at campsites for part of the trip, so that you can splurge on more luxurious accommodations at other times. If you are coming in winter, make sure the site you select has heated cabins.

Israeli campsites offer water, bathrooms, showers, first aid, and telephones. Some sites rent equipment such as tents and sleeping bags, but many do not. Others provide cooking facilities or barbeques, but you may want to use a portable gas cooker or take advantage of restaurants on the premises.. Almost all sites have grocery stores. There are often beaches nearby, and most campgrounds have pools, playgrounds, and evening entertainment.

Bungalows: Most campsites also rent cabins, called "bungalows," which offer beds and bedding and the use of common cooking facilities and bathrooms. If you stay in a bungalow, you don't have to carry bulky camping equipment.

Caravans: A few sites also offer "caravans," small, stationary mobile homes These include kitchenettes (but no utensils) and are usually air-conditioned.

Specific camp sites are noted in appropriate geographical sections.

FIELD SCHOOLS

Most of SPNI's 26 field schools have overnight accommodations. You get a large family room with up to six beds (often including bunk beds) and a private bathroom. Most field schools have kosher meal options. Their advantage is a relatively low price, fabulous locations for hiking, and the possibility of hiring a guide who knows the area well. In Tel Aviv, **PHONE:** (03) 638-8666; **FAX:** 377-695; in Jerusalem, **PHONE**: (02) 244-605; **FAX:** 254-953

HOLIDAYS HOLY DAYS

Experiencing the holidays in Israel is a treat. On Rosh Hashanah, the sound of the shofar echoing from dozens of synagogues is inspiring. On Yom Kippur, the suspension of traffic and commerce communicates a sense of the "Sabbath of all Sabbaths." On Sukkot, thatched huts appear overnight on balconies and courtyards. A week before Purim, children begin wearing holiday costumes. After feverish cleaning for Passover, the country celebrates the Feast of Freedom and the beginning of spring with spirited seders and matzah picnics.

Tourist sites observe Friday schedules the day before a holiday (holiday eve). Passover, Sukkot, and Shavuot are celebrated for a day less than in the Diaspora.

The Sabbath (Shabbat)

Shabbat is traditionally considered a taste of the world to come. Observant Jews attend synagogue, eat festive meals, take walks, study, and rest. For the non-observant, Shabbat is a family and recreation day.

Friday newspapers list Sabbath services. Synagogues welcome visitors. Remember, prayerbooks are in Hebrew, so if you want one with English, bring your own. (See *Appendix* for a list of religious movements to contact about services and programs.)

> If a site you plan to visit on Saturday charges admission, find out if you need to buy tickets in advance. Some places are open, but will not sell tickets.

The Biblical prohibition against work on Shabbat includes all activities used to build the Holy Temple. Among them are riding in vehicles, writing, lighting fires, using money, and planting or harvesting. Most communities in Israel have an *eruv*, a "fence" surrounding the city, which obviates the prohibition against carrying in a public place. Therefore, you can carry a package and push a stroller, even in the most religious neighborhoods.

Before you accept an invitation for Shabbat, ask your hosts if they object to your riding to their home. And remember that electrical toys and writing tools are put away on Shabbat. If you have such gifts, save them for another time.

Newspapers list the emergency hospitals and pharmacies that are open on Shabbat. You can also get this information from the Magen David Adom. PHONE: 101

Moslems follow a Lunar calendar, and the dates of Moslem holidays change from year to year. The most important holidays are the **New Year, Mohammed's Birthday, Ramadan** (one month), **Id El Fitre** (conclusion of Ramadan), and **Id El Adha** (Sacrificial Festival). The Moslem Sabbath is on Friday.

JANUARY - FEBRUARY

New Year's Day is not an official holiday, but banks are closed.

Epiphany (Catholic and Orthodox churches)

Christmas (Armenian Orthodox)

Tu B'Shevat: New Year for Trees. This is the time to plant trees. Contact a Plant-A-Tree office of the Jewish National Fund (JNF).

FEBRUARY-MARCH

Purim: The victory over the Persian enemy Haman is celebrated on the 14th of Adar, except in the walled cities of Jerusalem and Safed where it is celebrated the following day (*Shushan Purim*). Festivities include reading the *Megillah*, holiday meals, giving gifts of food (*mishloach manot*), and colorful *Adloyad*a parades. Some people begin the celebration on the 14th and then travel to Jerusalem or Safed to continue the merriment. Children have both days off from school, but most adults work, and buses run. Make sure your child has a costume for the Purim events. You can buy inexpensive disguises, masks, and groggers at street corner kiosks.

International Birdwatching Conference: Eilat

MARCH-APRIL

Palm Sunday, Good Friday, and Easter: Check with the Christian Information Office for a listing of religious and cultural activities. There are special services and pageants at the Church of the Holy Sepulchre.

Pesach (Passover): This is a major school holiday period for children (2-3 weeks), and many organizations sponsor week-long camps. Check the newspapers.

Pesach is high season in Israeli hotels. Some require that you book full board for the holiday week. Reserve at least three months in advance and expect to pay more than usual.

Most hotels have communal seders, which are usually expensive. If you are traveling with a large group, ask if you can rent a private dining room for your own seder. Israelis celebrate only one seder. Some hotels offer a second seder for those following the Diaspora tradition.

Maimouna: On the day after Pesach (which corresponds to the 8th day in the Diaspora), *Maimouna* celebrations take place. This was a custom of Moroccan and Tunisian Jews, but today Israelis of all backgrounds join in the picnics and folklore celebrations. In Jerusalem, these festivities take place in Sacher Park. Pack a picnic and join in the fun.

Jerusalem March: Groups representing cities, settlements, businesses, organizations, and occasional tourists march through the city recalling the pilgrimage during Temple Days.

Ein Gev Music Festival: Kibbutz Ein Gev — Intermediate Days of Passover.

Flower Festival: Haifa

Acre Theater Festival: Alternative theater and street performances

Tel Aviv Marathon: For information contact Hapoel Sports Center. PHONE: (03) 561-3322

Children's Theater Festival: Haifa

Family Festival: Beit Guvrin Caves

APRIL-MAY

Jerusalem International Book Fair (Held every other year in odd years): Books from all over the world are exhibited. Children will enjoy the play corner, theater, and puppet shows.

Yom Hashoah (Holocaust Remembrance Day): Check newspapers for a schedule of memorial services and special television programs. All places of entertainment are closed. A memorial siren is sounded during the day.

Yom Hazikaron (Memorial Day): On the day before Independence Day, Israel mourns her war dead. Services are held in military cemeteries, and a siren is sounded for a minute of silence at night and in the morning.

Yom Ha'atzmaut (Independence Day): Look for the soft, squeaking plastic hammers (*patishim*) at street corner kiosks. Don't be insulted if you get bopped on the head. It's a way to wish you a Happy Independence Day. Good manners require that you strike back.

Many families begin Independence Day the night before with a festive communal meal. The day itself is the national picnic day at all parks and beaches. In major cities you may see fireworks and dancing in the street. Check newspapers for special events. Most stores and many restaurants are closed, so do your food shopping in advance.

World Bible Quiz for Youth: Jerusalem

Galilee Walkathon: For information contact Hapoel Sports Center. **PHONE:** (03) 561-3322.

MAY-JUNE

Lag B'Omer: The 33rd day of the Omer period between Pesach and Shavuot marks the end of a plague in Talmudic times. The holiday also honors the great teacher Rabbi Shimon Bar Yochai. Many travel to the town of Meron near Safed, the reputed site of his grave, for picnics and bonfires. Three-year-old Hassidic boys have their first haircuts. Stores are open, and buses run.

Jerusalem Festival: Dozens of cultural events for children and adults. Check the newspaper.

Hebrew Book Week (Shavuat Hasefer): Outdoor book fairs in most cities and town.

Shavuot: Seven weeks after Pesach, Jews commemorate the giving of the Torah. Shavuot is celebrated for one day in Israel. Traditional Jews attend all-night study sessions, which are held in many languages. Check the newspapers for a listing. The place to be at sunrise is the Kotel, the Western Wall, where families wait to catch a glimpse of the sun before beginning morning prayers. Bakeries feature cheese cake and other dairy delicacies.

Yom Yerushalyim (Jerusalem Day): The anniversary of the reunification of Jerusalem in 1967.

JULY-AUGUST

Tiberias Music Festival: Outdoor concerts.

Israeli Song Festival: Arad

Youth Festival: Haifa

Folkdance Festival: Carmiel

Klezmer Festival: Safed

Jacob's Ladder Folk Festival: Horshat Tal

Tisha B'Av: Beginning with the first of Av, traditional Jews mourn the destruction of the First and Second Temples, which occurred on the 9th of Av. Many refrain from swimming, movies, and festive activities, and eat only dairy foods, except on Shabbat. On the evening before the 9th of Av, the Scroll of Lamentations is read at synagogues. Many people go to the Kotel, where large crowds of tourists and Israelis mix. Movie houses and restaurants are closed, but buses run normally. Tisha B'Av is a fast day.

Kite Festival: Israel Museum, Jerusalem

Assumption: Christian holiday. Processions from the Church of the Holy Sepulchre to Gethsemane.

SEPTEMBER-OCTOBER

Rosh Hashanah (Jewish New Year) and Yom Kippur (Day of Atonement): The High Holidays are peak season in Israel. Synagogues are crowded. If you wish to order seats, contact one of the religious groups listed in the *Appendix* well in advance. Rosh Hashanah is celebrated for two days, just as in the Diaspora. Public transportation does not run, and businesses are closed on both days and on Yom Kippur.

Sukkot: Hotels and restaurants put up thatched booths, so patrons can celebrate this harvest holiday. It is fun to walk through religious neighborhoods, such as Meah Shearim in Jerusalem, to see the dozens and dozens of sukkot lining the narrow streets. Remember to dress modestly.

Many organizations sponsor evenings of song and entertainment to recall the festivities surrounding the water-drawing ceremony in the days of the Temple.

On the morning of **Hoshanah Rabah**, the seventh day of Sukkot, thousands gather at the Kotel to tap willow branches and recite the prayer for rain.

Shemini Atzeret/Simchat Torah: In Israel, these are celebrated as one holiday. There is great rejoicing as Torah scrolls from all the synagogues are paraded in the streets.

On the first day of Sukkot and on Shemini Atzeret stores are closed and buses do not run. On the intermediate days, government offices and some stores are closed half day. Children are on vacation the whole week, and SPNI and other organizations run camps.

Tabernacle Festival: Week-long celebration for Christian tourists from many countries including children's events. Contact the Christian Embassy, 10 Brenner Street, Jerusalem. **PHONE:** (02) 669-823

Swimathon: 3 miles across Lake Kinneret. Contact Hapoel Sports Organization, 8 Ha'arba'a Street, Tel Aviv. **PHONE:** (03) 561-3322

Haifa Film Festival. PHONE: (06) 767-630

Hanukkah (Festival of Lights): Hanukkah lamps (*hanukkiot*) adorn the windows and roofs of public buildings, and many hotels sponsor festive candle-lighting ceremonies. There are torch relays from the site of the Maccabees' graves in **Modi'in**. This is a good time to tour Modi'in (see *Between Jerusalem and Tel Avi.*). *Sufganiot* (jelly donuts) and *latkes* (fried potato pancakes), the traditional delicacies, are available in bakeries and supermarkets. School is closed, but stores and transportation function normally.

Christmas: Celebrations focus on the city of Bethlehem. The Ministry of Tourism arranges visits there on Christmas Eve. If you want to stay overnight, make your reservations at least six months in advance. Churches in Jerusalem sponsor family plays and puppet shows.

Bike Marathon: Sea of Galilee. Contact: Jordan Valley Regional Council. **PHONE:** (06) 757-630

JERUSALEM

Jerusalemites love their city. I am one of them. Just ask me about the city's timeless beauty, its spiritual aura, dramatic history, and exotic cultures, and I'll go on for hours.

Jerusalem is both the ancient city of the Bible and the modern, bustling capital of the State of Israel. Shrines holy to Jews, Moslems, and Christians stand side-by-side with museums, shopping malls, and government buildings. Children will find much to do in Jerusalem. It should be the focus of any visit to Israel.

You are your children's guide. If you take time to give them some background about the city, its geography and history, they will enjoy their visit more. Children might be confused, for instance, by the term Old City, which refers to the part of the city surrounded by walls. Many things in the New City look very old as well.

With children 8 and up, I would begin a visit by spending at least ten minutes with a time-line. Children will relate to many events which took place in Jerusalem.

SOME HISTORY

Biblical Time: According to tradition, about 2000 BCE Abraham brought Isaac to be sacrified on the site of the Temple Mount above the Kotel (Western Wall).

> Because the notations BC and AD refer to the birth of Jesus, Jewish historians use the notations BCE (Before the Common Era) and CE (Common Era).

First Temple: King David, whom we remember from his battle with Goliath, conquered Jerusalem about 1000 BCE. You can see the archeological remains of David's City outside the Dung Gate. His son, King Solomon, built the First Temple where the Temple Mount is today.

Hezekiah, one of the kings who followed Solomon, was counseled by the prophet Isaiah to protect the city against an Assyrian assault. He dug the famous water tunnel that runs through David's City, which you can visit.

In 586 BCE, under King Nebuchadnezzar, Babylonian forces exiled the inhabitants of Jerusalem and burned down the city, leaving it desolate for over 50 years.

Second Temple: In 540 BCE, Persian King Cyrus allowed the Jews to return to Jerusalem and to rebuild the Temple. Many archeological sites in the Old City are from the Second Temple period.

The Maccabeean victory and rededication of the Temple celebrated at Hanukkah took place in 164 BCE. You can visit Modi'in, the ancestral home of the Maccabees, not far from Jerusalem.

The Romans invaded Jerusalem in 63 BCE. King Herod rebuilt the city. As one of his building projects, he surrounded the Temple Mount with a wall of huge blocks. The Kotel or Western Wall has many Herodian stones.

The Jews rebelled again Rome, and in 70 CE, the Roman General Titus destroyed the Second Temple and burned the city. After an unsuccessful revolt in 132 by Bar Kochba, all Jews were exiled from the Roman-ruled city in 135.

Over the next 800 years, the city was ruled in turn by Byzantines, Arabs, Crusaders, Mamalukes, and the Ottoman Turks. The walls that surround the Old City today were built in the 1500s by Ottoman ruler Suleiman the Magnificent.

19th Century: Jerusalem began to expand in 1860, when British philanthropist Moses Montefiore paid citizens to move to an area outside the stone ramparts. You can visit the landmark windmill built by Montefiore to provide the settlers with a trade. Slowly, other new neighborhoods were established in Meah Shearim and downtown.

20th Century: In 1917, the ruling Turks surrendered to the British. Under a League of Nations mandate, Britain ruled Palestine until Israel gained independence in 1948. Visit the Old Court Museum in the Old City to learn about life during this period. The struggle for independence was marked by Jewish-Arab violence. Ben Yehudah Street and the King David Hotel were blown up. Full-scale war broke out on May 15, 1948. Shortly thereafter, the pipeline to Jerusalem was cut and water was rationed. Sites such as the Castel, the Cablecar Museum, the Hall of Heroism, and Mt. Scopus will help you learn the history of this period.

Jerusalem Divided: According to the UN decision to partition Palestine, Jerusalem was to become an international city, but at the end of the War of Independence, it had become a city divided by concrete walls and barbed wire. Visit the Tourjeman Post on the old border to see the exhibit of photos and maps from this period. The Old City and the Kotel were no longer in Jewish hands, and the University and Hadassah Hospital on Mt. Scopus were inaccessible. During those years, a new Hadassah Hospital was built, as well as the Givat Ram campus of the Hebrew University. So were Yad Vashem, the Israel Museum, Knesset, and the Center of the Chief Rabbinate, which houses the Wolfson Museum.

Jerusalem Reunited: In 1967, during the Six Day War, Israeli forces conquered the Old City and East Jerusalem. A movie at the Tourjeman Post and a visit to Ammunition Hill will help you understand this victory. The city was reunited. Since then, the Jewish Quarter was rebuilt, and the area around the Kotel expanded to accommodate the thousands of tourists who visit this holy site.

JERUSALEM TODAY

Some geography: The **Old City** in **East Jerusalem** is the ancient walled city with the world's major religious shrines: the Kotel (Western Wall), the Al Aksa Mosque and the Dome of the Rock, and the Church of the Holy Sepulchre. Mt. Scopus, the Mount of Olives, and several archeological sites are outside the Old City walls in East Jerusalem.

The **New City** or **West Jerusalem** includes downtown, the government and museum complex in Givat Ram, Mount Herzl, Yad Vashem, and residential neighborhoods. The new neighborhoods of Ramot, Gilo, Givat Ze'ev, Pisgat Ze'ev, Neveh Yaakov, and Maaleh Adumim have been built during the last 20 years.

In addition to visiting historic sites, let your children taste life as Jerusalem's kids do. Plan time exploring the Youth Wing of the Israel Museum, roller-skating or playing at Liberty Bell Park, sliding down the Monster in Kiryat Hayovel, and eating felafel on Ben Yehudah Street. In addition to all its other assets, Jerusalem is a city of fun.

CITY NOTES

Area Code: (02). If you are calling from out of town you must dial these numbers first.

> As this book goes to press, Jerusalem phone numbers are changing from 6 to 7 digits. The new digit is being added at the beginning of the number. If you dial an old number, you should get a recording with the new number.

Important Phone Numbers

Police Emergency: 100
Police (non-emergency) : 391-111
Municipal Hotline: 106, 666-666
Ambulance, First Aid: 101
Terem 24-hour drop-in medical care: 652-1748, 652-2607
Dental Emergency: 254-779
Fire: 102
Mental Health Hotline: 610-303
Yad Sarah Medical Equipment: 244-242
Egged Bus: 304-704 (local); (02) 304-555 (from out of town)
Train Station: 733-764
Tourist Police: 391-254

TOURIST INFO

Government Tourist Center
24 King George St.
PHONE: (02) 754-811

This center, open 24-hours a day, has user-friendly computers to tell you about the sites around the country.

Jerusalem Municipal Tourist Office — 17 Jaffa Rd.
PHONE: (02) 258-844
HOURS: Sun.-Thurs. 8 a.m.-4:30 p.m.; Fri. until noon

Jerusalem Municipal Tourist Office —Inside Jaffa Gate
PHONE: (02) 280-382, 280-457
HOURS: Sun.-Thur. 8:30 a.m.-6 p.m., Fri. until 2 p.m.

Along with information about tourist sites, pick up a brochure called *Events* with upcoming arts programs and festivals.

Jerusalem 3000 Events: **PHONE:** (02) 254-088

> **A City Visitor's Center** opening in Safra Square in 1996, will feature audio-visual materials and computer terminals.

Christian Information Office
Inside Old City
PHONE: (02) 272-692; Pilgrim's Office: 272-697
HOURS: Monday-Saturday 8:30 a.m.-1 p.m.

Up-to-date information on Christian sites, hospices, church services, classes, and children's activities for all denominations. You can get tickets for Christmas Mass in Bethlehem here. Tourists who want pilgrimage certificates can purchase them at the Franciscan Pilgrim's Office in the same building.

Meet Israelis for coffee and cake. The Tourism Department will try to find a family with kids the same ages, or who shares your occupation or interests. PHONE: (02) 754-877

Shabbat in an Orthodox Home. For home hospitality call Jeff Seidel. PHONE: (02) 288-338, 282-634, (050) 344-341(mobile phone); or Meir Schuster. PHONE: (050) 218-534

RESOURCES

Newspapers: The Friday *Jerusalem Post* and the *In Jerusalem* supplement have advertisements of special events as well as the week's TV schedule. The *Jerusalem Report* bi-weekly magazine has a lively news update and interesting features.

If you can read Hebrew, buy the Friday *Kol Ha-ir*, the city paper, for an excellent list of events. Film names are printed in English as well as Hebrew.

Ask for free copies of brochures such as *Hello Israel, In Jerusalem,* and *Jerusalem Menus,* along with a listing of cultural events. They're available in hotel lobbies and from tourist offices. Look at the posters on billboards.

The Israel Museum publishes a monthly calendar of events which includes films, special tours, lectures, and exhibition openings. It's available at the museum and tourist offices.

Maps: Make sure you have a good city map. They are free at tourist offices and many hotels, or can be purchased at bookstores and gift shops.

Bus Routes: You can get bus routes and schedules at the Central Bus Station (Egged). An abbreviated list is in tourist booklets available at hotels.

TICKET AGENCIES

Bimot. 8 Shamai St. PHONE: (02) 240-896
Ben Naim. 38 Jaffa Road. PHONE: (02) 254-008
Klaim. 12 Shammai St. PHONE: (02) 256-869

These agencies have tickets to concerts, plays, museums, and sports events, including tickets for events on Shabbat. Tickets, often with discounts, are also for sale at the campus ticket office of the Hebrew University on Mt. Scopus. You can buy tickets over the phone with a credit card, but you often have to wait in line to pick them up, so allow time before the performance.

CIRCLE LINE

Bus 99— The Circle Line

For about $5, you can ride an air-conditioned tourist bus to 37 focal points in the city. You can get off the bus at any stop and reboard when you have finished viewing that particular site. The bus gives you an overview of the city at low cost, and allows you to reach the more remote tourist sites with ease. The same bus will take you to Mt. Scopus, the Model of the Second Temple at the Holyland Hotel, and Yad Vashem. One-or two-day unlimited tickets also are available.

Bus 99 begins its route on Haemek Street ouside the Jaffa Gate Sunday-Thursday at 10 and 11a.m., noon, and 1, 2, and 4 p.m.; on Friday it leaves at 10 and 11a.m. and at noon. But you can board anywhere along the route. Signs at each site list the times the bus stops there. The round trip takes about two hours. The driver announces the stops, but there is no narration. PHONE: (02) 304-422

WALKING TOURS

Self-Guided Walking Tours. Several walking and jogging tour books are available in bookstores (see *Bibliography).*

Guided Walking Tours. Numerous groups conduct walking tours. In our experience, children under 8 are generally bored by historical tours, unless there is a gimmick, such as wading through a tunnel, walking on a roof, or interacting with nature or animals. Try to find one geared for children, such as certain tours sponsored by the SPNI. If you have a small child, take a light stroller or baby carrier. Don't forget your canteens and hats!

Free walking tours in English offered by the Jerusalem Municipality meet Saturday mornings at 10a.m. at the entrance to the Russian Compound, 32 Jaffa Rd. Each tour in the series takes about three hours. PHONE: (02) 280-382

City Hall Tours are given in English Mondays at 9:30 a.m. This new complex has a fascinating model of Jerusalem and great views from the balcony. Meet in Safra Square under the palm trees for an hour's walk. There is a nominal cost. PHONE: (02) 241-379

Religious Walking Tours of the Old City are run by Young Israel Sunday, Monday, and Tuesday mornings by appointment.. The tour is free, but a small donation may be solicited for Young Israel. Modest dress is requested. PHONE: (02) 287-065

Zion Walking Tours specializes in the Old City and Meah Shearim. Tours of the Old City quarters and excavations leave each morning from inside the Jaffa Gate opposite the police station. Students and children get a 25% discount on most tours. PHONE: (02) 287-866

Archaeological Seminars, Ltd. offers superb morning tours of the various quarters of the Old City, excavations of the Western Wall Tunnels, and the City of David, including Hezekiah's Tunnel. Tours begin with a slide show and background talk. Children under 8 are free. A 2½-hour tour costs $15. Tours leave from 34 Chabad Street in the Old City. PHONE: (02) 273-515

SPNI (Society for the Protection of Nature) offers walking tours (in English, French, German, Spanish) of Jerusalem and the surrounding areas with an emphasis on history and nature. These may include tours led by important military figures or experts in archeology, geology, and history. There is a family-friendly tour of the Old City every Thursday. Pick up a brochure at SPNI headquarters, 13 Helena Hamalka St. There are lovely, shaded gardens and a gift shop where you can buy posters. SPNI also offers hiking and bus tours out of the city. PHONE: (02) 252-357, 244-605

SPECIAL TOURS

Plant a Tree. From 8 a.m.-2 p.m. you can plant a tree with your own hands in a JNF Forest. The cost is $10 per tree. You get a certificate and a pin. PHONE: 177-022-3484 (Toll-free)

Hadassah Hospital. See *Ein Kerem*

Shaare Zedek Hospital. Children 13 and older can join a tour of one of Jerusalem's busiest hospitals. PHONE: (02) 655-5434

Hebrew University. See *Mt. Scopus* and *Givat Ram*

Knesset (Parliament) and **Supreme Court**. See *Givat Ram*

ORT will show you its technological schools. **PHONE:** (02) 754-666

WIZO will show you its childcare centers and other projects. **PHONE:** (02) 256-060

B'nai Brith Women Children's Home can be visited daily between 8a.m.-noon. **PHONE:** (02) 429-238

Na'amat has morning tours of its educational and social service institutions. **PHONE:** (02) 244-878

The **General Israel Orphans Home for Girls** has a morning tour of its facilities. **PHONE:** (02) 652-3291

Emunah, the National Zionist Women's Organization, has a free tour of its childcare centers and schools. **PHONE:** (02) 662-468

Amit Women has a tour of its schools and children's homes. **PHONE**: (02) 619-222

BUS AND JEEP TOURS

Egged Tours. PHONE: (02) 304-868, 304-422; **United Tours. PHONE:** (02) 252-187; and **Galilee Tours. PHONE:** (02) 258-866 offer half-day tours of the Old and New Cities. You can arrange to be picked up at any of the major hotels. Children usully get a 20% reduction. Galilee will take children on Old City tours only if they can walk a full three hours. United Tours offers 10% discount and doesn't take children under 5. These companies also offer tours out of the city.

Desert Tours. Ne'ot Hakikar. PHONE: (02) 236-262 and **Avi Jeep Tours. PHONE:** (02) 991-8855 will take you on a wide range of tours to the desert and the Judean Hills, as well as to Jordan and the Sinai. Avi charges about $300 to take a group of up to seven on a day-long jeep tour.

On Fridays, **Archaeological Seminars** runs **Dig-for-a-Day** at Tel Marisha between Jerusalem and Tel Aviv. Pick up is at 8 a.m. from major hotels, followed by a jeep ride to the site and digging, sifting, and washing pottery. The program ends with cave crawling and a visit to completed dig areas. The cost is $50 per person. Children 12 and under get a 10% discount. This firm can also arrange a private guide to take you around the country for about $250 per day. **PHONE:** (02) 273-515

Eshel Desert Tours has one and two-day jeep tours for families to Christian and Jewish sites in the Judean desert. They will pick you up at your hotel. This firm also has self-drive dune buggies, but you must be 18 or older and have a driver's license. They're located in Mishor Adumim, about a 20-minute ride out of Jerusalem. **PHONE:** (02) 355-655

Kids Jerusalem Adventures. David Schoenfeld leads family tours on a daily or weekly basis. **PHONE:** (02) 361-477

Happy Trails, run by Sharon Morgenstern, a former NYC school teacher, offers family-oriented private tours. Write Shalom Yehudah 38/19, Jerusalem. **PHONE:** (02) 733-987

Mazada Tours has a wide variety of travel packages, including tours to Egypt, the Sinai, and Jordan. 4 King Solomon St. **PHONE:** (02) 235-777

Airplane Tours. See Jerusalem, the Judean desert, and Masada from the air for about $40 for half an hour. **Nesher. PHONE:** (02) 834-345 and **Kanfei Jerusalem.** PHONE: (02) 831-444

OLD CITY

The Old City is divided into four quarters: the **Jewish Quarter, Moslem Quarter, Christian Quarter,** and **Armenian Quarter.** The names can be confusing, because religious sites are not always in what one might consider to be the "appropriate" Quarter.

There are eight gates in the Old City Wall: **Jaffa Gate, Zion Gate, Dung Gate, Golden (Mercy) Gate, Lion's (St. Stephen's) Gate, Herod's Gate, Damascus Gate,** and **New Gate.** The Golden Gate is closed. According to tradition, it will not be opened until the Messiah comes.

Strategies

Don't attempt to see the entire Old City in one day. Children quickly become saturated with the unusual sites, smells, and rocky walkways. If you have only two days, here is a suggested itinerary:

First Day: Begin at the Jaffa Gate exploring David's Tower including the multi-screen presentation. Walk on the ramparts toward the Kotel (Western Wall). After you've experienced the Kotel, climb up to the Jewish Quarter. To encourage your children up the long stairways, promise them a popsicle at the top! There are many cafes where you can have something to eat and drink. If your children are interested in archeology, choose an easy activity such as visiting the Burnt House. Or your may wish to shop at the Cardo.

> **A Note on Safety:** Because of continuing political unrest, many areas of the Old City should be toured only in organized groups. These include the Shuk, the Moslem Quarter, Hezekiah's Tunnel, Zedekiah's Cave, the Roman Square Excavations, and the Rampart's Walk, except for the area from David's Tower to the Kotel.

Second Day: Take a walking tour of the Jewish or Christian Quarters or of the tunnels underneath the Kotel. Then try an audio-visual show such as Voice of the Wall, To You Jerusalem, or the Temple Institute. Try to resist shopping until you're heading for your hotel or apartment. Otherwise, you'll have to carry your purchases while you tour. Later in the day, take the walk through Hezekiah's Tunnel.

WHAT TO SEE

The Tower (Citadel) of David/ Jerusalem City Museum

Outside Jaffa Gate
BUSES: 3, 19, 20, 30, 99
PHONE: (02) 283-394, 283-273; 24-hr. info: 274-411
HOURS: Sun.-Thurs. 10 a.m.-5 p.m.; Fri., Sat., holidays until 2 p.m.
　　　Guided tours in English Sun.-Fri. 11 a.m.
ADMISSION: You can buy combined tickets for the museum and shows.
　　　Tickets are sold on Shabbat.

This fabulous museum is a great place to launch your visit to the Old City. A variety of multi-media exhibits show Jerusalem during each period of Jewish history. Children can explore walls from the days of the Maccabees, and towers from the time of Herod. Don't miss the model of 19th century Jerusalem, the Dolls of Jerusalem exhibit, and the spectacular view from the tower. The museum offers family activities on the theme of exploring history. Call to find out what's on. You also can schedule a Bar/Bat Mitzvah celebration here. In summer, there are concerts in the courtyard. Check the newspaper for listings.

Sound and Light Show at the Tower of David

HOURS: Several nights a week; check times for English
ADMISSION: Fee

An impressive, 45-minute story about Jerusalem throughout history, with music, readings, and illumination. The show is held outside in the Citadel courtyard. Dress very warmly. Currently there also is an historical mystery show on Saturday nights.

TEENS

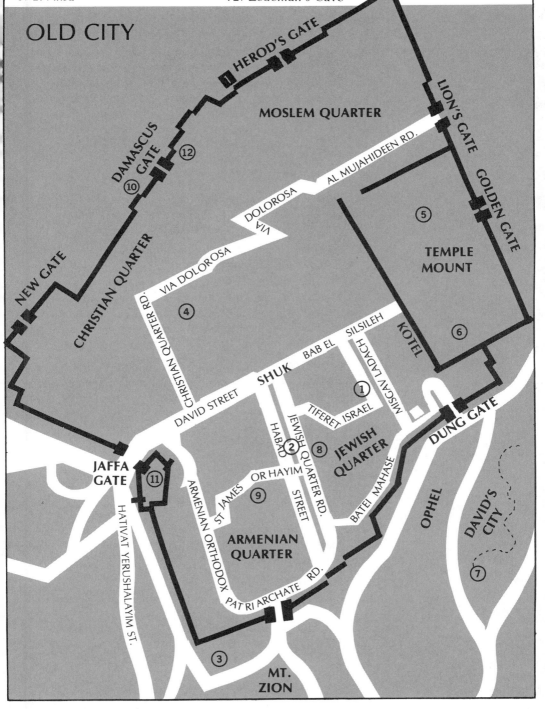

OLD CITY

HEROD'S GATE

MOSLEM QUARTER

LION'S GATE

DAMASCUS GATE

GOLDEN GATE

VIA DOLOROSA

AL MUJAHIDEEN RD.

NEW GATE

CHRISTIAN QUARTER

VIA DOLOROSA

CHRISTIAN QUARTER RD.

TEMPLE MOUNT

BAB EL SILSILEH

SHUK

KOTEL

DAVID STREET

TIFERET ISRAEL

MISGAV LADACH

DUNG GATE

HABAD

JEWISH QUARTER RD.

JEWISH QUARTER

JAFFA GATE

OR HAYIM

ST. JAMES

BATEI MAHASE

OPHEL

DAVID'S CITY

ARMENIAN ORTHODOX

ARMENIAN QUARTER

HATIVAT YERUSHALAYIM ST.

PATRIARCHATE RD.

MT. ZION

Ramparts Walk — Old City Walls
BUSES: 1, 38
PHONE: (02) 254-403
HOURS: Sat.-Thurs. 9 a.m.-4 p.m.; Fri. until 2 p.m.
 Watch the newspaper for notices about special night group tours
ADMISSION: Fee. Your ticket is for two days. You can walk one section
 and come back later that day or the next day to walk more.

These massive fortifications, designed for watchmen and city defenders, are now open to the public. You can ascend and descend at the Damascus and Jaffa Gates and the moat at the Tower of David. Only a quarter-mile stretch north of Lion's Gate is inaccessible because it borders mosques and burial grounds. From the Tower of David to the Kotel is about a 20-minute walk. Walking the "whole" circumference takes several hours.

THE KOTEL

The Kotel (Western Wall)
BUSES: 1, 38
WALKING: From Jaffa Gate, the shortest distance is down David Street
 through the shuk. Follow the signs. You also can walk through
 the Armenian Quarter
HOURS: The Kotel is always open.
ADMISSION: Free

The Kotel, the holiest of Jewish sites, is a remnant of the outer wall of the Second Temple Courtyard. Here, Jews have come for centuries to mourn the destruction of the Temple and to pray. For 20 years the wall was inaccessible to Israel, when Jerusalem was a divided city. In 1967, when the city was reunited, the plaza area was enlarged to accommodate more visitors and worshippers.

You should dress modestly to visit the Kotel. You can borrow shawls and paper *kipot (yarmulkes)* from the guard at no cost. Be prepared with small change, because you probably will be approached by charity-seekers. We like to give our children coins to share, so they can learn the value of *tzedakah* (giving to the needy). The little pieces of paper in the cracks of the wall are prayers that people write and leave there. Children like to write their own thoughts and stuff them into the crevices.

Friday night is the busiest time at the Kotel. Throngs of tourists gather to welcome Shabbat and to watch the yeshiva students and Hassidim dance and sing. A good time to visit the Kotel is early on a Monday or Thursday morning, when young Israelis and others celebrate their Bar Mitzvah.

Western Wall Tunnels
BUSES: 1, 38
PHONE: (02) 271-333. You must reserve ahead of time.
ADMISSION: Fee

Excavations have uncovered the entire length of the Western Wall and over 2,000 square yards of rooms, halls, and passageways. A visit here (best with a guide) gives new dimensions to your understanding of the Wall. There's an amazing mechanical model of the Second Temple where the ground falls away and you can see the city at its level of 2000 years ago. This site is wheelchair accessible.

JEWISH QUARTER

The Jewish Quarter lies above the Kotel, and you must climb several flights of steps to reach it. **BUS 38** stops at the Quarter's parking lot. You also can take **BUS 1** and walk from Mt. Zion or the Kotel, or take a bus to the Jaffa Gate and walk through the shuk or Armenian Quarter. In addition to historic sites, the Quarter has restaurants, cafes, galleries, and shops. It's a good place to buy a Bar Mitzvah tallit, hallah cover, or hanukkiah. There are maps and signs posted to help you find your way, as well as clean, attended public restrooms.

Temple Models (Atara Lyoshna)
29 Misgav Ledach St.
PHONE: (02) 894-466
HOURS: Sunday-Friday 9a.m.-4p.m.
ADMISSION: Fee

Small children will like the model of Noah's Ark, while older siblings, if they've studied about the Temple, will like the models of the ark and tabernacle built according to the specifications in the Torah and Talmud.

To You Jerusalem
1 Hayehudim St.
PHONE: (02) 276-625
HOURS: Daily 10 a.m.-5 p.m. and by appointment.
ADMISSION: Fee

This is a 45-minute audio-visual show about Jerusalem. Decide if your child can sit that long!

Voice of the Wall
PHONE: (02) 272-355
HOURS: Sun.-Thurs. 10 a.m., noon, 2:30 and 4:30p.m.; Fri. 9 and 11 a.m.
ADMISSION: Nominal fee

This is a great place to take photos. The half-hour tour includes a multi-media show about the Jewish connection to the area.

Genesis Jerusalem-The Jerusalem Experience Center
70 Hayehudim Street
PHONE: (02) 894-488, 894-489
HOURS: By appointment.
ADMISSION: Fee

Children five and older can dress in costumes from Jerusalem's rich past and "live the life" of the period. Birthday parties and Bar/Bat Mitzvahs also can be arranged here.

Cardo Maximus

The Cardo, from the Latin word for heart, was Jerusalem's main street in the 6th century. Excavations have revealed a street below, which Hadrian laid out in the 2nd century when he rebuilt the city after the Bar Kochba revolt. He called Jerusalem *Aelia Capitolina*, and tried to wipe out any signs of its Jewish origins. You can walk down steps and see even further, to a part of the city from the time of the Maccabees. As in Roman days, today's Cardo is a shopping mall with exclusive galleries and boutiques. The Cardo is always open; stores generally open at 10 a.m.

The Last Day
PHONE: (02) 282-005, 288-767
HOURS: Sun.-Thurs. 9 a.m.-5 p.m.; Friday until 1 p.m.
ADMISSION: Nominal fee

Dramatic *Life Magazine* photographs taken by John Phillips at the Jewish surrender of the Old City in 1948 are displayed in the Cardo. News clips from the time are shown on closed-circuit TV.

Old Yishuv Court Museum
6 Or Hayim Street
PHONE: (02) 284-636
HOURS: Sunday-Thursday 9 a.m.-4 p.m.
ADMISSION: Fee

You will feel as if you walked back a century when you enter this unusual museum. Clothing and household items such as a baby's cradle, laundry tub, and kitchen utensils are attractively displayed. Two synagogues of the time have been restored. The courtyard has hand pumps, rain gutters, and areas for growing medicinal herbs and vegetables.

Siebenberg House
6 Hagitit Street
PHONE: (02) 282-341
HOURS: Groups only; call ahead.
ADMISSION: Fee

Imagine digging up ruins in your basement! When the Siebenbergs began renovating their house in the Jewish Quarter., they found artifacts and construction dating back 3000 years. A brief slide show precedes a tour of the excavations.

The Burnt House
PHONE: (02) 287-211
HOURS: Sun.-Thurs. 9 a.m.-6 p.m.; Fri. until 1 p.m. English audio-visual
    shows every two hours beginning at 9:30 a.m. Hebrew shows
    every two hours beginning at 10:30 a.m. German and Spanish
    by appointment.
ADMISSION: Fee; you can get a combined ticket to this and the Wohl Museum

A short sound-and-light show tells the story of this home, uniquely preserved during the fire in the year 70, when the Second Temple was destroyed.

Herod's Mansions — Wohl Museum
Hakaraim Street
PHONE: (02) 283-448
HOURS: Sun.-Thurs. 9 a.m.-5 p.m.; Friday until 1 p.m.
ADMISSION: Fee; combined ticket availble with Burnt House

This large archeological park, recently opened to the public, will interest older children and their parents.

Ramban Synagogue
Jewish Quarter Road
ADMISSION: Free

When there were no Jews left in Jerusalem in the 13th century, the eminent rabbi and scholar Nachmanides paid Jews from Hebron to live and study here.

Hurva Synagogue
Jewish Quarter Road
ADMISSION: Free

The large arch that dominates the Jewish Quarter was rebuilt from the ruins of the Hurva Synagogue, destroyed in 1948. A photo exhibit tells the story. Some youth groups gather here to pray on Friday evenings.

First Temple Model (Rachel Ben Zvi Center)
Shonei Halahot St., corner of Plugat Hakotel (near Hurva Square)
PHONE: (02) 286-288
HOURS: Sun.-Thurs 9 a.m.-4 p.m. Call for program times in English.
ADMISSION: Nominal fee

Kids will like putting on 3-D glasses to see the model of Jerusalem during First Temple times. The audio-visual show is good, and there's a family treasure hunt.

Temple Institute Museum
24 Misgav Ledach St.
PHONE: (02) 894-119
HOURS: Sunday-Wednesday 9 a.m.-5 p.m.; Friday until 1p.m.
ADMISSION: Nominal fee

Audio-visual show and exhibits show the work of this serious research institute seeking to know what the Temple trumpets, menorah, and priestly clothing were like. Ask for an English-speaking guide to tell you the story.

THE SHUK

The Shuk (Arab Market)
HOURS: Daily from 9 a.m.-sundown

Hundreds of stalls line the narrow streets and alleyways of the Old City. Here you can buy Middle Eastern trinkets, clothing, pottery, rugs, olivewood carvings, spices, and food. The streets are crowded. Don't carry a lot of baggage, and hold on to your purse, camera, and pockets. Bargain hard for what you buy, but be polite while you offer 50% less than the asking price. Many stalls are closed on Friday, when Moslems observe their Sabbath. Stalls owned by Christians are closed Sunday. Because of the political situation, some people are uncomfortable shopping in the shuk.

TEMPLE MOUNT

Temple Mount
Up the staircase from the Kotel plaza
HOURS: Sat.-Thurs. 8:30-11 a.m., 12:15-3 p.m. Closed to the public on Fridays and Moslem holidays.
ADMISSION: There is no charge to enter the compound, but you have to pay to enter the mosques. You can buy a combined ticket to the Dome of the Rock, El Aksa, and the Islamic Museum, a small, domed building next to El Aksa.

The **El Aksa Mosque** is Islam's holiest shrine after Mecca and Medina. **The Dome of the Rock** (Mosque of Omar) is built around the spot upon which Abraham is said to have prepared to sacrifice Isaac, and Mohammed is said to have ascended to heaven. You must leave your shoes and parcels outside. Robes are available at no cost to tourists in shorts, short sleeves, or other immodest dress.

MOSLEM QUARTER

Via Dolorosa
FREE TOUR: Friday at 3p.m. from the Tower of Antonia near the Lion's Gate

Beginning at the Lion's Gate in the Moslem Quarter, you can follow the 14 **Stations of the Cross**, the route followed by Jesus to his crucifixion. The stations are marked by plaques. Of particular interest is the **Sisters of Zion Convent**, in which you can see excavations down to the Roman street level and underground pools that were part of Jerusalem's ancient water system. Nearby are the **Pools of Bethesda**, where the sheep were washed before being sacrificed in the Holy Temple.

CHRISTIAN QUARTER

Church of the Holy Sepulchre
ADMISSION: Free

The last five Stations of the Cross are at the Church of the Holy Sepulchre. The nuns and monks will be happy to show you around. Several Christian denominations claim ownership of parts of the church and its grounds. There are daily masses and processions and special services and pageants on Easter. If you climb to the small, Ethiopian monastery on the roof, the monks who live there will show you a chapel commemorating the meeting between King Solomon and the Queen of Sheba.

ARMENIAN QUARTER

The Armenian community in Israel numbers about 4,000, and if you walk to the Jewish Quarter via the Armenian Quarter you will pass many of their churches, museums, homes, and courtyards. Most buildings are closed to tourists.

DAMASCUS GATE

Zedekiah's Cave — King Solomon's Quarry
HOURS: Daily 9 a.m.-5 p.m.; Friday until 3 p.m.
ADMISSION: Nominal fee

Stones from this quarry, just outside the gate, were used for important public buildings in Jerusalem during the First Temple period, the days of the Maccabees, Herod's reign, and in modern times. This is a great place to explore. There are illuminated paths, and it's always cool.

Roman Square Excavations
PHONE: (02) 254-403
HOURS: Daily 9 a.m.-4 p.m.; Fri., Sat. until 2 p.m.
ADMISSION: Free

Below the gate is a plaza with huge stones, possibly taken from the Temple, but certainly dating back to the time of the Bar Kochba rebellion in 135. The huge, ancient olive press explains why the road leading from the plaza has been called Olive Street.

HEROD'S GATE

Rockefeller Museum
Sultan Suleiman St.
BUSES: 27, 23
PHONE: (02) 282-251
HOURS: Sun.-Thurs. 10 a.m.-5 p.m.; Fri., Sat., holidays until 2 p.m.
ADMISSION: Fee

Check newspapers for archeological exhibits of interest to children. Guided tours are on Sunday and Wednesday at 11a.m.

Ophel Gardens Archeological Park

Inside the Dung Gate
PHONE: (02) 254-403
HOURS: Sunday-Thursday 9 a.m.-4 p.m.; Friday until 2 p.m.
ADMISSION: Fee or Combined Site Ticket

This is only for children who really enjoy archeology, but teens would enjoy it with a guide. Continuing excavations reveal 25 layers of settlement back to the 18th century BCE. Highlights from the Second Temple period include Gihon Spring and excavated walls and towers.

David's City and Warren's Shaft

PHONE: (02) 288-141
HOURS: Sun.-Thurs. 9 a.m.-5 p.m.; Fri. until 1 p.m.
ADMISSION: Fee

Yoav, King David's chief of staff, may have entered the city through this shaft in the ground from which water from the Gihon Spring was brought into the city. It's worth the effort to climb the 70 steps down and up, but leave strollers at home. Bring water. Currently there are no water fountains or bathrooms on site.

Hezekiah's Tunnel (Siloam Tunnel)

DIRECTIONS: You can walk from the Kotel is less than 15 minutes via
a foot path from the City of David. If you are driving, follow
signs to Siloam Tunnel. A taxi will deliver you to the tunnel entrance,
and you can arrange to be picked up later at the exit.
HOURS: Open all the time, but it's best to walk in summer or early fall
before the rains begin.
ADMISSION: Free

During the First Temple period, King Hezekiah was preparing to defend the city against a massive Assyrian invasion, and decided to redirect the water from the Gihon Spring to supply the city of Jerusalem. (Read *Chronicles II, 32,* for a description.) The 1600 foot-long tunnel still exists, and you can walk through it in about 45 minutes. Wear old shoes or sneakers, and prepare to get your feet wet. The water is 10-16 inches deep. Bring a flashlight — it's dark! If you forget one, you can buy long candles at the kiosk near the entrance. This is a favorite site for children, and it's free!

There are several places of interest here, including **King David's Tomb**, the **Room of the Last Supper**, the **Dormition Abbey**, and the **Chamber of the Holocaust** (see *Holocaust*). The **Diaspora Yeshiva,** located on the mount, has a band which performs lively Hassidic shows on Saturday nights at 8:30 p.m. in winter, 9:30 p.m. in summer. **PHONE:** (02) 716-841, 717-112

THE NEW CITY

Downtown Jerusalem is the business and shopping center of the new city. There are several museums and historic sites and dozens of restaurants and kiosks for snacks and meals. Some artists have their workshops nearby (see *Artists at Work).*

Ben Yehudah Street

It's fun to walk through **Ben Yehudah Street Mall** (closed to traffic) in the center of town. After you enjoy a soft drink, ice cream, or felafel and listen to the street musicians play, you can shop for t-shirts, army paraphernalia, and other tourist favorites. **Nahalat Shiva**, an early neighborhood nearby, has lots of outdoor restaurants, craft and book shops.

If you've run out of reading material, or don't want to carry already-read books home, stop at **Sefer v'Sefel**, 2 Yavetz St. They're happy to buy and sell you used books (and new ones, too). You can get a cup of coffee there while you browse. **PHONE:** (02) 248-237. Another used book store, **Book Maven**, is on Agrippas St. near Machane Yehudah.

Hall of Heroism
Russian Compound behind Jaffa Road
BUSES: 18, 20
PHONE: (02) 233-166
HOURS: Sunday-Thursday noon-4 p.m.; Friday 10 a.m.-1 p.m.
ADMISSION: Fee

This unusual museum is located behind the court building. If you come in the morning, do not be surprised to see handcuffed criminals being escorted to and from trial. The building was a hostel for Russian pilgrims, but in 1917, the Russian Revolution left the church without funds. It was leased to the British and became the maximum security prison for the entire country.

You can visit the prison yard, the cells, and the gallows. Of special interest is an escape tunnel used by Jewish underground fighters. The museum is cool, even on hot days. A snack bar is located nearby, across from the main Jerusalem police station.

Rav Kook's House
9 Harav Kook Street, off Jaffa Road
PHONE: (02) 232-560
HOURS: Exhibit and audio-visual show: Sunday-Thursday 9 a.m.-3 p.m.
Friday until 1 p.m.
ADMISSION: Nominal fee

The beloved spiritual leader and the first Chief Rabbi of Israel, Rabbi Abraham Isaac Hacohen Kook, lived here and founded Mercaz Harav Yeshiva on this site, now a museum. The rabbi's study and yeshiva have been restored. The audio-visual show is good, but aimed toward older children interested in Jewish history and learning. Classes and seminars are given here.

Anna Ticho House
7 Harav Kook Street
BUSES: 6, 11, 15, 18, 21
PHONE: (02) 245-068
HOURS: Sun., Mon., Wed., Thurs. 10 a.m.-5 p.m.; Tues. until 10 p.m.
Fri. until 2 p.m.
ADMISSION: Free

The artist Anna Ticho and her ophthalmologist husband lived in this house, one of the first built outside the Old City walls. The gallery, now a branch of the Israel Museum, displays Anna Ticho's paintings. It's a good place to rest while you are downtown. Order a hot chocolate, cold drink, or lunch in the cafe. Children will enjoy Dr. Ticho's extensive collection of Hanukkah lamps upstairs. There is a small Museum Gift Shop. Check times for the Hebrew story hour for children ages 6-10.

Tourjeman Post (*Emdat Tourjeman*)
Intersection of Shivtei Yisrael and Shmuel Hanavi Streets
BUSES: 1, 2, 11, 27, 99
PHONE: (02) 281-278
HOURS: Sunday-Thursday 9 a.m.-5 p.m.; Friday until 1 p.m.
ADMISSION: Fee includes movie

The Tourjeman house was built in the early 1930's on land owned by Hassan Bey Tourjeman. During the War of Independence, and the years 1948-1967 when Jerusalem was divided, it served as a military post on the border. You can see the original positions from which the Jewish soldiers fought. An audio-visual display, *Jerusalem — A Divided City Reunited*, and a movie about the 1967 battle for Jerusalem are shown. Students can gather information about Jerusalem in the library.

Meah Shearim
BUSES: 1, 11, 15

If you wish to walk through Meah Shearim and the other nearby Hassidic neighborhoods of Beit Yisrael and Geula, dress modestly. Men and older boys should wear long pants; women and girls, skirts or dresses and sleeves that reach the elbow. There are many good places to shop for a Bar Mitzvah kipah, tallit and tefillin, silver candlesticks, kiddush cups, and shofars.

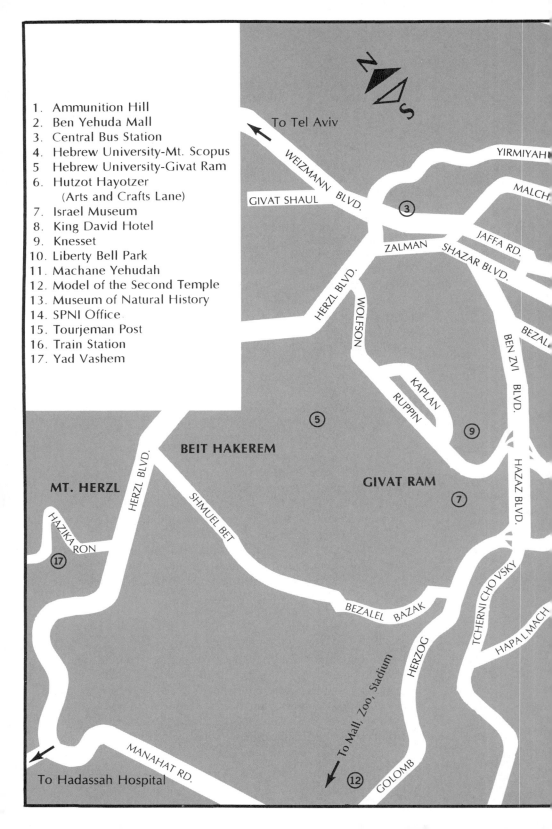

1. Ammunition Hill
2. Ben Yehuda Mall
3. Central Bus Station
4. Hebrew University-Mt. Scopus
5. Hebrew University-Givat Ram
6. Hutzot Hayotzer
   (Arts and Crafts Lane)
7. Israel Museum
8. King David Hotel
9. Knesset
10. Liberty Bell Park
11. Machane Yehudah
12. Model of the Second Temple
13. Museum of Natural History
14. SPNI Office
15. Tourjeman Post
16. Train Station
17. Yad Vashem

To Tel Aviv

YIRMIYAH

MALCH.

WEIZMANN BLVD.

GIVAT SHAUL

③

JAFFA RD.

ZALMAN

SHAZAR BLVD.

HERZL BLVD.

WOLFSON

BEN ZVI BLVD.

BEZAL

KAPLAN

RUPPIN

⑤

⑨

BEIT HAKEREM

GIVAT RAM

HAZAZ BLVD.

MT. HERZL

HERZL BLVD.

SHMUEL BET

⑦

HAZIKARON

⑰

TCHERNICHOVSKY

BEZALEL BAZAK

HAPALMACH

HERZOG

To Mall, Zoo, Stadium

MANAHAT RD.

To Hadassah Hospital

⑫

GOLOMB

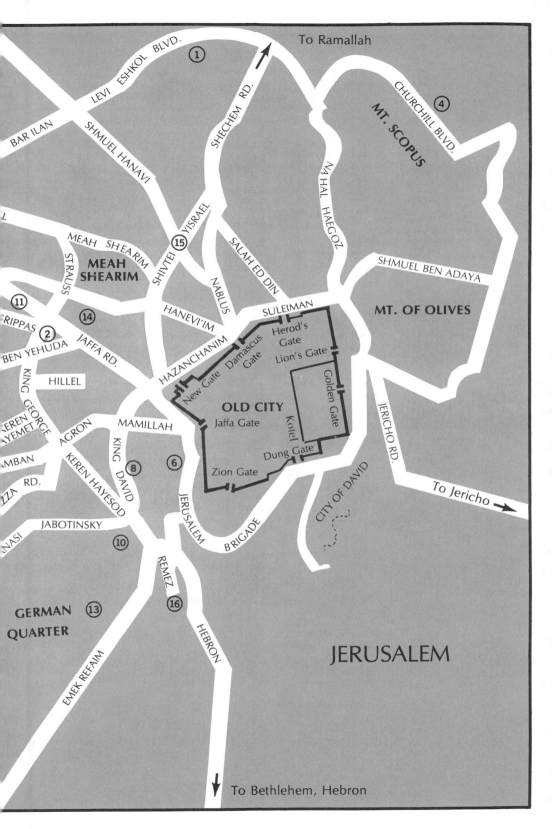

Kikar Davidka

One long block past the intersection of Jaffa Road and King George Street, you can see Israel's earliest weapon, the *davidka*, a home-made machine gun, displayed in a small park.

Machane Yehudah
Jaffa Road west of King George
BUSES: 6, 15
HOURS: Sunday-Friday 7 a.m.-sunset

Bring or buy a basket, and fill it with wonderful fruits, vegetables, and baked goods at this busy market where many Jerusalemites do their weekly shopping. Nearby are a dozen simple, kosher grill restaurants with delicious homemade humus and felafel.

Wolfson Museum — Heichal Shlomo
58 King George Street, across from Plaza Hotel
BUSES: 4, 9, 7, 31, 32, 45, 99
PHONE: (02) 247-112
HOURS: Sunday-Thursday 9:30 a.m.-1 p.m.
ADMISSION: Fee

Unusual items of Judaica, including Torah scrolls, maps, coins, and ceremonial objects are displayed here. Children will enjoy the collection of Purim groggers, the micrography, and dioramas of scenes from Jewish history. You will even see the morning prayers written on a kernel of wheat. Take the elevator up; the four flights of stairs are steep.

Taxation Museum
1 Agron Street, corner Rabbi David Ben Shimon Street
BUSES: 6, 15, 18, 20, 22, 30
PHONE: (02) 703-333
HOURS: Mon., Thurs. 10 a.m.-noon; Sun., Tues., Thurs. 1-4 p.m.
ADMISSION: Free

This museum warrants a short visit. Children like the still for making illegal whiskey, the uniforms of the customs collectors, and the cigarette-making machine. The museum has excellent materials on the taxation system since Biblical times.

Artists' House
12 Shmuel Hanagid Street
BUSES: 17, 19, 22
PHONE: (02) 252-636
HOURS: Sun.-Thur. 10 a.m.-1 p.m. and 4-7 p.m.; Fri. 10 a.m.-1 p.m.
        Sat. 11 a.m.-2 p.m.
ADMISSION: Free

If your child is a budding artist or wants to see what is happening in the Israeli art scene today, drop by here while you are downtown. Paintings and sculptures of over 400 member artists are displayed. There are lectures and concerts in the evenings and an art shop.

King David Hotel
23 King David Street
BUSES: 6, 15, 21
PHONE: (02) 251-111

Sit in the lobby, walk the magnificent grounds, or treat yourself to a drink or dessert (expensive) in this historic hotel. It served as British Headquarters before Independence, and in 1947, was blown up by the Irgun Zvai Leumi, a Jewish underground organization.

YMCA and Bell Tower
26 King David Street
BUSES: 6, 18, 15, 21
PHONE: (02) 257-111
HOURS: Monday-Saturday 9:30 a.m.-6 p.m.
ADMISSION: Small fee for access to the tower.

This building was designed by the same architectural firm that did the Empire State Building. Ride the elevator or walk the 207 steps to the bell tower for a wonderful aerial view of the city. The YMCA has a snack bar and restaurant, and there are carillon concerts on summer evenings. Members of any YMCA can use the facilities here, including tennis courts, weight room, and pool.

Skirball Museum of Biblical Archeology
Hebrew Union College, 13 King David Street
BUSES: 15, 18, 21
PHONE: (02) 203-333
HOURS: Sun.-Thurs. 10 a.m.-4 p.m.; Sat., holidays until 2 p.m.
ADMISSION: Free

Discoveries from the excavations of several Biblical sites are on display. This center for the Reform movement in Israel also offers lectures, courses, concerts, and ulpan classes.

Yemin Moshe and the Windmill
Plummer Square
BUSES: 4, 6, 7, 8, 14, 48
HOURS: Windmill: Sunday-Thursday 9 a.m.-4 p.m.; Friday until 1 p.m.
ADMISSION: Free

Yemin Moshe, the first Jewish settlement built outside the Old City walls, was financed by British philanthropist Moses (Moshe) Montefiore, for whom it is named. The area is now an artist colony with attractive galleries and gardens. Montefiore built the windmill to give the settlers a livelihood in agriculture. It now houses a museum in his honor. Montefiore's carriage was on display until vandals burned it down in 1968. Children can play in the **Mitchell Gardens** nearby or across the street at **Liberty Bell Park** (see *Where to Play)*. The **Zionist Confederation House,** a 1500 year-old structure behind the King David Hotel, has a lovely restaurant with a spectacular view.

Cable Car Museum
17 Hebron Street
BUSES: 21, 48
HOURS: Sunday-Thursday 9 a.m.-4 .m.; Friday until 1 p.m.
ADMISSION: Fee

If you look out the window you can see the cable car used during the War of Independence to sneak supplies to Jewish soldiers on Mt. Zion and to take out the wounded. It's a small museum with an interesting story.

GERMAN COLONY

Emek Refaim Street in this lovely residential neighborhood, has several outdoor cafes and fast-food restaurants.

Museum of Natural History
6 Mohilever Street
BUSES: 4, 14, 18
PHONE: (02) 631-116
HOURS: Sun.,Tues., Wed. 9 a.m.-1 p.m.; Mon., Thurs. until 6 p.m.
ADMISSION: Fee

The beautiful, shaded grounds are perfect for a picnic, or for small children to romp. Inside, their older siblings will enjoy the small, well-chosen collection of preserved animals and the push-button displays about anatomy. Learn what the various parts of the brain do, take your blood pressure, or move the bones on a skeleton.

The museum sponsors a two-week summer camp for children 6 and up, usually in mid-July. Registration takes place in June and must be done in person. During the year, after-school nature clubs study topics such as wildlife and astronomy. Combine this visit with a stop at the Doll Collection.

Doll Collection—ICCY (International Cultural Center for Youth)
12A Emek Refaim Street
BUSES: 4, 14, 18
PHONE: (02) 664-144
HOURS: Sunday-Friday 8 a.m.-3 p.m.
ADMISSION: Free

A large collection of dolls in national costumes from all over the world is on display.

The **L.A. Mayer Institute of Islamic Art** nearby features changing exhibits of jewelry, carpets, battle gear, and an unusual collection of clocks. Some exhibits may interest older children. If you organize a group of ten, the museum will provide a guide and arrange age-appropriate activities. **PHONE:** (02) 661-291.

EAST TALPIYOT

Tayelet (Sherover and Haas Promenades)
Hebron Road
BUS: 6

This is a beautiful place to view the Old City, especially at sunset. Children will enjoy the grassy play area. There are concerts in summer. The restaurant and snack bar serve a variety of food.

The Magic Road

You need a car for this. Ask a native to direct you to the road — on the other side of the UN compound from East Talpiyot. The unusual geological structure of the road makes it seem as if you are driving uphill, when in fact you are driving downhill — and vice-versa. Kids love it!

TALPIYOT

Rav Mecher
17 Ha'oman St.
PHONE: (02) 794-881

This complex has movie theaters, coffee houses, and **Fun-Fun**, a play area with a child care program where kids can even get help with homework!

MT. HERZL AREA

Mt. Herzl Museum, Memorial Park, and Military Cemetery
Herzl Blvd., just past Beit Hakerem
BUSES: 18, 20, 27
HOURS: Museum: Sunday-Thursday 9 a.m.-6:30 p.m.; Friday until 2 p.m.
Park/ Cemetery: Summer: 8 a.m.-6:30 p.m.; winter until 5 p.m.
PHONE: (02) 651-1108 (Museum); 437-257 (Cemetery)
ADMISSION: Free

If your child is a history fan and has learned about Theodore Herzl, stop in the **Museum** to see his study from Vienna, recreated as originally furnished with his personal belongings.

Hundreds of Israel's leaders and war heroes are buried in the **Military Cemetery**. Most children will have studied about some of them: Hannah Senesh and other parachutists who died trying to rescue Jews from the Nazis; soldiers killed defending Gush Etzion during the War of Independence; the sailors of the Dakar submarine; Entebbe hero Yonatan Netanyahu; and Prime Minister Yitzhak Rabin. You may wish to bring a book of Psalms to recite a memorial tribute.

Yad Vashem Holocaust Memorial is nearby (see *Holocaust*).

Model of the Second Temple
Holyland Hotel, Bayit Vegan
BUS: 21, 21A, 99
PHONE: (02) 437-777
HOURS: Sun.-Thurs. 8 a.m.-9 p.m.; Fri., Sat. until 5 p.m.
ADMISSION: Fee

This large model of Jerusalem during the time of the Second Temple shows how the Temple dominated the city. It's a toss-up if you should come before or after touring the Old City. I think it makes more sense to see it after at least one visit to the Kotel. Children 6 and over will appreciate the detail and accuracy of the work. You can borrow a guidebook from the cashier or purchase one at the snack bar. The miniature golf course at the hotel is set in a cool garden area.

Hadassah Hospital
Ein Kerem
BUSES: 19, 27, 52
PHONE: (02) 416-333
HOURS: Guided tours Sun.-Thurs.at 8:30 a.m.-2:30 p.m. on the half hour (except for 1:30 p.m.); Friday at 9:30, 10:30, 11:30 a.m.
ADMISSION: Nominal fee

There are hourly tours of the Chagall Windows in the chapel. The Yael Gift shop at the hospital is a good place to buy inexpensive souvenirs. Half-day tours of all Hadassah facilities (Ein Kerem, Mt. Scopus, and educational institutions) are held Sunday, Tuesday, and Thursday and cost $15 per person.

Havat Nokdim Experiential Farm
PHONE: (02) 434-280
HOURS: Programs at 9:30 a.m., 12:30 and 3 p.m. during summer and school vacations
ADMISSION: Fee; discount for adults!

The 2½-hour program for children ages 3 and up includes hands-on activities, such as milking sheep, bottle-feeding lambs, wool work, and making butter and pita.

GIVAT RAM

This section of town is where you will find the science campus of the **Hebrew University**, the **Knesset** (Israel's Parliament), the **Supreme Court**, the **Prime Minister's Office,** and several major museums.

The Hebrew University
BUSES: 9, 24, 28
PHONE: (02) 658-5376

The **National Library** is a good place to do research if one of your children has a project to complete. All information personnel on the ground floor speak English. Walk up one flight to see the Ardon Window depicting Isaiah's vision. It's one of the two largest stained-glass windows in the world. Albert Einstein's archives are on exhibit, as are old Biblical manuscripts. The Library is open from 10 a.m.-6 p.m.

In the **Berman Building** you can see models of hundreds of fish from the Red Sea. The **Levi Building** has an exhibit on bird and animal migration. How **do** those birds and animals know where to go and how to get back? Stop to see the geology collection in the **Earth Sciences Building**. There are fossils and a model of a dinosaur that lived in the area and left its footprints in Beit Zayit (see *Between Jerusalem and Tel Aviv).*

You can get bargain lunches at the Administration Building (*Binyan Hahanhala*) and at the *Menza,* the student cafeteria. Fancier meals are served at Belgium House. The Book Store has moderately priced gifts and souvenirs.

Botanical Garden
Ruppin St., at the edge of campus
BUSES: 9, 24
PHONE: (02) 636-342; Restaurant 584-551
HOURS: Open all day.
ADMISSION: Free

A beautiful place for a walk, a picnic, or lunch.

The Knesset
BUSES: 9, 24, 28, 99
PHONE: (02) 753-333
HOURS: Free tours Sunday and Thursday 8:30 a.m.-2 p.m.
   In session Monday-Wednesday 4-9 p.m. during winter
ADMISSION: Free

When the Knesset is in session, you can watch from the visitor's gallery. Even if you don't know Hebrew, you will enjoy the very animated lawmakers. Bring your passport for identification.

The Supreme Court

BUSES: 9, 24
PHONE: (02) 759-612
HOURS: Tours Sun.-Thurs. 11 a.m. in Hebrew, noon in English
ADMISSION: Free

Opened in 1992, this striking building blends contemporary and Middle East motifs. Older children may enjoy the 45-minute tour, which includes a 20-minute film and background on Israel's legal system.

Coin Exhibit

Bank of Israel, 20 Kaplan Street
PHONE: (02) 655-2845, 655-2828
HOURS: Sun, Tues, Thurs. 8:30 a.m.-1 p.m.
ADMISSION: Free

Ancient and modern Israeli coins, bank notes, and commemorative medals are displayed.

The Israel Museum

BUSES: 9, 28, 24, 99; there is a free shuttle to the main entrance for the elderly and disabled
PHONE: (02) 708-811; Library: 708-886; Youth Wing: 708-835
HOURS: Sun., Mon., Wed., Thurs. 10 a.m.-5 p.m.; Tues. 4-10 p.m.
Fri. 10 a.m.-1 p.m.; Sat. 10 a.m.-4 p.m.
Museum Highlights in English: Sun.-Fri. 11a.m., Tues. 4:30 p.m.
ADMISSION: Fee

The Israel Museum is more than a museum. It is the major cultural center of Jerusalem and features a variety of programs for children.

On Fridays the museum takes out an advertisement in the *Jerusalem Post*, listing the coming week's activities Permanent exhibits include a model of a synagogue from Cochin, India, Jewish costumes from different countries, Hanukkah and Shabbat lamps, and well-displayed archeological finds. Slide shows, recorded explanations, and reconstructed models of what life was like in the past help children enjoy and understand the significance of what they see. The **Dead Sea Scrolls** are exhibited in an unusual building called the **Shrine of the Book.** You can take a free museum tour or explore by yourself.

Recent children's exhibits in the **Ruth Youth Wing** have included, "Meet the Israeli Artist," "Heroes," and "Mirrors." Touching is encouraged. There are computers to play with in the multi-media corners. The **Recycling Room** is a pleasant place to try your hand at creating items out of industrial refuse. The **Children's Library** has puzzles and picture books in many languages. On Wednesdays there is a Mother Goose program in English for 2-4 year olds. Tuesday afternoons are for hands-on family programs. Hebrew and English storytellers perform several times a week, and children's films are shown. There are after-school activities, summer camp, holiday workshops, and entertainment featuring magicians, puppets, and music. Children's concerts are given in the museum courtyard.

Outside, there are wonderful playgrounds. My children have always enjoyed climbing and fantasizing in the **Billy Rose Sculpture Garden.**

In addition to a restaurant, there are ice-cream and drink vendors outside in summer. At the **Museum Shop** you can buy unusual (though not inexpensive) gifts, including games and puzzles. Members get reductions for special events, are eligible to take museum courses, and get a discount in the Museum Shop. Family membership is about $50 for half a year.

Bar/Bat Mitzvah/Birthday Bonus: For a fee, the museum will arrange a "happening" to celebrate a child's Bar or Bat Mitzvah or birthday.

Bible Lands Museum
25 Granot Street
BUSES: 9, 17, 24, 99
PHONE: (02) 611-066
HOURS: Sun.-Thurs. 9:30 a.m.-5:30 p.m.; Wed. until 9:30 p.m.
   Fri. until 2 p.m.; Sat. 11a.m.-3 p.m.; Daily guided tours.
ADMISSION: Fee

Ask to participate in a **Family Treasure Hunt,** and a guide will take you through the museum and make archeology an adventure geared to the ages of your children. During week-long school holidays, the museum runs creative arts and exploration programs, and there is a day-camp in summer. The museum will also organize theme birthday parties and has a Bar/Bat Mitzvah program.

Bloomfield Science Museum
Ruppin Road, next to Hebrew University campus
BUSES: 9, 24, 28
PHONE: (02) 618-128
HOURS: Mon., Wed., Thurs. 10 a .m.-6 p.m.; Tues. until 8p.m.
   Fri. until 1 p.m.; Sat. until 3 p.m.; closed Sunday.
   Extended summer hours.
ADMISSION: Nominal fee

The new science museum offers a range of hands-on activities with explanations in Hebrew, English, and Arabic. Check the day's program as you come in. There are permanent exhibits where you can use pulleys, levers, and wave machines, as well as frequent demonstrations of scientific principles with audience participation.

On holidays and vacations, do-it-yourself workshops in areas such as printing and rocketry are scheduled. Sometimes there is science story-telling; other times you may bump into a guide dressed as Newton. The museum is always expanding and experimenting. The **Youth Wing** has activities for children ages 3-9. You can celebrate a birthday at the museum with a program of scientific fun. The cafeteria serves lunch, snacks, and drinks.

MALHA AREA

Eyn Yael Living Museum
Refaim Valley
BUS: 26
PHONE: (02) 413-257
HOURS: Saturday and Sunday 9 a.m.-3 p.m.
ADMISSION: Small entrance fee plus activity fees.

This stunningly beautiful outdoor, living museum specializes in old-fashioned arts and crafts activities for children from pre-school through teen-age. They can weave, create mosaics and pottery, milk sheep, make cheese, bake bread, and more! There are hikes and donkey rides "up to Jerusalem" to celebrate Jerusalem 3000. You can come for an hour or a whole day. There also is a lovely picnic area.

Tisch Family Zoological Gardens
BUS: 26
PHONE: (02) 430-111
HOURS: Sat.-Thurs. 9 a.m.-6 p.m.; Fri. until 3 p.m.   Ticket office closes
        one hour before the zoo.
ADMISSION: Fee

A modern, open space zoo with many rare animals native to Israel and mentioned in the Bible. The petting section is quite unusual. You can even hold a boa constrictor and an iguana. The small animal house features a rain forest. This is a lovely place for a walk and a picnic. There are seasonal pony rides. There's a gift shop and snack bar. Ask about the special nature and art courses for children.

 TEENS

The Jerusalem Mall (*Canion Yerushalayim*)
BUS: 6, 24, 31
PHONE: (02) 335-416; **Children's services**: 363-177
HOURS: Mon., Wed., Thurs. 9:30 a.m.-9 p.m.; Tues until 10 p.m.
        Fri. until 2:30 p.m.; Sat. opens one hour after end of Shabbat
        Restaurants and cafes open until midnight.

This mall is cool in summer, warm in winter. Jerusalemites spend many hours here shopping, eating, seeing movies, and strolling. You can leave your children at **Playland** or **Shvung**, two centers with climbing areas, slides, and games, while you shop or have a quiet lunch. The playlands also do birthday parties.

MT. SCOPUS

Ammunition Hill (*Givat Hatachmoshet*)
Eshkol Blvd., Ramat Eshkol
BUSES: 4, 9, 25, 26, 28, 39, 99
PHONE: (02) 829-132
HOURS: Sun.-Thurs. 9 a.m.-5 p.m.; Fri. until 1 p.m.; closed Sat.
ADMISSION: Fee for museum

This park is the site of a major Six Day War battle in which Israeli forces took the "unconquerable" Jordanian outpost controlling the approaches to Mt. Scopus. Guided tours in English, Spanish, Russian, and Yiddish are available on request. The **museum**, one large bunker, is a memorial to those who died fighting for Jerusalem. Firearms from Israel's wars, and photos and memorabilia from the Battle for Jerusalem are displayed. A short film plays continuously in English and Hebrew. Ouside, bunkers are open for imaginative play. Picnics are not permitted.

Hebrew University
BUSES: 4A, 9, 23, 26, 28, 46, 99
PHONE: (02) 882-819, 882-933
HOURS: Tours daily at 11 a.m.
ADMISSION: Free guided tours in English leave from the Bronfman
Visitor's Center in the Administration Bldg. Sun.-Thurs. at 11a.m.

This campus houses the humanities, social science, and law faculties of the university. You can see the old buildings (including the amphitheater where the University was dedicated) and the new complex built since 1967. Kids enjoy the computerized library. The **Botanical Garden** features a section for the blind with plants of special fragrance and texture labeled in braille. The restaurant in the Education Building has great humus and felafel, and the **Maiersdorf Faculty Club** serves breakfast and lunch. The view from the Club's roof is among the best in town.

MOUNT OF OLIVES

Don't miss the beautiful view of Jerusalem from the **Intercontinental Hotel** on the edge of the oldest Jewish cemetery in the world. You can usually find a camel driver willing (for a fee) to take your picture atop a friendly camel. You can ride bus 42 or 43 up from the Damascus Gate.

HOLOCAUST

Parents may want to visit these museums ahead of time to determine which exhibits are appropriate for their children. We feel it is important to take our children to Holocaust memorials, but not all parents agree.

Yad Vashem
Off Herzl Boulevard
BUSES: 13, 17, 17a, 20, 21, 23, 27 to Mt. Herzl (plus a half-mile walk)
   Bus 99 goes all the way.
PHONE: (02) 751-611
HOURS: Sun.-Thurs. 9 a.m.-5 p.m.; Fri., holiday eves until 2p.m..
   Closed Sat. **Guided tours in English** of the Historical
   Museum: Sun. and Wed. 10a.m.
ADMISSION: Free

This monument to the victims of the Holocaust contains photos, documents, memorabilia, and art in several museums and archives. Make sure to see the striking **Memorial to the Children,** the children's art from Thereisenstadt, the cattle car from Poland used to transport Jews to the camps, and the boat from Denmark that ferried Jews to freedom in Sweden. The new **Valley of the Communities** has the names of 5,000 destroyed European communities engraved on massive boulders.

If you want to search for lost members of your family in the **Hall of Names**, bring as much information as possible. You may wish to prepare a prayer for your family to recite at the **Hall of Remembrance.**

Yad Vashem is a powerful place. Set atop the Mountain of Remembrance overlooking the Jerusalem hills, its tree-lined avenues of tribute, inspiring sculptures, and evocative architecture communicate a sense of awe. Children will be moved by a visit to the grounds, even if you decide not to take them into the museums.

Holocaust Seminar
Men's Heritage House, 2 Ohr Hahayim St., Jewish Quarter
PHONE: (02) 272-224 after 5 p.m. (Must register in advance.)
HOURS: Friday 8:30 a.m.-2:30 p.m.
ADMISSION: Fee includes transportation and light refreshments

A serious tour of Yad Vashem with expert Asher Wade. The film *Genocide* is shown...very moving but heavy-going.

Chamber of the Holocaust

Mt. Zion
BUSES: 1, 38, 99
PHONE: (02) 715-105
HOURS: Sun.-Thurs. 8:30 a.m.-5:30 p.m.; Fri. until 1 p.m.
ADMISSION: Free. A donation may be solicited.

Memorial plaques for destroyed communities, and artifacts from the Holocaust are displayed in a dark hall and open courtyard. If you phone first and arrange to come in the morning, you can see a film, *Children of the Holocaust.*

MUSIC AND THEATER

Check newspapers for English story hours at community centers, museums, and theaters:

Jerusalem Music Center. Mishkenot Sha'ananim. **PHONE:** (02) 234-347

Binyanei Ha'uma Convention Center. Shazar St. Home of the Israel Philharmonic. **PHONE:** (02) 655-8558

Jerusalem Theater. 20 Marcus St. Sherover Theater and Henry and Rebecca Crown Halls. **PHONE:** (02) 610-011, 617-167

Khan Theater. 2 Kikar David Remez. **PHONE:** (02) 718-281

Train Puppet Theater. Liberty Bell Park. **PHONE:** (02) 618-514

Habamah. 4 Yad Harutzim. **PHONE:** (02) 733-814

Gerard Behar Center (Beit Ha'am). 11 Bezalel St. **PHONE:** (02) 251-139

Pargod. 4 Bezalel St. They often have jazz and theater for young adults. **PHONE:** (02) 231-765

Beit Shmuel. 6 Shama St. **PHONE:** (02) 203-456

LIBRARIES

Central Library—Beit Ha'am

PHONE: (02) 254-158
HOURS: Children's wing: Sun., Mon., Wed. 12:30-7 p.m.
Tues. until 6 p.m.; Thurs. 2-7 p.m.

This is the best library for books in English.

American Cultural Center Library

PHONE: (02) 255-755
HOURS: Sun.-Thurs 10 a.m.-4 p.m.; Fri 9 a.m.-noon
Closed Jewish and American holidays

Only Israeli citizens can check out books, but anyone can come in to read and watch videotapes. The collection includes books on nature, education, and culture.

Hebrew Union College Library
13 King David St.
PHONE: (02) 203-333
HOURS: Sunday-Thursday 8:30 a.m.-5 p.m.

Extensive collection of English books about Jerusalem.

British Council Library
3 Shimshon St., Baka
PHONE: (02) 736-733, 736-737
HOURS: Mon.-Thurs 10 a.m.-1 p.m. and 4-7 p.m.; Fri. 10 a.m.-1 p.m.

Israel Museum Library. See *Israel Museum*

ARTISTS AT WORK

Jerusalem House of Quality
12 Hebron Street
BUSES: 4, 6, 7, 18
PHONE: (02) 717-430
HOURS: Daily except Shabbat 10 a.m.-6 p.m., but many artists leave by 4 p.m.

In addition to viewing the permanent exhibition of many of Jerusalem's artisans, you can see glass blowers, sculptors, potters, and silversmiths at work in the galleries above the museum. Unusual items of high quality are for sale.

Hutzot Hayotzer — Arts and Crafts Lane
14/16 Hativat Yerushalayim St., across from the Citadel
BUSES: 13, 19, 20, 23
HOURS: Sun.-Thurs 10 a.m.-5 p.m.; Fri. until 2 p.m.
 Sat. eves in spring and summer 8:30-11 p.m.

Watch weavers, glass blowers, musical instrument makers, and silversmiths at work in their studios. Beautiful, but expensive items are for sale. There are restaurants on the grounds.

Nekker Glass Factory
6 Beit Yisrael St., opposite Mir Yeshiva, Meah Shearim
BUSES: 27, 40
PHONE: (02) 829-683
HOURS: 8:30 a.m.-5 p.m.

Glass blowers make delicate vases, perfume bottles, wine cups, and dreidels. Items are for sale.

Yad Lekashish (Lifeline for the Aged)
14 Shivtei Yisrael St.
BUS: 3, 13, 1
PHONE: (02) 287-829
HOURS: Workshops: Sun.-Thurs. 8:30 -11:45 a.m.
 Gift Shop: Sun.-Thurs. 9 a.m.-6 p.m.; Fri. until 1 p.m.

Senior citizens are productively engaged in bookbinding, metal-work, needlework, silk painting, and ceramics in this cluster of workshops.   Their handiwork is for sale in the gift shop. They enjoy visitors.

Kuzari
10 Bucharim Street
BUSES: 9, 36, 35
PHONE: (02) 826-632
HOURS: Sun.-Thurs. 9 a.m.-5 p.m.; Fri. until 12:30 p.m.
   Workshop: 9 a.m.-12:30 p.m.

Watch local women create embroidered ethnic religious items and clothing.   There are handmade gifts for sale.

JUST FOR FUN

Angel Bakery
BUSES: 6, 24, 5
PHONE: (02) 658-0555
HOURS: Book ahead for day or evening tour.
ADMISSION: Fee

This huge bakery supplies bread and cake to much of the city. Groups of 10 or more can book a 20-30 minute tour to watch rolls being made. The smells are delicious and you get to taste!

Jerusalem Fire Fighters

If they're not busy, the firemen will show you around their **Givat Mordechai Firehouse.** Or stop at the **East Jerusalem Station** (on the road to Mt. Scopus) to see the Trenkle, the only fire engine in the world that can walk stairs.

Beit Shmuel
7 Shema St.
BUSES: 21, 18, 13, 15
PHONE: (02) 203-456
ADMISSION: Fee

Children's craft activities, holiday shows, and story hours are held in this center run by the Reform movement. Phone for schedule.

Kol Haneshama
57 Harakevet
PHONE: (02) 724-878

Workshops for parents and children on Jewish themes through movement, dance, and storytelling.

MITZVAH PEOPLE

Stop by and meet these mitzvah heroes, and see the good work they are doing. Often, they'll invite you to stay and help! They will also welcome your tzedakah money.

Noam Shabbat
18 Ezra Street
PHONE: (02) 825-129

Free kitchen and wedding hall. On Passover and Rosh Hashanah, there's a huge shoe give-away.

Yad Sarah Workshop
43 Hanevi'im St.
PHONE: (02) 244-242

This lending station for medical equipment welcomes volunteers. Maybe you can help build a wheelchair.

Tova's Kitchen
11 Joseph Caro
PHONE: (02) 822-789

Every Wednesday Tova Cohen prepares hot meals for 30 elderly people.

Rabbanit Bracha Kapach
12 Lod Street
PHONE: (02) 249-296

If you brought a new or gently-used wedding dress, or clothes, toys, and games (see *Plan Ahead*), drop them off, and the Rabbanit will find them good homes.

WHERE TO PLAY

Liberty Bell Park
Kikar Plumer
BUSES: 14, 18, 15
PHONE: (02) 735-029; **Train Puppet Theater:** (02) 618-514

A roller-skating rink forms the center of this park, which is one of the most popular family spots in Jerusalem. Climbing toys (including Jerry, a large green dragon), a sandbox, nice lawn, lots of shade, and paths for strollers make it a natural attraction. In the summer, the city offers various sports programs and skating lessons. Live entertainment, folk-dancing, musical groups, and storytellers perform in the outdoor amphitheatre. The park is an easy walk from the Laromme, King David, Sheraton, Windmill, and Moriah hotels.

The **Train Puppet Theater** gives regular performances. Tickets can be purchased at the door. Check the newspaper for the week's schedule. A **roller-skating** concession is open Sunday-Thursday 4-7 p.m. You can leave an I.D. or passport to rent skates.

> Almost every neighborhood has a community park, plus several little vestpocket parks with play equipment and benches.

Sacher Park
Ben Tzvi Blvd.
BUSES: 9, 24

Come for an afternoon picnic, ball game, or just to tumble in the grass. A fitness track and skating rink have been added. To rent skates, you must leave an I.D. or passport. The AACI Little League plays here.

San Simon Park
Shai Agnon Street across from the supermarket.
BUSES: 15, 24

This large, pretty park marks the spot of one of the dramatic battles of the War of Independence. Bring along a copy of *O Jerusalem* if you want historical background. In addition to a bunker, the park has a real tank to play on, along with a basketball court, sandbox, nice grass, and clear paths for strolling.

Ramot Parks. You need a car to reach the large park in the forest with climbing toys. A smaller park in the residential section has "Kippi Kippod," a large porcupine who stars in Israel's *Sesame Street.* Kids who have seen *Shalom Sesame* will love him.

The Monster in Kiryat Hayovel is a popular spot for kids. Super slides come out of the monster's mouth!

Jerusalem Forest on Herzl Boulevard is a good place for picnics, playing, and exploring.

Gilo Park, a superb park set in a forest, has wonderful wooden climbing toys, picnic benches, and a terrific view of the hills.

Efrata Street in Talpiyot has a small, but tasteful park with creative climbing toys. Bring shovels, spoons, and plastic containers to play in the sand. There's lots of shade on a hot day.

Musrara, one of the least posh neighborhoods in the city, has a small, pleasant park with a nice, wooden climbing toy.

WHERE TO SWIM

Hotel Pools

Many of the large hotels have pools and will allow non-registered guests to swim for a fee (about $15 per person). The pool areas often include small playgrounds. These hotels have pools:

Jerusalem Renaissance. 6 Wolfson St. PHONE: (02) 652-8111
King David. King David St. PHONE: (02) 208-888
Laromme. 3 Jabotinsky St. PHONE: (02) 756-666
King Solomon. 32 King David St. PHONE: (02) 695-555
Holyland Hotel. Bayit Vegan. PHONE: (02) 437-777
Hyatt. 32 Lehi St. PHONE: (02) 331-234
Jerusalem Plaza. 47 King George St. PHONE: (02) 298-666
Paradise. 4 Wolfson St. PHONE: (02) 651-1111
Holiday Inn Crowne Plaza. City entrance. PHONE: (02) 658-8888

Community Pools

Some local pools require purchasing a season's membership; others are open to the public. A number accommodate religious families by offering separate swimming hours or days for boys/men and girls/women. Only very small children can swim with the opposite sex. Most pools are open seven days a week.

Jerusalem Swimming Pool
43 Emek Refaim
PHONE: (02) 632-092

There's a 50-yard pool, separate children's pools, and a water slide right in Jerusalem. Your ticket will give you a discount at a nearby burger place. On certain evenings, there are separate hours for men and women. If the pool is open to members only, show them your copy of *Kids Love Israel*, and you can buy a day ticket.

Taylor (pronounced "Tyler")
Zangville Street, Kiryat Hayovel
BUS: 18
PHONE: (02) 414-362

The pool has a water slide. There is separate swimming for girls/women and boys/men in the afternoons.

Dgannogly Pool in Ramot is a covered, municipal pool with hours for separate swimming and hours for adults only. When the pool is crowded, only members may enter. PHONE: (02) 868-055

Kibbutz Ramat Rachel's pool is heated in winter and has a water slide and nice grassy areas. Often the pool is open to members only. PHONE: (02) 702-920

Jerusalem Forest Recreation Center pool has separate swimming on certain days. **PHONE:** (02) 416-060

YMHA Pool, 105 Rehov Herzog, is for members only. **PHONE:** (02) 789-441

YMCA pools in East and West Jerusalem are for members only, but you can use your Y card from abroad. **PHONE:** (02) 257-111

Blind Institute Pool, 6-8 Degel Reuven St., is a covered pool, open to the public with separate swimming hours for men and women. **PHONE:** (02) 652-0923.

Philip Lown Community Center in Kiryat Hayovel has a covered pool. **PHONE:** (02) 414-8996, 429-363.

On the Outskirts:

Beit Zayit has separate swimming on certain days. **PHONE:** (02) 346-217

Shoresh, 10 miles from Jerusalem, has a children's pool, water slides, nice grass, and a snack bar. **PHONE:** (02) 341-477

Moshav Neveh Ilan's pool is covered in winter. Show your copy of *Kids Love Israel* and you can buy day tickets. There also are tennis courts and a small zoo. On Monday evenings in summer, there's a flea market. **PHONE:** (02)343-359, 348-236

Kibbutz Ma'alei Hahamisha has adult and children's pools open to the public, as well as tennis, ping pong, volleyball, a children's playground, and grassy areas. **PHONE:** (02) 342-591

Neveh Yaakov has open and enclosed pools. Call for separate swimming hours. The complex also includes sports and cultural activities. **PHONE:** (02) 830-597

Gal Gai. See *Between Jerusalem and Tel Aviv*

TENNIS

Jerusalem Tennis Center
7 Almaliach St., Katamonim
BUSES: 4, 18, 99
PHONE: (02) 792-716
HOURS: Sun.-Thurs 7 a.m.-3 p.m and 7-10 p.m.
Fri. 7 a.m.-6 p.m.; Sat. 8 a.m.-4 p.m.

This 19-court center offers year-round lessons. Children up to age 18 can use the courts during the day for free. If you leave your watch or another valuable as a deposit, you can borrow racquets and balls. Courts are assigned on a first-come, first-served basis.

Other Courts

Moadon Haoleh. 5 Alkalai St. PHONE: (02) 633-718

Jerusalem Sports Club. Hatzfira St. PHONE: (02) 632-125

Beit Taylor. PHONE: (02) 414-362

Mitzpeh Rachel. Ramat Rachel. PHONE: (02) 702-920

If you're a **YMCA** member, you can use the courts at the two Jerusalem Y's. The **Holiday Inn, Holyland, Renaissance,** and **Hyatt** hotels have courts.

SPORTS

Information on sports clubs and lessons in Jerusalem is available at the **Berlin Center,** open Sun.-Thurs. 8 a.m.-3 p.m. PHONE: (02) 241-379

Miniature Golf. The course at the **Holyland Hotel** is open day and night; at the **Holiday Inn**, admission to the pool includes use of the golf course.

Gymnastics. The **Goldberg Gym** in Malha has organized basketball and gymnastics classes. In summer, there's a 3-week summer gymnastics camp. PHONE: (02) 431-331

Bowling. Talpiot Mall, 18 Yad Harutzim St. PHONE: (02) 732-195

Scuba. The first part of **Siam Diving's** 6-day course for kids ages 12 and over is held in Jerusalem. Part Two is in Eilat. A student completing the course will be certified as a one-star diver for open water. You need a medical exam and x-ray which can be arranged through Siam or a health service. PHONE: (02) 257-808

Roller Skating. See *Where to Play* for information on Liberty Bell and Sachar Parks.

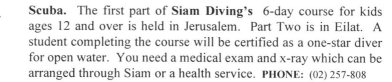

Soccer. Betar Jerusalem is one of Israel's top soccer teams. Hapoel Jerusalem is in the second division. Both play at the **Teddy Stadium** in Malha. You can get tickets at the gate or through agents. PHONE: (02) 788-376

Biking. **Neve Ilan** runs bike tours for beginners and experienced riders. You can order box lunches. PHONE: (02) 343-359, 348-236. There's also a **Jerusalem Biking Club.** PHONE: (02) 342-572

My Hobby Club has a model airplane group. PHONE: (02) 242-086 from 4-7 p.m.

Desert Shooting Games
PHONE: (02) 355-665
HOURS: Daily 8 a.m.-sunset, but you need to reserve ahead
ADMISSION: Fee

There are laser guns, infra-red hunting guns, blow guns, and an archery court — something for everyone age 3 and up.

Folkdancing. Check the newspaper for classes at **Liberty Bell Park**, the **ICCY**, and at community centers. Folklore evenings of ethnic dancing and singing take place at the **YMCA** Monday through Thursday and Saturday nights. PHONE: (02) 257-111

HORSE AND DONKEY RIDES

Hama'ayan Ranch. 12 Lower Lifta, an easy walk from the Central Bus Station. Children age 7 and over can take a scenic guided ride from one hour to a full day. The charge is by the hour. They also have ponies.

Kfar Adumin. Bus 173 from the Central Bus Station. Ponies for small children, and hillside tours for children six and over. They also give riding lessons. PHONE: (02) 354-769

Oz Horses and Dogs International. Behind the TV building and in Lifta. Children from age 2 and up can ride a pony. Children 11 and up can tour the hillsides of Jerusalem. PHONE: (02) 380-296

Amir Riding School. Mei Niftoah, Ramot. PHONE: (02) 824-769

Moshav Neveh Ilan. PHONE: (02) 340-535

Donkey Tours. PHONE: (02) 244-605.

SPNI also runs donkey tours. PHONE: (02) 244-605

SHOPPING

T-shirts and **army surplus** clothes and equipment are for sale at stores along Jaffa Road and in the Ben Yehudah Mall. On Jaffa Road, teens can find a selection of **funky clothes** at low prices. **Baby equipment** is sold in many stores in the Talpiot Industrial area as well as at the malls.

> **Buyer beware!** Shopping in Israel — even in stores — is like dealing in a middle-eastern bazaar. Prices are rarely fixed, merchandise is not returnable, and refunds are unheard of. Before you buy, check prices at a couple of stores. As a rule, you get better bargains in the Jewish Quarter of the Old City than on Ben Yehudah Street.

If your 2 year-old has just fallen asleep on the couch, or you can't face dinner out with cranky pre-teens, call **Lazy Deliveries!** If you order from one of their regular restaurants, the charge is about $2.50. If you want them to pick up at a restaurant not on their list, or if you're staying in a neighborhood far from the center of town, the charge could be as high as $7. **PHONE:** (02) 733-369

Downtown has a variety of fast food restaurants. Agrippas Street and Machane Yehudah feature grill restaurants. The Ben Yehudah Mall has cafes for light dairy meals, such as grilled cheese and omelets. There are felafel places on almost every block. New restaurants are opening all the time. Here are a few we like:

Fast Food: The **Kosher Food Court** at the Malha Mall has separate sides for milk and meat. There's also a **Pizza Hut** in the mall, a **Bagel Nosh**, and several coffee shops. The bakeries on the ground floor serve hot baked goods.

Burger Ranches:
Emek Refaim St. PHONE: (02) 666-990
Central Bus Station. PHONE: (02) 233-766
18 King George St. PHONE: (02) 233-766

Pizza Places With Free Delivery:
Big Apple. PHONE: (02) 233-888
Home Pizza. PHONE: (02) 618-111
Trevi Pizza. PHONE: (02) 722-249
May Pizza. PHONE: (02) 639-450
Pushka Pizza. PHONE: (02) 780-593

Kafe Kafit. 35 Emek Refaim. This terrific outdoor cafe is shaded in the summer and has outdoor heaters in winter. You can order a half-salad for the kids. Baked potato dishes are terrific. Try an off hour. Israel's writers and artists gather here, and it's often crowded. **PHONE:** (02) 635-284

Stop by a tourist office or hotel desk and pick up one of the *Jerusalem Menu* booklets, containing menus and discount coupons for several of the city's unusual ethnic restaurants.

Off the Square. 6 Yoel Salomon St. A vegetarian restaurant that serves large portions. **PHONE:** (02) 242-549

Ima. 178 Agrippas. You can share the huge portions at this grill restaurant. They also deliver. **PHONE:** (02) 246-860

Mifgash Ha'esh. 23 Yirmiahu. Grill. **PHONE:** (02) 388-888

Mamma Mia. 38 King George. Italian food. **PHONE:** (02) 248-080

Shor-Habar. 3 Yavetz St. Steaks and burgers with a South African flavor. **PHONE:** (02) 244-395

The 7th Place. 37 Hillel (in Beit Agron). Indian-vegetarian. **PHONE:** (02) 254-495

Village Green. Vegetarian. 10 Ben Yehudah (self-service); **PHONE:** (02) 252-007. 1 Bezalel (table service). **PHONE:** (02) 251-464

Norman's. 3 Hama'alot St. American burgers and ribs. Reservations recommended. Kids portions. **PHONE:** (02) 253-446

Rahmo. Machane Yehudah Market. Try their famous humus and soup. **PHONE:** (02) 234-595

Flamingo. 30 Pe'er Koenig, Talpiot. Steak, chicken, chips, and salad. **PHONE:** (02) 783-430

Angel Cafe. Bell Tower, 3 King George St. Light meals and pizza. **PHONE:** (02) 233-105; **PIZZA:** 231-428.

Rosemary. 28 King David St. Dairy and fish in a garden setting. **PHONE:** (02) 258-157

Cardo Culinaria. First century Roman restuarant (kosher) in the middle of the Cardo. Togas for all! They're open for lunch noon-2 p.m.; dinner is for groups. **PHONE:** (02) 894-155

For that Special Night Out:

Pavarotti. Zionist Confederation House, Emile Botta St. Call to reserve window seats. The view is fabulous and the food tops. **PHONE:** (02) 251-179

Monitin. 220 Jaffa Rd. Fabulous food and enormous portions. **PHONE:** (02) 383-222

WHERE TO STAY

Jerusalem has a hotel for every pocketbook. In addition, a number of kibbutz guest houses with spacious grounds and good recreation facilities are located on the outskirts of town. A disadvantage is that if you don't have a car, you have to plan your touring with the bus schedule in mind. For additional information, see *Where to Stay* in the General Section. The following hotels offer something special to families.

Holiday Inn Crowne Plaza. Entrance to Jerusalem. Kids are free in parents' room. There's a children's program and gifts for the little ones. PHONE: (02) 658-8888

Jerusalem Renaissance. 6 Wolfson Street. Special holiday packages include children's programs during school vacations. There are indoor and outdoor pools. PHONE: (02) 652-8111; FAX: 651-1824; U.S.: (800) HOTELS1

King Solomon. 32 King David Street. A well-located hotel with a family plan. PHONE: (02) 695-555

Hyatt Regency. 32 Lehi Street. One child free in parents' room. Children get a 50% discount in hotel restaurants. There's a full-day children's program in summer and activities on school holidays. PHONE: (02) 331-234; FAX: 815-947; U.S.: (800) 233-1234

Sheraton Plaza. 47 King George. A family plan provides discounts for children in their own rooms. Bar/Bat Mitzvah kids stay free in their parents' room. The family gets free upgrading and a welcome cake, and the child gets a gift from the hotel. Ask your travel agent to check out the combined program with the Tel Aviv Sheraton and Royal Beach. PHONE: (02) 298-666; FAX: 231-667; U.S.: (800) 325-3535; Canada: (800) 526-5343

King David Hotel. You pay for the ambience here, especially if you want your room to overlook the Old City. The grounds are superb, there's a beautiful pool and several restaurants. Part of the Dan Chain. PHONE: (02) 221-111

Moriah Plaza. Family plan allows up to two children in parents' room to pay for breakfast only. During summer and school vacations there are activities for children 4-12. PHONE: (02) 232-232; FAX: 232-411

Paradise. 4 Wolfson St. Modestly-priced, this hotel has the Kiskushim Club for kids ages 4-12 on holidays and Shabbat. Kids' movies are shown evenings. The indoor pool is open year-round and there are nice outdoor grounds. Rooms have refrigerators; suites have kitchenettes. **PHONE:** (02) 651-1111; **FAX:** 651-2266

Jerusalem Gate Hotel. A simple, moderately-priced hotel near the Central Bus Station. There are family suites and children's rates. The lobby is lovely! **PHONE:** (02) 383-101; **FAX:** 389-040

APARTMENT HOTELS

Itzik Hotel. 141 Jaffa St. Simple, inexpensive apartments in the heart of the city. **PHONE:** (02) 243-879

David's Village. 4 David Hamelech. Large rooms with private bathrooms and an Old City view. Breakfast is included. Food is not kosher. **PHONE:** (02) 250-075

YMCA. King David St. Family rooms and excellent sports facilities in a great location. **PHONE:** (02) 227-111.

Apartotel. Jaffa Road, near downtown. **PHONE:** (02) 318-221

Lev Yerushalayim. 18 King George St. in the heart of the city. **PHONE:** (02) 300-333; **FAX:** 232-432; **U.S.:** (718) 338-6537

YOUTH HOSTELS

There are nine official youth hostels in Jerusalem. Those with family rooms include:

Hadavidka. 67 Hanevi'im St. Talk about location. This is right downtown! **PHONE:** (02) 384-555; **FAX:** 388-790

Beit Shmuel. 13 King David St. Another terrific location, next door to the King David Hotel. This is run by Judaism's Reform Movement. **PHONE:** (02) 203-466; **FAX:** 203-446

Beit Bernstein. 1 Keren Hayesod. Also right downtown, this hostel is affiliated with the Center for Conservative Judaism. Shabbat dinners are served. In summer it's often reserved for groups and closed to individuals. **PHONE:** (02) 258-286

Jerusalem Forest. **PHONE:** (02) 413-065; **FAX:** 416-060. Less central, but set in a forest with a pool and a magnificent view.

Beit Meir. Ramot Shapira, on the road to Tel Aviv. Lovely country location and religious atmosphere. **PHONE:** (02) 342-691; **FAX:** (02) 343-797

Kiryat Anavim. Swimming pool. **PHONE:** (02) 348-999

Teens and young adults can stay absolutely FREE at the **Heritage House** in the Old City. It's a great place for Jewish networking. No reservations are necessary. The Women's Hostel is at 2 Hamalach Street. PHONE: (02) 281-820; the Men's Hostel is on Or Hayim Street. PHONE: (02) 272-224. If you're going to be in the Old City on Shabbat during the summer, there's a communal lunch; other times manager Jeff Seidel will arrange for home hospitality. PHONE: (02) 271-916

GUEST HOUSES

Maaleh Hahamisha. Swimming pool. PHONE: (02) 342-591; FAX: 342-144

Mitzpeh Rachel. Ramat Rachel. Swimming pool with water slide, playground, and tennis courts. PHONE: (02) 702-555; FAX: 733-155

Shoresh. Swimming pool and water slide. PHONE: (02) 341-171; FAX: 340-262

Neve Ilan. Swimming pool, small animal farm, excellent sports facilities. Some rooms have kitchenettes. PHONE: (02) 341-241

CAMPING

Beit Zayit. This camping site has expanded. In addition to cabins, there are air-conditioned rooms and RV hook-ups. You can use the moshav pool which offers separate swimming for men and women. Synagogue services are available in the moshav or in nearby Har Nof. PHONE: (02) 346-217

Mevo Betar. Southwest of Jerusalem. You can sleep in a tent, cabin, or caravan; there are RV hookups for mobile homes. Swimming pool and kosher restaurant on premises. PHONE: (02) 345-474, 333-574; FAX: 334-474

BED AND BREAKFAST

Jerusalem Inns. PHONE: (02) 611-745

Good Morning Jerusalem. PHONE: (02) 511-270

JUDEA AND SAMARIA

The central, mountainous area of the country, including Bethlehem, Hebron, and Nablus, is referred to as the West Bank, or by the Biblical names Judea and Samaria.

Seeing these areas by yourself is not recommended, because of the changing political situation and the poorly marked and confusing roads. Hire a private guide or take an organized tour. If there have been recent conflicts, don't go.

TOURS

Hebron Hills Excursions. Run by Hayem Ma'ageni of Kiryat Arba, this group specializes in tours that reflect early Judaic and Talmudic sources in Judea and Samaria. **PHONE:** (02) 996-1015

All the major tour companies go to **Bethlehem.** Most include a stop for buying souvenirs.

SITES

Rachel's Tomb
Hebron Road, shortly before Bethlehem
BUSES: 160, 161
HOURS: Sun.-Thurs. 8 a.m.-dark; Fri. 8:30 a.m.-1 p.m. Closed Sat.
ADMISSION: Free

This is the spot generally considered to be the burial place of the matriach Rachel. Many come here to pray. You may wish to stop for a few minutes on the way to other nearby sites.

Bethlehem
7 miles east of Jerusalem

Christians will be particularly interested in Bethlehem, the birth-place of Jesus. Sites include the **Church of the Nativity** and the **Milk Grotto.** Entrance is free. You will find a wide selection of Christian religious items in olive wood and mother-of-pearl in the shops around **Manger Square.** The **Tourist Center** is there also.
PHONE: (02) 741-581

Herodian
DIRECTIONS: You need a car or a private tour to see this site. Either turn left after Rachel's Tomb and follow the winding road, or drive past Bethlehem and turn right at the sign after Efrat.
PHONE: (03) 696-1212
HOURS: Sunday-Thursday 8 a.m.-5 p.m.; Friday until 4 p.m.
ADMISSION: Fee or National Parks Ticket

This lavishly-appointed fortress was built by King Herod. It's about 2500 feet above sea level. Like most archeological sites, it will be more interesting to kids if you have a good guide, or on days when family activities are offered.

Solomon's Pool
2½ miles past Bethlehem

A side road leads to three pools and a small, 17th century Turkish fortress called the Castle of the Pools. The pools, which go back to Herod's time, were part of an ancient system to supply water to Jerusalem. There's no swimming.

Kfar Etzion Water Tower and Museum
Off Hebron Road near Alon Shvut
PHONE: (02) 993-5160
HOURS: 9 a.m.-4 p.m.
ADMISSION: Fee

The story of Gush Etzion, whose settlers staged a valiant War of Independence battle ending in a tragic surrender, is a dramatic one. If you are seeing the area on your own, ask at the museum for some historical background. There is an audio-visual presentation. Climb to the top of the water tower for a superb view of the area! The kfar has a Youth Hostel. PHONE: (02) 935-133

There's a **swimming pool** on Yellow Hill, on the road to Kfar Etzion. Call for separate swimming hours. PHONE: (02) 993-1035

Efrat

The new city of Efrat was founded by modern Orthodox Jews, many of them Americans, under the leadership of New York Rabbi Shlomo Riskin. Stop and walk around. There are several nice parks and play areas, a pizza place, and a supermarket.

Call the Efrat Yeshiva, **Ohr Torah**, to reserve rooms at Herodian, their lovely guest house. Frequently there are interesting seminars. PHONE: (02) 993-1911

Tomb of the Patriarchs — Hebron
HOURS: Early morning-10 p.m.
ADMISSION: Free

Because the **Tomb of the Patriarchs** (*Ma'arat Hamachpelah*) is located here, Hebron is considered one of Israel's four holy cities. (The others are Jerusalem, Tiberias, and Safed.) The book of Genesis tells how Abraham bought the burial cave for his family. The graves of Abraham, Isaac, Jacob, Sarah, Rebecca, and Leah are housed in a fortress built by Herod. If there has been political tension in the area, postpone your visit.

You can arrange a tour of the holy places or Shabbat hospitality in Hebron. PHONE: (02) 992-9333

BETWEEN JERUSALEM AND TEL AVIV

The area between Jerusalem and Tel Aviv has a wide variety of family-friendly sites. While you can get to and from a single site by bus, getting from one site to another is hard without a car. With a car, you can plan delightful day trips mixing historical sites with recreation.

For hiking information, call the **Yoav Regional Council.** PHONE: (08) 583-501 or (07) 874-222. **Avi Desert Safari** does a jeep tour through this area. PHONE: (02) 991-2217

The Castel
Right at the Mevasseret Zion exit on the Jerusalem-Tel Aviv Highway
PHONE: (02) 330-476
ADMISSION: Free

To get a superb idea of what the War of Independence battle for the Jerusalem-Tel Aviv road was like, visit the Castel, ten minutes out of Jerusalem. Climb up the fortress and see what a great vantage point the attacking forces had. The Palmach captured the Castel on April 1, 1948, lost, and recaptured it.

On the way to the Castel, stop at the **Harel Canion**, a new shopping mall right at the highway exit. It has shops, restaurants, and the world's first kosher McDonald's!

Givat Haradar (Radar Hill)
Behind Kibbutz Ma'ale Hahamisha
ADMISSION: Free

The famous Harel Brigade of the Palmach (and later Israeli Army) is honored with a monument. There are tanks to climb on and a magnificent view of the Judean hills.

Dinosaur Footprints
Beit Zayit exit on Jerusalem-Tel Aviv Highway
HOURS: Daylight
ADMISSION: Free

Look behind the water tower for real dinosaur prints.

Globusland
Near Neve Ilan
PHONE: (02) 349-111, 200-221
HOURS: Sat. and school holidays: 10 a.m.-5 p.m.; Fri. until 2 p.m.
ADMISSION: Fee

Don't expect MGM or Universal, but there is a wild west show, an exhibit of fairy tales, a make-up demonstration, and (our favorite part) a mummy left over from a special-effects movie. Be sure to see the stunt man!

At the gas station on the way to Globusland, you'll find good ice-cream and — believe-it-or-not — a restaurant dedicated to Elvis Presley. The **Elvis Inn** boasts 700 pictures of the The King, and the stereo plays nothing but.
PHONE: (02) 341-275

Ein Hemed, five miles west of Jerusalem, is a pleasant park for picnics. **PHONE:** (02) 342-741

Avshalom Stalactite Caves
Beit Shemesh exit on Jerusalem-Tel Aviv Highway
PHONE: (07) 991-1117
HOURS: Sat.-Thurs. 8:30 a.m.-3:30 p.m.; Fri. 8 a.m.-12:30 p.m.
        Picture-taking is allowed on Friday only.
ADMISSION: Fee

A short movie introduces you to the world of stalactites and stalagmites before you visit the spectacular geological formations. There are well-planned, well-lit paths. Egged and Galilee tours will take you to the caves and nearby sites, and JNF runs a tour once a week in conjunction with a tree-planting stop at American Independence Park. **PHONE:** (02) 635-261, ext. 13

Nes Harim Water Park
PHONE: (02) 330-261
HOURS: Call ahead; often it is closed for groups.
ADMISSION: Fee

This moderate-size water park and pool are attractively set in the Judean Hills.

Speedy Kef
Via Ein Kerem toward Mevo Betar
PHONE: (02) 345-164
HOURS: Daily 9 a.m.-5 p.m.; an hour later in season.
ADMISSION: Fee

Slide down 800 meters of the Judean hills on a mini-car. This is a metal slide in the mountain, not a water slide. Little kids will love it; their older siblings may find it tame. There are bumper boats and trampolines, as well as a swimming pool. A snack bar offers light meals. During Sukkot, there is a sukkah for picnics.

Kibbutz Tzora

Beit Shemesh exit on Jerusalem-Tel Aviv Highway
PHONE: (02) 990-8231
ADMISSION: Fee

The kibbutz offers organized tours, or you can call ahead and book your own family tour. Emphasize that you have small children who would like to see the children's house and computerized cowshed.

Tzubah Animal Farm

Kibbutz Tzubah — past Castel and right at Sataf Junction
PHONE: (02) 347-952
HOURS: Spring and fall: 9 a.m.-5 p.m.; summer until 7 p.m.
winter until 4 p.m.
ADMISSION: Fee

See birds, rodents, deer, and impressive snakes and lizards, some of which you can touch in the petting corner. Call to arrange a tractor ride of the kibbutz or an underground archeological hike. There are pony rides and a children's play area.

If you are touring Avshalom Caves or Kibbutz Tzora, **Gal Gai Pools** and **Waterslides** are nearby.

Canada Park

Latroun exit on Jerusalem-Tel Aviv Highway
HOURS: Daylight
ADMISSON: Free

Here is one of JNF's nicest parks, with tadpole-filled ponds, streams, archeological artifacts, hiking trails, picnic places, and a food concession. You can even go pony and horseback riding. Bring a stroller, picnic lunch, or barbeque equipment for an outdoor experience. Signs indicate where you can light fires.

Mitzpe Masua

PHONE: (02) 991-2464

A good place for hiking. There are donkeys for rent and a convenient kosher restaurant with a great view.

Beit Guvrin National Park and Tel Maresha

27 miles south of Jerusalem via Beit Shemesh
PHONE: (07) 811-020 (Kibbutz Beit Guvrin Tourist Services)
HOURS: Winter: 8 a.m.-4 p.m.; Summer: Open until 5 p.m.
ADMISSION: Fee

These limestone caves feature a columbarium (for 200 pigeons), and there are lots of underground cisterns and baths to explore. Ask for a map at the entrance. There are stairs, so a baby carrier

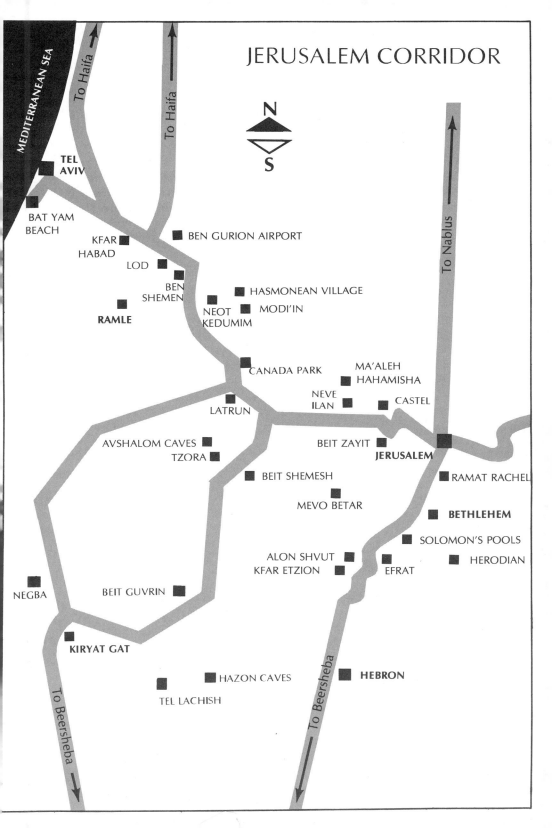

is better than a stroller. Music festivals have been staged here, and you can reserve a cave for a private party or Bar Mitzvah. There is a restaurant on the premises. To dig for a day here, call Archaeological Seminars in Jerusalem. **PHONE:** (02) 273-515

Tel Lachish
ADMISSION: Fee

Lachish was an ancient city destroyed and rebuilt by a series of rulers including Assyrians, Babylonians, and Persians. The original treasures found here are housed in the British Museum, but reproductions are being created as part of the restoration. On a cool day, families who like archeological sites will enjoy the hike up to the city from the parking lot.

Siurei Lachish Playpark
Near Moshav Lachish toward Beit Guvrin Caves
PHONE: (07) 889-514
HOURS: Currently open Shabbat, holidays, and vacations; phone ahead.
ADMISSION: Fee; adults pay half price and get a cold drink!

This amusement park offers mini-carts, laser guns, miniature golf, bikes, bumper-boats, and basketball courts for a day of leisure.

Armoured Forces Tank Park
Old Latroun Police Barracks
Latroun exit on Jerusalem-Tel Aviv Highway; look for a tank on a pedestal!
PHONE: (08) 255-268
HOURS: Weekdays 8 a.m.-4 p.m.; Fri. until 2 p.m.; Sat. until 4 p.m.
ADMISSION: Fee

What used to be an open field of tanks has been organized! It's a rustic, outdoor exhibit of 120 armoured fighting vehicles with steps to help you climb in. One tank has been cut open so you can see inside. Call ahead and request an English-speaking guide. There are two films; ask for the one designed for children.

Hazan Caves
Near Moshav Amatzia
PHONE: (07) 880-267
HOURS: Sun.-Thurs. 9 a.m.-5 p.m.; closes at noon Fri. and holiday eves.
ADMISSION: Fee

During the Bar Kochba revolt against the Romans (132-135 C.E.) these 35 caves were used as secret hiding places from which the Jews launched attacks. Only one person at a time can enter the narrow passageways. Inside are an olive press and storage rooms for 10,000 liters of olive oil. The name Hazan comes from the Arabic word *hazane* for closet.

Reservations must be made in advance. Specify that you want a tour in English. A videotape about the caves in English, Hebrew, or German precedes the tour. There is a snack bar and pony and camel rides. This area is particularly beautiful in spring, when abundant wildflowers bloom on the hillside.

Yoav's Post/Givati Museum
Kibbutz Negba
PHONE: (07) 752-004
ADMISSION: Nominal fee

Yoav's Post, the pock-marked building you see on the Beit Guvrin Road as you approach the kibbutz, was once British army headquarters. In 1948, the Arabs took it over, but later the Israelis captured the building and the Egyptian officers inside, including Gamal Abdul Nasser, the future president of Egypt. They were allowed to return to Egypt after the cease-fire that ended the war. The building is named for Yoav Dubnow, the commander of the Jewish forces, who lived in Kibbutz Negba.

Drive onto the kibbutz to see one of Israel's most impressive war memorials. You learn from the dates on the gravestones that some of the soldiers killed were only 16 years old.

A new military museum, dedicated to the Givati infantry, has been opened. A sound-and-light show depicts the battle for the site.

Barkan Castle
Kibbutz Negba
PHONE: (08) 774-312; rural accommodations: 774-799, 774-899

The castle is closed, but there are pony and donkey rides, a petting farm, Bedouin tent, a picnic area, and rural accommodations.

What's A Moshav?
Moshav Avigdor
PHONE: (08) 580-501
HOURS: Phone for arrangements.

The program introduces children to various farming activities, such as fruit picking, milking, and animal care. Guides speak Hebrew, English, and Italian. You can ride on a wagon through the orchards and bake your own pita for lunch.

Segulah Pool and Water Park
PHONE: (08) 585-757

This pool with water slides is sometimes open only to groups, so phone ahead. There is a good restaurant on the premises.

Shefela Museum
Kibbutz Kfar Menachem
PHONE: (08) 501-827
HOURS: Sun.-Thurs. 8:30 a.m.-12:30 p.m.; Sat. 10:30 a.m.-2 p.m.; closed Fri.
ADMISSION: Fee

This open air museum has a permanent exhibit of a kibbutz wall and tower, as well as changing exhibits on agriculture and archeology. A recent one traced the history of bread.

The Parrot's Nest
En route Kibbutz Na'an, a mile from the Bilu Junction towards Ramle.
PHONE: (08) 414-515
HOURS: 10 a.m.-4 p.m.
ADMISSION: Fee

You can play with and feed a wide variety of birds.

Kfar Habad

Airport exit on Jerusalem-Tel Aviv Highway
PHONE: (03) 960-7588
ADMISSION: Free

To make the Lubavitcher Rebbe (z"l) feel at home, his house at 770 Eastern Parkway in Brooklyn was reproduced at Kfar Habad, the center for the Lubavitcher Hassidim in Israel. If you would like to spend a Shabbat here as guests of the village, phone or write the Visitors Committee, POB 14, Kfar Habad; you and your family will be hosted, free of charge. Dress modestly, and remember that on Shabbat there is no driving, turning on lights, smoking, or writing. Your hosts will cheerfully explain the reasons for these laws and the Hassidic philosophy.

Behind the Honey

Kfar Habad
PHONE: (03) 960-6367
ADMISSION: Fee

This 3-hour program, run by the Lubavitcher Hassidim for children 6-12, includes meeting the beekeepers, a visit to the beehives, and a handicraft workshop using beeswax. At press time the program was available only in Hebrew.

Beit Halomoti (House of My Dreams)

Givat Brenner
PHONE: (08) 443-339
ADMISSION: Fee

There are thousands of Legos, blocks, bubbles, and games for small children to play with.

Mizkeret Batya Museum

40 Rothschild St.
PHONE: (08) 349-525
HOURS: Mon.-Fri. 8 a.m.-1 p.m.; Fri. until noon; Sat. 9:30 a.m.-1:30 p.m.

You can tour this old settlement from 1884. The museum is located in one of the six original buildings.

Gedera Settlers Museum

29 Habiluim Street
PHONE: (08) 593-316
ADMISSION: Nominal fee

An 1894 settlement featuring old agricultural tools and home furnishings.

Moshav Me'or Modi'in
PHONE: (08) 232-635
ADMISSION: Small fee

The residence of the late Rebbe Shlomo Carlebach (z"l) offers Shabbat family hospitality. Call ahead to visit the health food factory (closed on Pesach).

Hasmonean (Maccabean) Village
Between Modi'in and the Holon junction
PHONE: (08) 261-617
HOURS: Call ahead; the village does not have regular hours.
ADMISSION: Fee

This reconstructed village displays living styles in the time of the Maccabees. Allow an hour or two for the many hands-on activities, including reaping with scythes, writing old Hebrew calligraphy, baking pita, minting coins, and making pots from the abundant clay. The restaurant features home cooking! PHONE: (08) 264-510

Neot Kedumim — The Bible Landscape Reserve
Ben Shemen exit on Jerusalem-Tel Aviv Highway towards Mevo Modi'in
PHONE: (08) 233-840
HOURS: Sun., Mon., Wed., Thurs. 9:30 a.m.-sunset; Tues. until 6 p.m.
　　　Fri. and holiday eves until 1 p.m. Last admission is two hours
　　　before closing; closed Sat. and holidays.
　　　Guided tours in English: Tues 3:30 p.m., Fri. 9:30 a.m.
ADMISSION: Fee

Over 550 acres of flora are displayed in settings which recreate the wilderness of ancient Israel. There are self-guided trails, but I recommend you call ahead and request one of the superb English-speaking guides for a family tour that includes children's activities at the wine press, threshing floor, and olive garden. The Reserve specializes in a creative Bar/Bat Mitzvah Day program featuring a Biblical meal, Torah reading, mezuzah treasure hunt, and nature tour. The reserve is wheel-chair accessible.

Ramle
Off the Jerusalem-Tel Aviv Highway
PHONE: (08) 227-911 for City information.

The city is a mixture of old and new, with car repair stations next door to very old mosques. On Wednesday a huge, day-long open-air market draws Jews and Arabs from all over the country. Ramle's **Fischer Auditorium** is one of the best in the country. Check the performance schedule. You may be able to catch a play or musical group there. Across from **Haganah Park** you can take a short, but interesting boat ride in the city's underground lake.

TEL AVIV

Tel Aviv advertises itself as the city that never stops. It is the heart of big business, serious shopping, theater, and sports in Israel. This sprawling metropolis was started in 1909, when a group of 60 families from the port town of Jaffa settled on the sandy tracts of land they called "Hill of Spring," or Tel Aviv. Today, Jaffa is a small part of the busy metropolitan area, but it is being redeveloped into a picturesque center of galleries, cafes, and antique shops.

Suburbs to the south include the resort community of Bat Yam, the industrial city of Holon, and the posh area of Savyon. Suburbs to the east are Ramat Gan, a community of private homes and the campus of Bar Ilan University, and Bnei Brak, an orthodox enclave with many yeshivot. Ramat Aviv to the North is home to Tel Aviv University, the Diaspora Yeshiva Museum, and the Ha'aretz Museum and Planetarium.

GETTING THERE

From **Jerusalem,** take one of two express buses: #405 takes you to the new Central Bus Station; #480 takes you to Arlosoroff Bus Station (near the train station). Buses run from about 6 a.m. until 11:40 p.m. They board from the very last gate at the Jerusalem Bus Station, and leave as soon as they fill up.

In the early morning, buses also leave from several Jerusalem neighborhoods. Call Egged in Jerusalem to ask if there is one near where you're staying. **PHONE:** (02) 304-555. All buses on the Jerusalem-Tel Aviv line are air-conditioned and many are double-deckers. Buses from **Haifa** to Tel Aviv leave every 15 minutes.

With the improvement of bus service between cities there are fewer shared taxis (*sherut*), but you can still find them in the area of the Jerusalem and Haifa bus stations. Taxi Aviv/Yael Daroma leaves frequently from 12 Shammai Street in Jerusalem. **PHONE:** (02) 257-366. Other sherut service to Tel Aviv leaves from Rav Kook Street.

After many years in construction, Tel Aviv's new bus station has replaced the sprawling, disorganized station of the past. Now in one building you can get a bus to anywhere in the country. You can buy a ticket at the booth on each platform or, after hours, from the driver. There are many stores in the building including an indoor clothing market.

CITY NOTES

The area code is **(03)**. If you are calling from out of town you must dial these numbers first.

Important Phone Numbers

Police: 100
Fire: 102
Magen David Adom (Red Cross): 101
Mental Health Hotline: (03) 546-1111; Children: 696-1113
Egged Bus Information: (03) 537-5555
Dan Bus Information: (03) 639-4444
Arlosoroff (Northern) Train Station: (03) 638-3946
National Parks 24-hour Info (Hebrew): (03) 696-1212

Municipal Tourist Center
Central Bus Station, 6th floor, room 6108
PHONE: (03) 639-5660; **FAX:** 639-5659
HOURS: Sun.-Thurs. 9 a.m.-6 p.m.; Fri. closes at 1:30 p.m.; closed Sat.

Ticket Agencies

Contact these agencies for tickets to plays, concerts, museums, and major tourist sites:

Hadran. 90 Ibn Gavirol. **PHONE:** (03) 527-9955
Kastel. 153 Ibn Gavirol. **PHONE:** (03) 604-7678
Le'an. 101 Dizengoff. **PHONE:** (03) 524-7373
Rococo. 93 Dizengoff. **PHONE:** (03) 522-3663
Kanaf. 91 Allenby. **PHONE:** (03) 629-3838

Festivals:

Internationl Street Theater Festival — end of June
Cinematic Theater Jazz, Movie, and Video — February
Music Festival in Old Jaffa — Passover
Night Festival in Old Jaffa — first week in July
Beaches Festival on the Board Walk — July and August
Storytelling Festival — Dallal Center — August and Sukkot

GETTING AROUND

You'll get **to** Tel Aviv on an Egged bus, but the city of Tel Aviv has its own bus company, different from that in the rest of the country. **Within** Tel Aviv you'll ride **Dan** buses, and won't be able to use your Egged tickets or passes. Dan sells its own bus passes if you'll be staying in the city and riding the bus frequently.

TOURS

Egged Tours. 78 Ben Yehudah St. **PHONE:** (03) 527-1212

Galilee Tours. 42 Ben Yehudah St. **PHONE:** (03) 546-6333

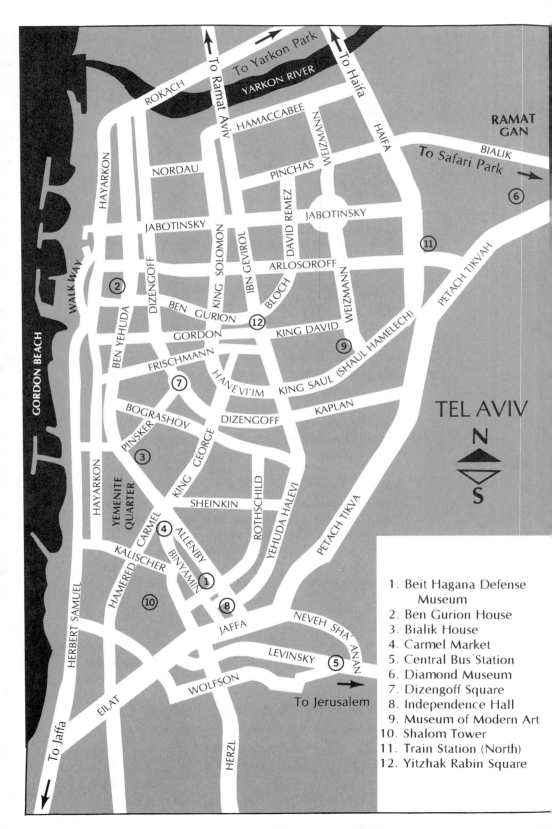

TEL AVIV

N
S

1. Beit Hagana Defense
   Museum
2. Ben Gurion House
3. Bialik House
4. Carmel Market
5. Central Bus Station
6. Diamond Museum
7. Dizengoff Square
8. Independence Hall
9. Museum of Modern Art
10. Shalom Tower
11. Train Station (North)
12. Yitzhak Rabin Square

United Tours. 113 Hayarkon St. **PHONE:** (03) 693-3404

Ne'ot Hakikar. **PHONE:** (03) 522-8161

SPNI. Main Office. 4 Hashfela St. **PHONE:** (03) 638-8677

Boat Tours take you from the port of Jaffa to the Tel Aviv Marina and back again with no stops, in under an hour. If your kids don't get seasick, bring a snack and a pad and pencil for doodling, drawing, or tic-tac-toe. Contact **Kef.** **PHONE:** (03) 682-9070; or **Sababa.** **PHONE:** (03) 682-5753

Walking Tours:

Eretz Israel Museum sponsors three-hour walking tours in Tel Aviv and Jaffa. Call for schedule. **PHONE:** (03) 641-5244, ext. 6267

Jaffa. Free two-hour walking tour every Wednesday. Meet at the Clock Tower at 9:30 a.m.

Tel Aviv University campus tours led by Friends of Tel Aviv University. **PHONE:** (03) 640-8055

Bar Ilan University. Tour the campus and see a film about this fast-growing university. **PHONE:** (03) 635-7461

ORT Technological High Schools. **PHONE:** (03) 520-3222

Naamat/Pioneer Women. Tour of day care centers and other facilities. **PHONE:** (03) 691-0791

Amit Women. Tour of schools and children's homes. **PHONE:** (03) 523-3154

SITES

Shalom Tower Rooftop Observatory
1 Herzl Street
BUSES: 4,5
PHONE: (03) 517-7304
HOURS: Sun.-Thurs.: 10 a.m.-5:30 p.m.; Fri. closes at 1:30 p.m.
ADMISSION: Fee

A wonderful view from one of the tallest buildings in the Mideast.

Silent World
Dolphinarium Bldg. behind Carmel Market
PHONE: (03) 510-6670
HOURS: Summer: Daily 9 a.m.-5 p.m.; Winter: Daily 9 a.m.-4 p.m.
ADMISSION: Fee

The aquarium holds a large variety of fish, snakes, and seals. Often on school holidays there are shows, and children may feed the seals. Nature films in English are shown. Call ahead.

Beit Eliahu/ Beit Haganah Defense Museum

23 Rothschild Boulevard
BUSES: 4, or other Allenby Road buses
PHONE: (03) 560-8624
HOURS: Sunday-Thursday 8 a.m.-4 p.m.; Friday closes at noon.
ADMISSION: Nominal fee

This small museum includes audio-visual programs about the pre-state defense forces, the dramatic Night of the Bridges, and the Yom Kippur War, in addition to fascinating displays of early army dress and weapons. Models of Palmach soldiers in a primitive defense post, and an arms cache in the form of a book are particularly interesting.

Lehi Museum

8 Stern Street
BUSES: 26
PHONE: (03) 682-0288
HOURS: Sunday-Thursday 9 a.m.-4 p.m.; closed Friday and Saturday.
ADMISSION: Nominal fee

Audio-visual dioramas depict the life of Lehi founder Yair Stern and the revisionist movement.

Independence Hall

16 Rothschild Boulevard
BUSES: 4, 5
PHONE: (03) 517-3942
HOURS: Sunday-Thursday 9 a.m.-2 p.m; closed Friday and Saturday.
ADMISSION: Fee

Ben Gurion read Israel's Declaration of Independence from this hall, which is still set up as it was that day, May 14, 1948.

Educational Center for Games

10 Rehov Israel Bak, near Hamasgir and Hashmoni'im
BUSES: Egged 73, 74, 75, 86, 274; Dan 51, 54, 59, 60
PHONE: (03) 561-0149
    Or call founder Margolit Akavya at home: 523-8530

Volunteers have put together this collection of 1000 board games. Some are on exhibit, but many are available to play with. Look for the picture made from 33,000 matchsticks and the 28 hand-made doll houses filled with miniatures. Volunteers will get you started on new games. It's warm in summer; choose a cool day.

Kikar Malachei Yisrael at the intersection of King David and Ibn Gavirol Streets, the site of the tragic assassination of Prime Minister Yitzhak Rabin, was renamed **Rabin Square**. Visitors often leave notes and flowers in his memory.

Beit Bialik

22 Bialik Street
BUS: 4
PHONE: (03) 525-4530
HOURS: Sun.-Thurs. 9 a.m.-4:45 p.m.; Sat. 11 a.m.-1:45 p.m.; closed Fri.
ADMISSION: Free

If your child is interested in Hebrew language and poetry, stop by the home of one of Israel's greatest poets, the late Hayim Nahman Bialik. Children may be familiar with his poems set to music in children's songs such as *The Bird's Nest* and *Parash.*

Tel Aviv Museum of Modern Art

27 Shaul Hamelech Street
BUSES: 18, 70
PHONE: (03) 695-7361
HOURS: Sun.-Thurs.10 a.m.-6 p.m.; Tues. until 11 p.m.; Fri., Sat. noon-10 p.m.
ADMISSION: Fee

The museum sponsors special children's tours and programs and has a children's activity room. Call for update.

Ben Gurion's House

17 Ben Gurion Street
BUSES: 4
PHONE: (03) 522-1010
HOURS: Sun.-Thurs. 8:30 a.m.-3 p.m.; Mon. until 5 p.m.; Fri. until 1p.m.
   Call ahead for Sat. hours
ADMISSION: Free

The library and personal effects of Paula and David Ben Gurion will be of interest to children who have studied Jewish history.

Etzel Museum

38 King George Street
BUSES: 6
PHONE: (03) 528-4001
HOURS: Sun.-Thurs. 8 a.m.-3 p.m.; Fri. until 1 p.m.; closed Sat.
ADMISSION: Small fee

An audio-visual presentation describes the history of the Etzel and Lehi underground movement before the creation of the State. There are displays of weapons and a permanent exhibit about the life of Revisionist leader Vladimir Jabotinsky.

Harry Oppenheimer Diamond Museum

Diamond Exchange, Ramat Gan
BUS: Any bus going to the Arlosoroff Train Station; you can walk from there
PHONE: (03) 576-0219
HOURS: Sunday-Thursday 10 a.m.-4 p.m.; closed Friday and Saturday
ADMISSION: Fee

Set aside at least an hour for this interesting tour and movie about the history and use of diamonds. If you call ahead, you can get a family guide. The exhibit shows how diamonds form and are mined, and there's a hands-on section about the properties of diamonds. Need to do a term paper? Use the diamond library! One of every two polished diamonds in the world is polished in Israel. Sorry, no free samples.

Man and His World Natural History Museum
Ramat Gan Park
PHONE: (03) 631-5010
HOURS: Sun.-Thurs. 9 a.m.-2 p.m.; Fri. until 1 p.m.; Tues., Wed. 4-7 p.m..
Saturday until 5 p.m. in July and August
ADMISSION: Fee

Special exhibits show how bats use radar and how the animal nervous system works. The museum specializes in educational (and fun) programs for elementary school children during school holidays. There's also a summer camp. Three-hour courses are given on "A Baby Is Born," "Senses and Communication," "Reptiles and Dinosaurs," "Flight, Sound, and Light," and "Food, Reproduction, and the Desert." Call for the latest schedule.

Ha'aretz Museum and Planetarium
University Street, Ramat Aviv
PHONE: (03) 641-5244
HOURS: Sun., Mon., Thurs. 9 a.m.-2 p.m.; Tues., Wed. until 7 p.m.
Shabbat 10 a.m.-2:30 p.m.; closed Friday
ADMISSION: Fee; combined ticket for Museum and Planetarium is available.

The Man and His Work Center is an appealing exhibition of Israeli folk crafts and techniques, including knife-sharpening, woodworking, glass-blowing, and ceramics. Live demonstrations take place in the **Domes of the Craftsmen.** Coin collectors will enjoy the **Numismatic Pavilion.** An old-fashioned flour mill was opened recently, and sometimes children can bake pita. There are story hours in the olive press room, and crafts workshops on school holidays. The museum is located on the **Tel Quasile Excavation** and you can take a self-guided walk around the dig.

Lasky Planetarium
PHONE: (03) 641-3217
HOURS: Same as museum; *Journey Through the Universe* is shown in
English Wednesday afternoon. Call for times.
ADMISSION: Fee; combined ticket with museum is available.

The solar system, The Copernican Revolution, and black holes are among the subjects introduced through a number of good programs. These days there are more programs in English and Arabic, so call for current schedule.

Beit Hatefutzot — The Diaspora Museum

Tel Aviv University Campus, Ramat Aviv
PHONE: (03) 646-2020
HOURS: Sun.-Thurs. 10 a.m.-5 p.m.; Wed. until 7 p.m.; Fri. 9 a.m.-2 p.m.
  Closed Saturday.
ADMISSION: Fee

The world of Jews outside Israel is brought to life through three floors of outstanding audio-visual displays depicting Jewish family, community, culture, faith, history, and aspirations over the last 2,500 years. Older children will enjoy the dioramas, models, movies, slide-shows, and computer games; younger children may be bored. You can use the museum computer to check your family's roots.

Plan a 1-2 hour visit with children, who become saturated and tire quickly. Break up the visit with snacks at the convenient cafeteria, or stretch out on the lovely lawns of the university campus, where the kids can play. You will enjoy this museum and may wish to return without your children.

If you are part of a group of 12 or more, you can take part in family-centered programs through the Museum's Seminars Dept. Call for information. You also can hire a family-friendly private guide to take you through the museum. The museum sponsors children's summer and holiday camps on museum themes.

OLD JAFFA

The "Jaffa" stamped on your oranges refers to the port of Old Jaffa, the town from which Tel Aviv grew. The area is colorful, rich in history, and fun for shopping and entertainment. There are quaint artists' studios, boutiques and galleries, and lots of nightclubs and restaurants.

Flea Market (*Shuk Hapishpishim*) is a favorite place for teens looking for cheap, off-beat clothing and earrings. You also can bargain for used furniture and antiques. It's open every day.

The Collection Houses

35 Eilat Street, corner Elifelet
PHONE: (03) 517-2913
HOURS: Sunday-Thursday 8:30 a.m.-3:30 p.m.; Closed Friday and Saturday
ADMISSION: Nominal fee

Weapons and military enthusiasts will enjoy the display of rare arms, as well as weapons collected from all over the world used by the new Israel Defense Forces to fight the War of Independence. Our favorites are Ben Gurion's car, the armor plated "sandwich" vehicle he used for driving to Jerusalem in 1948; and the milk cans used to smuggle arms. There are old Sherman tanks and even the two canons positioned by the Egyptians to guard the Tiran Straits in 1956. A variety of movies are shown. Currently there is one on the Yom Kippur War and another about Israel's armed forces.

OUTSIDE THE CITY

Babylonian Jewry Museum
83 Haganah St., Or Yehudah
PHONE: (03) 533-9278
HOURS: Sun.-Thurs. 9 a.m.-3 p.m.; Tues. until 7 p.m.; closed Fri. and Sat.
ADMISSION: Fee

Exhibits show the glorious history of Iraq's Jewish community.

Mikve Yisrael Agricultural School
PHONE: (03) 503-0489
HOURS: Sun.-Thurs. 8 a.m.-4:30 p.m.; open Fri. for groups; closed Sat.
ADMISSION: Fee

If your children are interested in early Israeli history, you can visit the country's first agricultural school. This is where the *kova tembel,* the trademark kibbutz hat, was created. The original buildings from the 1870's are still in use, including the oldest wine cellar in the country which the Haganah used for secret training. You can bring a picnic lunch, but include drinks. There's no kiosk on the grounds. An audio-visual show tells the history of the school.

THEATERS

Mann Auditorium. Huberman St. Home of the Israel Philharmonic Orchestra. PHONE: (03) 528-9163

New Opera House. Leonardo DaVinci St. PHONE: (03) 692-7777

Susanne Dellal Center for Dance and Theater. 6 Yechieli St.
PHONE: (03) 510-5656, 510-5319

Habimah National Theater. PHONE: (03) 526-6666

LIBRARIES

Beit Ariella
25 Shaul Hamelech St., near Tel Aviv Museum
BUSES: 18, 32 (Ibn Gabirol stop)
PHONE: (03) 691-0141
HOURS: Children's Library: Sun.-Thurs.10 a.m.-7 p.m.; Fri. 9 a.m.-noon.

Children are welcome to come in and read books in Hebrew, English, French, and Italian. Story hours in Hebrew for children ages 5-9 are held Tuesdays at 5:15 p.m. Watch the newspaper for Children's Theater schedule. Tickets usually sell out on the first of each month when the new listing is published.

נא לא
לנגוע

WALKING AND DOING

Dizengoff Street. Buy ice cream and watch the parade of fashions and folks along the country's best known street. (In Israeli *Monopoly* this street is Boardwalk!) Stop at **Dizengoff Square** and watch the computer-operated **Fire and Water Sculpture** by artist Yaakov Agam. On most days at 9 and 11 a.m., 1 and 9 p.m., it erupts in an extravaganza of fountains, flame, and color. Then walk to **Dizengoff Center**, an air-conditioned mall for shopping, eating, and entertainment. On Friday afternoons from 2-4 p.m., book, newspaper, and music vendors peddle their wares, while musicians entertain the crowds.

Tel Aviv Walkway. Start at the Sheraton Hotel and walk north along the beach as far as you wish. There are many outdoor eating places, particularly for ice cream and felafel.

Carmel Market. Our children love the shouting and bustle of this outdoor market. Underwear, sun hats, watermelons, and fresh bread are among the goods hawked at dozens of stalls. At the end of the market, across from the parking lots, is a great felafel stand, with unlimited salad to fill up your pita. Behind the market is a park with swings and climbing toys.

Neveh Tzedek, an old neighborhood south of the Carmel Market, has small streets, tiny factories, boutiques, and cafes. You might want to stop at **Beit Rokah**, the oldest house in the neighborhood, which today is a sculpture gallery. PHONE: (03) 516-2531

Tnuva welcomes teens at any of their 40 different courses in baking, cooking, and candy-making. But...they're taught in Hebrew. PHONE: (03) 524-3157

YARKON PARK

Yarkon and Yehoshua Parks
BUSES: 21, 48
PHONE: (03) 642-2828

This large, lovely park, the setting for a variety of activities, includes good climbing toys, bike rentals, boat trips, and a world-class aviary. If you come by car, you'll have to pay for parking, but you can cross the street and go to the Luna Amusement Park and fairgrounds from here, also. There are many places to buy drinks, but no water fountains, so bring your canteens. The park also has cactus, rock, and tropical gardens that will interest adult horticulturalists. Highlights include:

Tzapari Bird Center

PHONE: (03) 642-2888
HOURS: Sun.-Thurs. 9 a.m.-4 p.m.; Fri. until 2 p.m.; Sat. until 5 p.m.
Phone ahead to find out when the bird show is.

An extraordinary collection of colorful and exotic birds from all over the world. Some speak Hebrew. Ask for a guide to show you around and tell you stories about the birds. One toucan was so depressed when his mate died, he had to see a psychologist! Late afternoon is usually less crowded and the birds are livelier. Sometimes amusement rides are set up.

Boat Rides

PHONE: (03) 642-0541
HOURS: Daily 9 a.m.-7 p.m

Reasonable rates for row boats, paddle boats and motor boats.

Bicycles-Built-for-A-Family

PHONE: (03) 642-5286
ADMISSION: Rentals by the half-hour.

You can rent a bike or go-cart for everyone. A family bike seats five (the driver must be 15 or older), there are side-by-side bikes for two, electric carts, pedal carts...in short, wheels for all!

Golfitek

PHONE: (03) 699-0229
HOURS: Weekdays 4 p.m.-evening; Shabbat and holidays 10 a.m.-evening
ADMISSION: Fee; tell the attendant at the Yarkon parking lot that you're going to play golf, and you'll get a discount.

This family-friendly site has two miniature golf courses for ages 6-adult, and a special course for children 3-6. There are trampolines, bumper cars, and a coffee shop. Bring drinks. They're expensive, and playing on a hot day, you're sure to get thirsty.

Luna Amusement Park

PHONE: (03) 642-7080
HOURS: July and August, Shabbat and holidays daily 4 p.m.-midnight
ADMISSION: Fee

One of Israel's largest amusement parks has a variety of rides highlighted by a roller coaster. Summer entertainment includes rock concerts. The Atlas Hotel Chain is currently offering their guests free tickets to the park. Member hotels include Basel, Grand, Top, Tal, City, and Center.

Nearby is the Convention Center which hosts interesting exhibitions and trade shows on computers, coins, stamps, and furniture.

MORE PARKS

Safari Park
Ramat Gan
BUSES: 30, 34, 35 from Tel Aviv Central Bus Station
     55 from North Tel Aviv; Egged 400 from Jerusalem
PHONE: (03) 631-2181; Education Dept.: 631-2806
HOURS: Mar.-June, Sept.-Oct.: Sun.-Thurs. 9 a.m.-4 p.m.; Fri. until 1p.m.
     Jul.-Aug.: Sun.-Thurs.9 a.m.-5 p.m.; Fri. until 1 p.m.; Sat. until 3 p.m.
     Nov.-Feb.: Check for winter hours.
ADMISSION: Fee

1600 animals live and wander free in this wonderful park. The African section has hippos, oryx, gnu, zebra, rhinos, and lions. The primate section has apes, lemurs, gorillas and the like. There are carnivores such as wolves, bears, and leopards, and a new reptile section. If you don't have a car, you can ride in a zoo vehicle. There is also a walking trail where you can see monkeys and other tamer animals. Pack a picnic lunch!

Special events on the holidays include a Purim carnival with face-painting and balloon animals, and a "from sheep to sweater" activity on Shavuot. Summer camps and special workshops take place on themes relating to animal families. Children 13 and older can learn about zoo-keeping. You also can celebrate your birth-day or Bar/Bat Mitzvah here. Contact the Education Department. The busiest times of the year are Pesach vacation and August.

Hamifuzar B'Kfar Azar Play Center
Misubim Junction
BUSES: 36, 37 from Tel Aviv
ADMISSION: Fee

Trampolines, cars, and a petting zoo aimed at children 1-6.

Ramat Gan National Park
PHONE: (03) 631-2004, 681-8497
HOURS: The park is always open.

You can ride in row, motor, paddle, or bumper boats or play on the trampoline at this 700-acre park.

Charles Clore Park on the seafront, a short walk from the end of the Carmel Market, offers a place to fish.

Independence Park is a small park near the Hilton Hotel.

Hasportek on Rokach Blvd. at the northern entrance to the city has large expanses of grass, climbing toys, and courts for basket-ball, tennis, soccer, and roller skating.

Meir Park is a nice park near King George Street.

SWIMMING

The Beach

Most of Tel Aviv's numerous free public beaches are suitable for children. You can reach the beach easily from just south of the Hilton Hotel, near the Sheraton Hotel, near the Plaza Moriah (close to Gordon Pool), south of the Dan Hotel, and near Charles Clore Park. The West Beach, just beyond the Dan Panorama, has a restaurant that comes out to the water. The Sheraton Beach has separate swimming days for men and women. Buses 18, 19, and 10 go to the beach in Bat Yam.

Tel Aviv's public beaches are open as follows:

April, May, September: 7 a.m.-5 p.m.
June: 7 a.m.-6 p.m.
July and August: 7a.m.-7 p.m.

Only beaches at **Hatzuk, Tel Baruch, Nordau, Frishman**, and **Borgrashov** are open other months — from 7 a.m.-2:30 p.m.

Swimming Pools:

Gordon Pool. Kikar Atarim, behind Moriah Hotel. PHONE: (03) 572-1555

Galit Pool. Near Yad Eliahu. PHONE: (03) 537-5031

Kiryat Ono Pool. 4 Keren Kayemet St. Indoor and outdoor pools, plus children's pool and slides.

Ilan Pool. 123 Rokah St., Ramat Gan. PHONE: (03) 575-4466

Many hotels allow non-guests to use their pools. Sometimes you must buy a package that includes lunch. Check the following:

Ramada Continental. PHONE: (03) 527-2627
Dan Panorama. PHONE: (03) 519-0190
Dan Tel Aviv. PHONE: (03) 520-2525
Holiday Inn Crowne Plaza. PHONE: (03) 520-1111
Carlton. PHONE: (03) 520-1818
Country Club Hotel. PHONE: (03) 699-0666
Metropolitan. PHONE: (03) 519-2727
Tel Aviv Hilton. PHONE: (03) 520-2222
Yamit Towers. PHONE: (03) 519-7111

Maymadion Water Park
Across from Luna Park
BUS: 23, 27
PHONE: (03) 642-2777
HOURS: 9 a.m.-5 p.m.
ADMISSION: Fee

A wide variety of water slides, a wave pool, and kiddie pools can turn a muggy Tel Aviv day into lots of fun.

> **Baby Swimming Lessons.** If you're staying for at least three months, you can enroll your infant at Israel's national baby swimming center at Maccabi Ramat Gan. **PHONE:** (03) 574-6869

Neveh Avivim Country Club
3 Levitan St., Ramat Aviv
PHONE: (03) 641-5521
HOURS: Daily 6 a.m.-8 p.m.
ADMISSION: Fee

Tennis, swimming pool, kiddie pool, gym.

Yamit 2000
Har Hatzofim St., Holon
BUSES: Egged 74, 94 from Tel Aviv
PHONE: (03) 556-6527
ADMISSION: Fee

An indoor water park and swimming center.

WATER SPORTS

Octopus Marina on Gordon Beach. You can take underwater diving courses here — from beginners to advanced. Courses begin every Friday and Sunday and the shortest is five days. But you can also sign up for a single dive to see if you like it. Children ages 12-15 can dive to a depth of 60 feet; ages 15 and up can dive to 90 feet. **PHONE:** (03) 527-3554, 527-1440

Leonardo Diving Club at the Dolphinarium. Diving courses for ages 12 and up, but younger children can take a single dive with an instructor. **PHONE:** (03) 510-5871

Diving Center. Courses and underwater tours. **PHONE:** (03) 546-3226

Water-Skiing. Park Hadarom. Water-skiing behind cables for kids ages 9 and up. **PHONE:** (03) 391-168

Para-Gliding. Sea Palace Beach, Jaffa. Teens with permission slips from parents can take courses on the beach between Tel Aviv and Bat Yam. **PHONE:** (03) 506-7467

Sailing. You can rent boats and wind-surfing equipment on the Tel Aviv Marina.

SPORTS

Hapoel Sports Organization for information on upcoming sporting events. 4 Brenner St. **PHONE:** (03) 567-0961

Ilan Sports Center for the Physically Handicapped
123 Rokah Street, Ramat Gan
PHONE: (03) 575-4444
HOURS: Call ahead
ADMISSION: Nominal fee

A swimming pool and other sports equipment for the physically handicapped.

TEENS

Israel Roller Blade Center
Tel Aviv Port
BUSES: 4 to last stop and walk
PHONE: (03) 604-2759
HOURS: Currently Friday and Saturday; call to confirm
ADMISSION: Free

Kids ages 4 and up can skate to music. Skates are for rent on the premises or from the **Roller Blade Store**, 250 Ben Yehudah in Tel Aviv. **PHONE:** (03) 604-5034

TEENS

Laser in the Forest
Between Morasha and Yarkon Junctions; there are no buses on weekends, so you need to take cab or walk.
PHONE: (03) 924-0960
HOURS: Currently open Saturdays and school holidays.
ADMISSION: Fee

Younger children can ride tractors, while their older siblings fire away with laser guns.

Miniature Golf and Play. Ramat Gan Park. **PHONE:** (03) 631-4126

Tennis Centers:

Kfar Hayarok. PHONE: (03) 645-6666

Jaffa. PHONE: (03) 683-0038

Yad Eliahu. PHONE: (03) 631-1023, 631-1024

National Tennis Center. Ramat Hasharon. **PHONE:** (03) 645-6666

Many hotels have tennis courts, including the Hilton, Country Club, and the Maccabiah Village.

Bowling:

American Center: 299 Abba Hillel, Ramat Gan. PHONE: (03) 570-0836

Ramat Gan Bowling: Nat'l Stadium. PHONE: (03) 570-0834

Ice-Skating. 2 Ben Gurion St., Ramat Gan. PHONE: (03) 752-0345

Heichal Hakerech Ice-Skating. Bat Yam. PHONE: (03) 552-6655

SPORTING EVENTS

You can buy tickets for sporting events at the stadium, but it's wise to buy them in advance from one of the ticket agencies or by phone using a credit card. PHONE: (03) 527-9955

Bloomfield Soccer Stadium. Jaffa. PHONE: (03) 682-1275

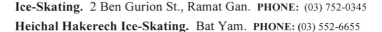

Yad Eliyahu Basketball Stadium
BUS: Dan 36, 37; Egged 475
PHONE: (03) 537-6376

This is where Maccabi Tel Aviv plays. If you want to be with "real" Israelis, attend a basketball game!

Ussishkin Basketball Stadium
Near Tel Aviv Port
PHONE: (03) 544-1076

Hapoel Tel Aviv plays here.

WHERE TO STAY

Tel Aviv has luxury hotels along the beach, as well as older hotels, pensions, and apartment hotels. Many have family plans and children's activities. See *The Coast* for nearby camping and kibbutz guest houses.

HOTELS

Holiday Inn Crowne Plaza. 145 Hayarkon. Indoor and outdoor pools and direct beach access. Children are free in parents' room. PHONE: (03) 520-1111; FAX: 520-1122

Dan Panorama. 10 Y. Kaufman Street. Pool, kids' club house, and full program for ages 4-14 with special events such as ice cream day and sports day. Family plan rates are available. PHONE: (03) 519-0190; FAX: 517-1777

Tel Aviv Hilton. A play room with arts and crafts activities is open during summer and holiday weeks. Family plan rates apply to most rooms. A child of any age can stay free in parents' room.

Children up to age 3 dine free in hotel restaurants, and children from 3-12 get a 25% discount. **PHONE:** (03) 520-2222

Moriah Plaza. 155 Hayarkon St. Children's program on weekends and during vacations. **PHONE:** (03) 691-1515; **FAX:** 527-1065

Maccabiah Village. Ramat Gan. This is the hotel and sports center for the Maccabiah games, held every four years. At other times the public can enjoy the facilities which include swimming pools, health club, workout rooms, water slides, and courts for volleyball, tennis, soccer, squash, and basketball. The village is a short bus ride from Tel Aviv. Under the family plan, children under 12 sharing the same room with their parents are free. **PHONE:** (03) 671-5715; **FAX:** 574-4678

APARTMENT HOTELS

Yamit Towers Hotel. 79 Hayarkon St. One or two-bedroom apartments with kitchenettes in a good location. **PHONE:** (03) 519-7111; **FAX:** 517-4719

Habakuk Apartment Hotel. 7 Habakuk St. Good location. **PHONE:** (03) 604-2222; **FAX:** 604-0022

Lusky Suites. 84 Hayarkon St. Moderately-priced 1-3 bedroom suites all with kitchenettes. **PHONE:** (03) 516-3030; **FAX:** 517-1047

Best Western Regency Suites. 80 Hayarkon. Centrally located, this relatively small hotel has one-bedroom suites with kitchenettes. Check into Best Western package deals such as "Tour As You Please." **PHONE:** (03) 517-3939; **FAX:** 516-3276; or book through Best Western in your home country.

Malonit Savoy. 5 Guela St. Near the beach, air-conditioned with washing machines available. **PHONE:** (03) 510-2923

Alexander All Suites Hotel. 3 Havakook St. 1-2 bedroom suites with kitchenettes. Expensive. **PHONE:** (03) 546-2222; **FAX:** 546-9346

Country Club. Gillot. This location is less convenient for city sites, but there are 1-2 bedroom suites and lots of sports facilities at reasonable rates. **PHONE:** (03) 699-0666; **FAX:** 699-0660

HOSTEL

Tel Aviv Youth Hostel. 36 Bnei Dan Street. Book well in advance for the family rooms. This is a bargain in a city where accommodations are expensive. **PHONE:** (03) 544-1748, 546-0719; **FAX:** 544-1030

WHERE TO EAT

Dizengoff Street is well known for its ice cream parlors and coffee houses.

Bezalel Market has several excellent competing felafel stands. You can get good mid-eastern food in the **Yemenite Quarter** near the Carmel Market.

Aboulafia is a famous hot pita stand. It's behind the Old Clock Tower in Jaffa at 7 Yefet Street. PHONE: (03) 683-4958

New York has inexpensive meat meals. 164 Dizengoff Street PHONE: (03) 522-2966

Pundak Shaul, one of the better known Oriental restaurants, serves children's portions. PHONE: (03) 517-7619

Tiv Restaurant features old-fashioned Jewish cooking. 130 Allenby St. PHONE: (03) 560-9125

These **pizza parlors** have free delivery:
Casa del Papa. PHONE: (03) 537-2688
Armon's (grilled pizza). PHONE: (03) 683-2101, 681-9303
Pizza Pitzakato (branches in Ramat Gan, Bnei Brak, Givatayim).
    PHONE: (03) 672-2736
Don't assume that a pizza chain that is kosher in Jerusalem is also kosher in Tel Aviv.

HAIFA

Haifa, Israel's major port and third largest city, is often compared to San Francisco because of its hills and its beauty. It is a center of industry and manufacturing, and is know for being well-organized. This "City of Flowers" hosts a number of festivals including a flower fair every Passover and a folklore festival in summer (see *Holidays and Holy Days*) .

CITY NOTES

Area Code: (04). If you are calling from out of town, dial these numbers first.

Police: (04) 354-444
Emergency: 100
Magen David Adom (Red Cross): (04) 512-233
Bus Information: (04) 549-555
Bat Galim Train Station: (04) 564-321
Mercaz Station: (04) 564-3154
Carmelite Subway: (04) 376-870

Municipal Tourist Information Office
Central Bus Station
PHONE: (04) 512-208
HOURS: Sun.-Thurs. 9 a.m.-5 p.m.; Fri. 9:30 a.m.-2 p.m.; Closed Sat.

Government Tourist Info. 18 Herzl St. **PHONE:** (04) 666-521

Haifa Tourism Board
106 Hanasi Boulevard, Carmel
PHONE: (04) 374-010
HOURS: 8 a.m.-6 p.m.

Ask for *Fun*, the family event and discount brochure. It's also available at many hotels.

GETTING THERE

From **Jerusalem**, a quick, air-conditioned bus, #940, will take you to Haifa in less than two hours. It runs every 30-45 minutes from 6:30 a.m.-7:15 p.m. You can drive via the coastal road or turn at Ben Gurion Airport and go via Petach Tikvah.

From **Tel Aviv**, Bus #900 leaves every 20 minutes from the Central Bus Station between 5:20 a.m.-11 p.m. The train, which leaves from north station, takes an hour and travels a scenic route.

GETTING AROUND

Haifa is built on three levels: the lower port level called *Ha-Ir,* the middle city called *Hadar,* and the upper city called the *Carmel,* after its majestic range of mountains. To climb from level to level you can walk, drive, take a bus, enjoy the cable car, or ride the **Carmelite,** Israel's only subway. The ride from the

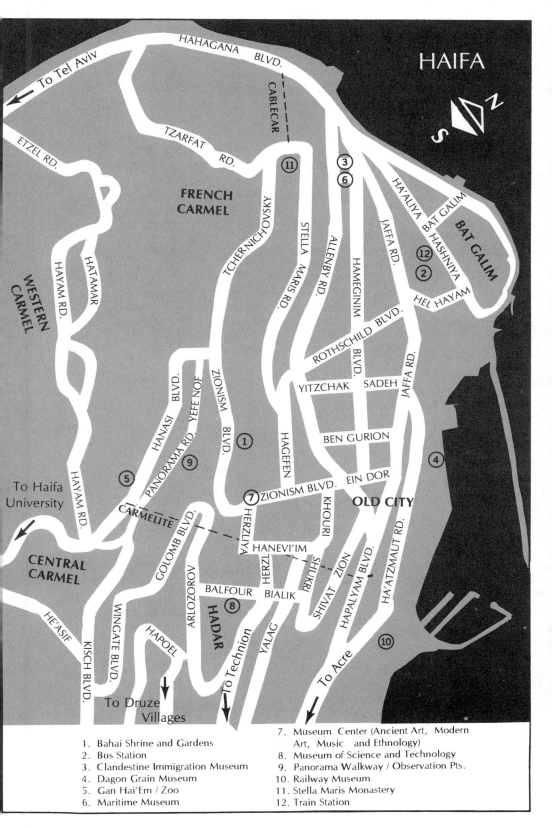

HAIFA

HAHAGANA BLVD.

To Tel Aviv

ETZEL RD.

TZARFAT RD.

CABLECAR

FRENCH CARMEL

TCHERNICHOVSKY

STELLA MARIS RD.

ALLENBY RD.

HAMEGINIM

JAFFA RD.

HA'ALIYA

BAT GALIM

HASHNIYA

BAT GALIM

⑪

③

⑥

⑫

②

HEL HAYAM

WESTERN CARMEL

HAYAM RD.

HATAMAR

ROTHSCHILD BLVD.

JAFFA RD.

YITZCHAK   SADEH

HANASI BLVD.

YEFE NOF

ZIONISM BLVD.

PANORAMA RD.

BEN GURION

①

⑨

⑤

④

HAGEFEN

EIN DOR

To Haifa University

CARMELITE

GOLOMB BLVD.

ZIONISM BLVD.   OLD CITY

⑦

HERZLIYA

KHOURI

HAYAM RD.

CENTRAL CARMEL

HANEVI'IM

HERZL

SHUKRI

SHIVAT ZION

HAPALYAM BLVD.

HA'ATZMAUT RD.

ARLOZOROV

BALFOUR   BIALIK

⑧

HE'ASIF

WINGATE BLVD.

HAPOEL

HADAR

YALAG

To Technion

To Acre

⑩

KISCH BLVD.

To Druze Villages

1. Bahai Shrine and Gardens
2. Bus Station
3. Clandestine Immigration Museum
4. Dagon Grain Museum
5. Gan Hai'Em / Zoo
6. Maritime Museum
7. Museum Center (Ancient Art, Modern Art, Music and Ethnology)
8. Museum of Science and Technology
9. Panorama Walkway / Observation Pts.
10. Railway Museum
11. Stella Maris Monastery
12. Train Station

bottom takes ten minutes, and there are six conveniently located stations. The Carmelite runs Sunday-Thursday 6:30 a.m.-midnight, Friday until 3p.m., and Saturday after sundown until midnight.

Buses run daily from 5 a.m.-11:30 p.m. There is no bus Friday night, but buses run on Shabbat from 9 a.m.-midnight.

Haifa Cable Car
You can buy a one-way ticket and ride **up** from Bat Galim in the Lower City,
        or **down** from Stella Maris Carmelite Monastery.
PHONE: (04) 335-970
HOURS: Winter: Sat.-Thurs. 10 a.m.-6 p.m.; Fri. closes at 2 p.m.
        Summer: Sat.-Thurs. 9 a.m.-9 p.m., Fri. 10 a.m.-2 p.m.

Enjoy a lovely ride up the mountain in this modern, transparent bubble. Don't worry, the doors will close before taking off! Turn the dial above your head to the language you understand best, and hear a description of the panorama. At the top, you can enjoy the vista and buy a cold drink or light meal (not kosher). If you wish to visit the monastery, dress modestly.

Take a pleasant walk along the sea on the **Bat Galim Walkway**. There are several restaurants, some very expensive!

CITY TOURS

Egged Tours. A panoramic tour of Haifa and a ride up the coast to Acre and Rosh Hanikra. PHONE: (04) 549-486

Galilee Tours. PHONE: 177-022-2525 (Toll-free)

SPNI. 18 Hillel St. PHONE: (04) 664-135, 664-136

Fly and Tour. You can book an hour air tour over Haifa and Acre, or hire a pilot/guide to take you around the country. Haifa's airfield is on an army base. You should call 2-3 days in advance to get entry permits from the Army. **Canfey Paz:** PHONE: (04) 724-474 (3 people minimum). **Aerobat.** PHONE: (04) 417-157

Little Haifa Trolley
Starts at Dan Panorama
PHONE: (050) 264-795 (mobile phone)

A pleasant half hour trolley ride around the Carmel to several tourist sites.

Walking Tour. A free tour in English leaves from Panorama Road Center, Saturdays at 10 a.m. A visit to the Bahai Shrine is included, so dress modestly.

Home Visits. To visit at home with Druze, Maronite Christians, and Ahmediyan Moslem families, or to stay at a Bed and Breakfast, call El Carmel. Teens can arrange to meet their Druze peers to discuss life styles and views. **PHONE:** (04) 390-125

Carmelite Boat Tour. A 50-minute coastal tour. Narration is usually in Hebrew. Call ahead for hours. **PHONE:** (04) 418-765

HA-IR LOWER CITY

Haifa's port area has several attractions of interest to children, as well as good Middle Eastern cafes and restaurants along Jaffa Road where you can eat with many of the people who work at the bustling port. You also can find souvenirs at reasonable prices.

Dagon Grain Museum
Plummer Square. Look for the grain silo. You can park at the railroad station.
BUSES: 12, 18, 17, 16, 15, 10
PHONE: (04) 664-221
HOURS: Sunday-Friday. Tour at 10:30 a.m. sharp; call for reservations.
ADMISSION: Free

This is the world's only grain museum, and exhibits show how grain has been cultivated throughout history. There are some 4,000-year-old grains on display. Ask to see a demonstration of how wheat is mechanically sorted and stored. The silo is Haifa's tallest building.

Railway Museum
Old Haifa Railroad Station, opposite 40 Hativat Golani Avenue
BUSES: 42, 21, 17
PHONE: (04) 564-293
HOURS: Sunday, Tuesday, Thursday 9 a.m.-noon.
ADMISSION: Nominal fee

Kids will love climbing on the old diesel locomotives and cabooses, ringing the railroad bell, and operating the ticket machine. A century of railroad memorabilia is displayed.

Combined Ticket: You can buy a ticket good for six Haifa museums: **Museum of Modern Art, Museum of Ancient Art,** and **Museum of Music and Ethnology** in the Haifa Museum complex, 26 Shabtai Levi St. The other three are the **Maritime Museum, Japanese Museum,** and **Prehistoric Museum.**

TEENS

The Edible Oil Industry Musem
Entrance to port, 2 Tuvin St.
BUS: 2
PHONE: (04) 654-340
HOURS: Sunday-Thursday 8:30 a.m.-2:30 p.m.
ADMISSION: Fee

This museum, the first of its kind in Israel, has 2000 year-old artifacts and exhibits on the manufacture of cooking oil throughout history. From October -April visitors can make their own oil.

Clandestine Immigration and Naval Museum

In the *Af Al Pi Chen* ship, 204 Allenby Street — walking distance from the
    Central Bus Station.
BUSES: 45, 44, 43, 26, 5
PHONE: (04) 536-249
HOUR: Sunday-Thursday 9 a.m.-4 p.m.; Friday closes at 1 p.m.
ADMISSION: Nominal fee

The actual illegal immigration ship *Af Al Pi Chen* ("In Spite Of It
All") houses a fascinating museum. You can visit the living
quarters of the refugees from Hitler's Europe who managed to
come to Palestine despite the British quotas, and see a movie
about this courageous effort.

National Maritime Museum

198 Allenby Street — walking distance from Central Bus Station
BUSES: 45, 44, 43, 5, 3
PHONE: (04) 536-622
HOURS: Sun.-Thurs. 10 a.m.-4 p.m.; Sat. and holidays closes at 1 p.m.
ADMISSION: Fee or Combined Museum ticket

Exhibits of ship models and artifacts obtained through underwater
archeology pertaining to seafaring in the area.

HADAR MIDDLE CITY

Hadar is the commercial heart of Haifa with stores, restaurants,
and movie theaters galore. Nordau Street is a pedestrian mall.
There are lots of places to snack along Herzl Street.

Museum of Music and Ethnology

26 Shabtai Levi Street
BUSES: 10, 21, 22, 28, 41, Carmelite
PHONE: (04) 523-255
HOURS: Tues., Thurs., Sat. 10 a.m.-1 p.m. and 5-8 p.m.
ADMISSION: Fee or Combined Ticket

Children interested in music will enjoy the colorful displays of
musical instruments in their ethnic settings. There is also a
Folktale archive with over 10,000 stories. The **Museums of
Modern Art** and **Ancient Art** are also in this complex.

Israel National Museum of Science

Historic Technion Building, Shmaryahu Levin Street
BUSES: 12, 21, 24, 28, 37
PHONE: (04) 628-111
HOURS: Monday-Thursday 9 a.m.-5 p.m.; Tuesday until 7 p.m.
        Friday 9 .am.-1 p.m.; Saturday 10 a.m.-2 p.m.; closed Sunday
ADMISSION: Fee

Inspired by San Francisco's Exploratorium, the old Technoda has
been revamped and expanded into an exciting science museum
with over 200 interactive exhibits focusing on Israel's achieve-

ments in science and technology. Budding scientists will especially enjoy the visual deceptions, mechanical puzzles, and challenging brain teasers in the **Game Room**, and they can explore the mysteries of light in the **Dark Room**.

Bahai Shrine and Gardens
Zionism Avenue
PHONE: (04) 358-358
HOURS: Shrine: Daily 9 a.m.-noon; gardens: 7 a.m.-5 p.m.
ADMISSION: Free

There is only one Bahai Temple built on each continent, and the one in Asia is in Israel. It is also the world headquarters of the Bahai movement. The gold-domed shrine is not particularly interesting to children, but it's one of those places you might not want to miss, simply because it appears on all postcards of Haifa. Kids do like taking off their shoes to enter the shrine. Visitors must dress modestly (no shorts). The grounds and gardens are beautiful.

For a lovely view of the city and a good place to stroll, follow the **Carmel Walkway** from the Central Carmel.

CARMEL
UPPER CITY

The Technion
BUSES: 17, 19
PHONE: (04) 320-664
HOURS: Koler Visitor Center: Sunday-Thursday 8 a.m.-3:30 p.m.
ADMISSION: Free

Israel's university of higher technology welcomes visitors. The huge campus is impressive, and the view from the Carmel hills is wonderful. A film narrated by Jack Lemmon, *The Technion Experience,* is shown as part of a 45-minute introduction to the work of this world-renowned scientific institution. While you are there, dine in one of the student cafeterias or at the Visitor Center.

Haifa University
BUSES: 24, 36, 37, 191, 192
PHONE: (04) 240-097; Hecht Museum: 257-773; observatory: 240-007
HOURS: Sunday-Thursday 8 a.m.-3 p.m.
ADMISSION: Free

The University has a free **Observation Tower** and lovely lawns to play on. A **Children's Library** is open Tuesdays and Thursdays. Paintings by artists killed in the Holocaust are displayed in the **Art Gallery**. You can take a student-guided tour of the campus Sunday-Thursday 10 a.m.-noon, starting from the Main Building.

The University's **Reuven and Edith Hecht Museum** has family and children's activities on historical and cultural themes, including treasure hunts and arts and crafts. In summer there are children's theater events. **PHONE:** (04) 257-773

ON THE OUTSKIRTS

TEENS

Druze Villages of Daliat El Carmel and Isfiya
BUS: 192 (The trip from Haifa's Central Bus Station takes about an hour.)

The Druze observe a secret religion, speak Arabic, and are loyal Israeli citizens. Many serve in Israel's defense forces. Walk around the village for a sense of the rural, small-town atmosphere in which the Druze bring up their children. Have a cup of Druze coffee with cardamom (called *hel* in Hebrew). Their village shops specialize in ethnic items and products made locally and in India.

Muhraka
A car or cab ride from the Druze Villages
HOURS: Saturday-Thursday 8 a.m.-1 p.m. and 4-6 p.m.

According to tradition, this is where Elijah the Prophet defeated the forces of Baal. Dress modestly if you want to visit the church. The view is magnificent. Stop for a picnic.

WHERE TO PLAY

Gan Ha'em
Central Carmel
BUSES: 21, 22, 23, 28, 37, Carmelite

This lovely park has play areas, a small amphitheater for outdoor concerts, and several museums, including the **Museum of Prehistory,** the **Natural History Museum,** the **Biological Institute,** and the **Zoo.**

The Haifa Zoo
Gan Ha'em
PHONE: (04) 372-886
HOURS: Sun.-Thurs. 8 a.m.-6 p.m.; Fri. until 1 p.m.; Sat. 9 a.m.-6 p.m.
ADMISSION: Fee

Young children will like the mini Noah's Ark at this small zoo in the heart of the park.

Carmel Park
South of Haifa University on Haifa-Osafia Road
BUSES: 24, 37, 37A, 191
PHONE: (04) 984-1750
HOURS: Always open
ADMISSION: Free

The park, near Haifa Univesity and Beit Oren, is the largest in Israel. It has numerous picnic sites and walking trails. Haifaphiles call it the city's "Switzerland." The animal reserve, open

March-May for groups of 25 or more, has deer, mountain goats and other hill animals.

Psalim Park
BUSES: 22, 23, 25, 26
ADMISSION: Free

22 bronze sculptures, a children's play area,   and a great view of the Bay of Haifa.

WHERE TO SWIM

Beaches

The pleasant public beaches of **Carmel, Dado,** and **Zamir** have lifeguards and changing facilities. There is an area for separate swimming at **Bat Galim.** You may wish to bring beach shoes; the beaches are pebbly.

The **Quiet Beach,** a private beach at the entrance to the city, charges a fee, but the breakwater makes the sea more manageable for children. There are kayaks and paddleboats for rent.

Swimming Pools:

Galei Hadar Pool. Hapoel St. **PHONE:** (04) 667-854

Maccabi Pool. Bikkurim Street. Separate children's and adults' pools are outdoors in summer, covered and heated in winter. **PHONE:** (04) 382-705

Beit Oren Pool. Water slides, too. **PHONE:** (04) 222-111

Sports Center Pool. Neve Shaanan. See *Sports.*

Haifa Diving and Surfing Club. **PHONE:** (04) 514-809

Hotel Pools:

Dan Panorama and **Dan Carmel** hotels permit non-guests to use their pools for a fee. You can buy a *cartisiya* which gives you a discount for multiple admissions.

SPORTS

Neve Shaanan Sports Center
BUS: 18 from Haifa Central Bus Station
PHONE: (04) 321-029
HOURS: Daily 6 a.m.-10 p.m. Closed Thursday
ADMISSION: Fee

Outdoor swimming pool with slides and waves, indoor pool, tennis, jacuzzi, sauna.

Haifa University offers tennis, karate, dance, and sports lessons for kids ages 8-14. **PHONE:** 904) 240-093.

Kfar Samir Tennis. PHONE: (04) 532-014

Sportan Squash. PHONE: (04) 539-160

Mitvahei Hatzafon Shooting Range. 38 Hanamal Street and at the Mall. For ages 16 and up.

The Recreation Center at Lev Hamifratz Shopping Mall has miniature golf, ice-skating, amusement park rides, and movies. PHONE: (04) 410-218. The **Bowling Center** is open from early morning to the wee hours. PHONE: (04) 720-529

WHERE TO STAY

Dan Panorama Hotel. 107 Hanassi Street. The Dan chain's family plans apply here. PHONE: (04) 352-222

Dan Carmel Hotel. 85-87 Hanassi Street. PHONE: (04) 306-211

Dvir Hotel (Dan Chain). 124 Yafe Nof St. PHONE: (04) 389-131

Nof Hotel. 101 Hanassi St. Junior suites are available. PHONE: (04) 354-311

Shulamit Hotel. 15 Kiryat Sefer St. Relatively low rates. PHONE: (04) 342-811

HOSTELS

Carmel Youth Hostel. Family rooms and a restaurant at the foot of Mt. Carmel close to the sea. PHONE: (04) 531-944; FAX: 532-516

Beth El Christian Hostel. 40 Hagefen Street. PHONE: (04) 521-110

Kibbutz Beit Oren Youth Hostel. PHONE: (04) 221-111

Aliya Hostel. Hechalutz St., Hadar. PHONE: (04) 623-918

Backpackers can stay at **Nesher.** 53 Herzl Street. PHONE: (04) 640-649; or **Talpiyot.** 51 Herzl Street. PHONE: (04) 673-753

See *The Coast* for nearby kibbutz guest houses and camping.

There are wonderful beaches along the more than 100 miles of Israel's coastline. Combine a day that begins or ends at the beach with visits to interesting cities and sites along the way.

KATIF

The ride to the Katif settlements and the lovely beaches that Israel still holds in Gaza goes by the Kisufim Junction which is controlled by the Israeli army. There are four beaches: one for men, one for women, one mixed but closed on Shabbat, and a fourth open to all on Shabbat. All are free.

Sports include exciting jeep rides in the sand, fishing, horseback riding, and tennis. For lake activities. **PHONE:** (07) 876-343

WHERE TO STAY

Youth Hostel Hadarom. East of the dunes of Gush Katif. A bungalow colony set up for families. Shabbat is observed. Children's activities. **PHONE:** (07) 847-597; **FAX:** 847-680

Hof Dekalim Hotel. Includes a miniature golf course. **PHONE:** (07) 847-910

Vacation Apartments. **PHONE:** (07) 847-240

TO ASHKELON

Eshkol Park
Near Ofakim
PHONE: (07) 985-110
HOURS: Sunday-Friday 7 a.m.-5 p.m.; Saturday 7 a.m.-3 p.m.
ADMISSION: Fees for parking and use of facilities.

A large park with a 10-mile nature trail (*Derech Habasor*), picnic areas, and Israel's largest swimming pool. There are campgrounds and bungalows for rent.

Yad Mordechai
Tel Aviv-Gaza Road, 7 miles south of Ashkelon
PHONE: (07) 720-528
HOURS: Daily 8 a.m.-4 p.m.
ADMISSION: Fee

During the War of Independence, the advancing Egyptian army, on its way to conquer Tel Aviv, was stopped by a tiny band of courageous soldiers at this kibbutz. The battle has been recreated with life-size cut-outs of soldiers, real tanks, and weapons. While you visit the battlefield, a recording (in Hebrew, English, and other languages) explains the events. The entrance fee also includes a visit to a small Holocaust/War of Independence Museum.

Kibbutz Magen
PHONE: (07) 983-080, 983-039
HOURS: 8 a.m.-4 p.m.
ADMISSION: Fee

During vacations, children's activities include a petting zoo and donkey rides.

ASHKELON

Ashkelon was a center of Philistine culture, as well as the city associated with Samson and Delilah. Archeology buffs will enjoy the ruins in the sunken sculpture garden at the National Park. Today, the city is a resort known for its wonderful climate and lovely beaches.

Tourist Office. Afridar Center. **PHONE:** (07) 770-173, 770-174

Central Bus Station. **PHONE:** (07) 750-221

National Antiquities Park
PHONE: (07) 736-444
HOURS: Apr.-Sept. 8 a.m.-6 p.m.; Oct.-Mar. until 4 p.m.
    Closes early Fridays and holiday eves
ADMISSION: Fee or National Parks Ticket

On the site of the ancient city, sculptures of Atlas, Nike, Isis, and others are set in a park of lush lawns and trees. Pick up a map at the entrance. Spring festival includes children's performances. There are activities on other holidays as well.

Public Beaches are free and rarely crowded. During the summer there are fashion shows and musical entertainment.

Delilah Beach. **PHONE:** (07) 736-929

Barena Beach. **PHONE:** (07) 732-605

Samson Beach. **PHONE:** (07) 711-765

TEENS

Ashkeluna Water Park
Delilah Beach
PHONE: (07) 739-970
HOURS: Apr.-Sept. Daily 8:30 a.m.-6 p.m. May stay open some nights.
ADMISSION: Fee

This is a place your children won't want to miss. Kids of all ages will enjoy the water slides — from gentle mini-slides to the "kamikaze," the scariest slide in Israel. There are two beautiful swimming pools and refreshment areas. Try to choose a weekday when the park is less crowded, and plan to spend all day.

Ashkelon Tennis Center, one of the country's largest, is open daily 9 a.m.-11 p.m. **PHONE:** (07) 722-286

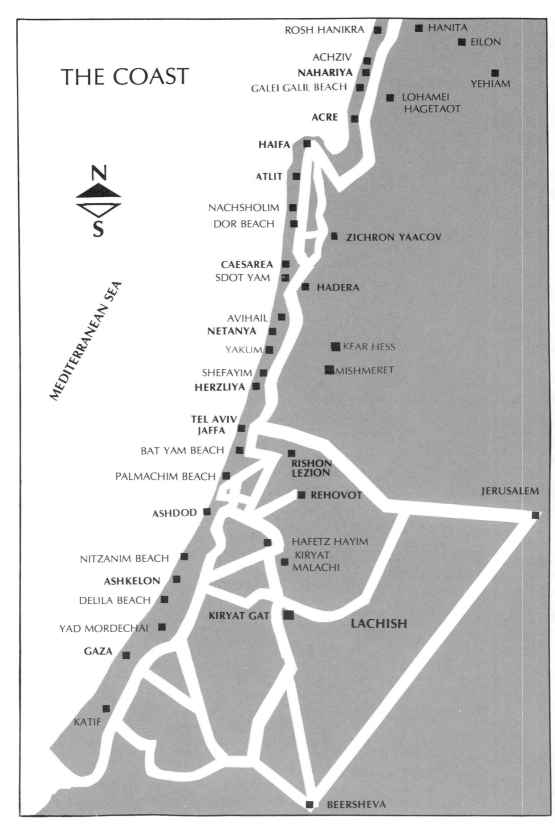

Delilah Beach Billiards Center is open daily in the afternoons and evenings. **PHONE**: (07) 734-794

Horseback Riding is at the City Stables. **PHONE::** (07) 726-608

Nitzanim Beach is a beautiful beach with a kids playground, auto karts, and tractor rides. **PHONE**: (07) 721-464

ASHKELON AREA

Malachim means "angels," and the **Malachim Forest** and nearby development town **Kiryat Malachi** were so named because they were built with donations from the Jewish community of Los Angeles. This is a good picnic spot.

Hafetz Hayim Kibbutz Water Park
PHONE: (08) 593-939
HOURS: Separate daytime and evening hours for boys/men and girls/women. Phone for latest schedule. Closed Shabbat and holidays.
ADMISSION: Fee

Water park designed for religious families, with slides and pools.

WHERE TO STAY

Ashkelon Campground. Campsites, bungalows, and caravans inside the National Park. **PHONE:** (07) 734-027

Vacation Village. This hotel on the sea has its own pool, horse-back riding, archery, fencing, and a children's program in season. PHONE: (07) 736-733, 736-111

Kibbutz Hafetz Hayim Guest House. The rooms are not fancy, but there is a nice religious atmosphere, and the water park is right there. **PHONE:** (08) 593-888; **FAX:** 593-958

ASHDOD

This rapidly developing town will one day be Israel's largest port and industrial center. From **Memorial Hall** you can look out at the harbor where big ships dock. There is building everywhere — residential areas, industrial plants, shopping centers, and hotels. Ashdod is also a lovely resort with sandy beaches.

Golfitek Miniature Golf
HOURS: Daily 4 p.m.-late at night. Shabbat, summer, and school vacations 9 a.m.-late.
PHONE: (08) 642-845

Miniature golf and trampolines.

Coal Terminal Center
PHONE: (08) 563-357 (Terminal); 512-060 (Refinery)
HOURS: Sun.-Thurs. 8 a.m.-3:30 p.m. or by arrangement
ADMISSION: Free

An hour-long presentation including a film about coal and how it's mined and used. You can view the mountains of coal at the terminal and if your Hebrew is good, call ahead and arrange to visit the Oil Refinery, too.

Ashdod Museum
16 Keren Hayesod, Rova Daled
PHONE: (08) 543-092
HOURS: Daily 9 a.m.-1 p.m.; Friday until noon.
   Sun.-Wed. evenings 5-10 p.m.   Also open after Shabbat.
ADMISSION: Fee

There are many children's art activities here. Call ahead for the schedule. A permanent exhibition on Philistine culture is opening soon. Open workshops held during holidays and vacations feature activities related to current exhibitions.

RISHON LEZION

This early settlement, literally "the first of Zion," was established in 1882 by Russian pioneers. When the farmers met hard times, the French philanthropist Baron Edmond de Rothschild sent money and experts to begin a winery. Poet Naftali Herz Imber wrote *Hatikvah,* Israel's national anthem, in Rishon.

Today there is a new cluster of family-friendly sites, and a large immigrant community. You hear so much Russian on the streets that the town has been nicknamed "Russian LeZion."

Open History Museum and the Well
Kikar Hamayasdim
PHONE: (03) 964-1621
HOURS: Sun., Tues., Wed., Thurs. 9 a.m.-2 p.m.; Mon. until 1 p.m.
ADMISSION: Fee includes tour in English

This excellent hands-on museum tells the story of the First Aliyah and recreates life in the old settlement. Make sure you see the schoolroom, where kids used erasers made from the native gum trees. The tour includes a walk along Pioneer's Way and a terrific light and sound show. Kids can dress up as kibbutz founders and take pictures at the town well.

Check out **Fun, Fun,** the play area in the Rishon Shopping Mall open 7 days a week. **PHONE:** (03) 962-5747

Rishon Zoo/Hai Kef

Left of Rishon interchange on Tel Aviv-Ashdod Highway
BUS: 11 from Rishon
PHONE: (03) 961-9402
HOURS: Daily 9 a.m.-6 p.m.; Friday until 4 p.m.
ADMISSION: Fee

A large selection of animals including roaring lions and hopping kangaroos. Watch your kids. The cages are a bit close for comfort!

TEENS →

Superland

Near Rishon Beach area
PHONE: (03) 961-9061
HOURS: Summer: Daily 10:30 a.m.- 1 p.m.; vacations 9 a.m.-midnight
ADMISSION: Fee

This is a very pleasant, medium-sized amusement park with rides for children of all ages. Even tiny tots can ride electric bikes or play in an area set off for them. Older kids will enjoy the roller coaster, the largest ferris wheel in the Middle East (over 100 ft. high), a pirate ship that turns over, and a river ride with an impressive splash — particularly welcome on a hot day! Unlike most amusement parks, Superland encourages you to bring lunch, and provides a picnic area. Drinks and ice cream are for sale.

Nevei Hadarim Country Club

PHONE: (03) 967-3335
BUS: For a small fee, Monit Ha-ir will take you to the club from anywhere in Rishon
HOURS: 5-9 p.m. Pool is closed Sunday night.
ADMISSION: Fee

Indoor and outdoor pools, children's pool, and waterslides. Additional fee for squash and tennis court. Two restaurants on premises.

Carmel Winery

25 Hacarmel Street
PHONE (03) 964-2021
HOURS: Sunday-Thursday 9 a.m.-3 p.m.; Friday until 1 p.m.
ADMISSION: Fee

Rothschild's winery has blossomed into one of Israel's major industries and exports. Visit the cellars, see the 3-D sight-and-sound show, and taste local wines. Each visitor receives a small bottle of wine.

Beaches:

You must pay a fee to use the Rishon public beach, which can be reached by bus from the Central Rishon Bus Station. There is a trampoline park and separate swimming in one section. Nearby is a free beach with handicapped access by car to the water. Another public beach is located at **Palmachim** on the coast between Ashdod and Rishon.

REHOVOT

Founded in 1890 by immigrant farmers, Rehovot is a center for citrus plantations. But it is most famous as the home of one of the world's finest scientific research institutes.

Weizmann Institute of Science

BUSES: 200, 201 from Tel Aviv Central Bus Station with a stop in Rishon.
Bus 435 from Jerusalem runs less frequently.
PHONE: (08) 343-852 (Public Affairs); 483-587 (Science Park)
343-487 (Weizmann House)
HOURS: Sunday-Thursday 9 a.m.-3 p.m.
ADMISSION: Free

Budding scientists may be interested in touring the beautiful campus with modern buildings, lush lawns, and colorful gardens. A documentary film of the Institute's activities is shown Sunday-Thursday at 11 a.m. and 2:45 p.m. The Youth Activities Department runs a hands-on outdoor science museum for children 10 and up. It's free! You also may visit **Chaim Weizmann House,** where Israel's first president lived, and groups can arrange a visit to Weizmann's laboratory. Lunch is served at San Martin Guest House on the campus. There's also a Burger Ranch nearby.

Underground Bullet Factory/Ayalon Institute

Kibbutz Hill, Science Park
PHONE: (08) 406-552
HOURS: Saturday-Thursday 8:30 a.m.-4 p.m.; Friday until noon
ADMISSION: Fee

Camouflaged by a laundry and bakery, this factory was so secret that many kibbutzniks who lived above it didn't even know it existed! The museum and audio-visual presentation give the history of the factory and the manufacturing process. More than 2 million bullets were produced for the sten submachine guns used in the War of Independence. Call ahead to arrange an English-speaking guide.

Further north is **Bat Yam Beach,** a nice beach with a swimming pool. There's also an ice-skating rink, **Heichal Ha-kerach.** PHONE: (03) 552-6655. You can reach Bat Yam by bus from Tel Aviv.

HERZILYIA

Israel's most famous beach resort is also home to many diplomats and wealthy families. United Tours runs buses from Tel Aviv.

At **Herziliya Country Club,** short-term memberships and daily entrance fees are available so tourists can use the wide range of sports facilities. Herziliya's public beach charges a fee. For separate swimming schedule, **PHONE:** (03) 699-9999. For the handicapped, there is a beach with access to the water by car.

Herziliya Miniature Golf at Neve Amirim has miniature golf, trampolines, and a coffee house. **PHONE:** (09) 554-402

WHERE TO STAY

Sharon and Sharon Towers has a salt-water pool and health club. The hotel has a family plan and children's programs during the summer and holidays. **PHONE:** (09) 575-777; **FAX:** 572-448

Eshel Inn charges by the room rather than by the person, and is moderately-priced. Up to four can share a room. The hotel provides free athletic equipment for children. Breakfast is served on the lawn. If you want a unit with a kitchenette, order it well in advance. **PHONE:** (09) 570-208; **FAX:** 570-797

The Daniel, one of the country's most luxurious and expensive hotels, has elegant public areas, easy access to the beach, and a large pool and kiddie pool. Children's activities are scheduled throughout the day. **PHONE:** (09) 544-444; **FAX:** 544-675

Dan Accadia's family plan rates are even better off-season, but it's still very expensive. **PHONE:** (09) 566-677; **FAX:** 562-141

Marine Heights Hotel has 1-3 bedroom suites with kitchenettes and a swimming pool. **PHONE:** (09) 508-787; **FAX:** 580-320

ON TO NETANYA

Yakum Park
Right off Herziliya-Haifa Road
PHONE: (09) 524-4422
HOURS: Daily 8 a.m.-3 p.m.; Friday until 1 p.m.
ADMISSION: Cars can park free every day but Saturday; fee for activities.

At the Poleg nature reserve, Kibbutz Yakum has created a park where youngsters can hike, go cliff rappeling with ropes, and learn to navigate paddleboats with the help of a map and compass (supplied). There is also a playground and wonderful flowers.

Shefayim Water Park
BUS: 60 from Tel Aviv
PHONE: (09) 595-757
HOURS: April-November daily 8 a.m.-9 p.m.
ADMISSION: Fee

A pool with wild waves and many water slides will interest the young and young at heart. There is a snack bar on the premises. You can spend a whole day here!

NETANYA

This beachside resort has dozens of hotels clustered around the shore. In the town center there is a pedestrian promenade with cafes, discos, movies, and shopping. A ferris wheel and bumper cars provide amusement. Horse and buggy rides (pricey) are available. During Sukkot there are folklore evenings, and in May and June the Israeli Chess Federation sponsors tournaments. In the summer, there are weekly programs for children, with magicians, clowns, and entertainment, as well as community folk-dancing every Saturday night. In July there is a week-long art exhibit on the mall.

Tourist Information Office
Kikar Ha'atzmaut
PHONE: (09) 827-286
HOURS: Sun.-Fri. 8:30 a.m.-2 p.m.; summer also 4-7 p.m.
Closed Saturday and holidays.

Central Bus Station. 59 Smilansky. PHONE: (09) 827-884

Gan Hamelech Park
North of Kikar Ha-atzmaut

Community sing-alongs, films, and concerts during the summer.

Orah Handweaving Workshop for the Blind
PHONE: (09) 653-356

Linens and clothing for women and children are made and sold.

National Diamond Center
90 Herzl Street
PHONE: (09) 624-770

An audio-visual presentation and a demonstration of diamond cutting and polishing. Call for a free tour.

Yemenite Culture Museum
PHONE: (09) 331-325
HOURS: Sunday-Thursday 8 a.m.-4 p.m.; closed Friday and Saturday.

Exhibit of Yemenite culture and folklore.

Therapeutic Riding Club of Israel
PHONE: (09) 967-705.
Call in afternoon to find out best time to come.

Anita and Giora Shekdi provide horseback riding as rehabilitation for those injured by war, disease, or accidents. You can visit and see their wonderful work.

Beaches:

The public beaches are free. **Herzl Beach** has a water slide, basketball court, and gymnastics field. **Kiryat Sanz Beach** has separate swimming. There is another public beach at **Michmoret** and a private beach at **Beit Yannai.**

NETANYA AREA

Pet-A-Pet
Moshav Havatzelet Hasharon
PHONE: (09) 663-275, 663-098
HOURS: Call for hours
ADMISSION: Fee

English immigrants Peter and Craig Myers have set up this low-key petting farm with genuine Welsh ponies for small children to ride. Adults can enjoy a cup of espresso while the kids play.

Israel Defense Forces Museum - Beit Hagedudim
Moshav Avihail
PHONE: (09) 822-212
ADMISSION: Fee

This museum focuses on the Hebrew Brigade (Hagedud Haivri) which fought with the British against the Turks. Many of Israel's early military leaders got their practical experience there. The 12-minute audio-visual presentation is interesting, but the rest of the museum is old-fashioned. Groups can arrange to see an excellent collection of historical-military films in the cool auditorium. There is a lovely picnic ground across from the museum, and you can swim in the moshav pool for a fee.

The Ranch
North of Netanya
PHONE: (09) 663-525
HOURS: 8 a.m.-sunset
ADMISSION: Fee

Horseback riding for children ages 8 and up. Smaller children can have corral rides while their siblings take lessons, or if they are experienced, head out to the beach. The scenery is stunning. Teens should check out the night riding.

These next two sites, off the beaten path, are worth it!

Parrot Farm
Kfar Hess
PHONE: (09) 961-773, 961-957
ADMISSION: Fee

Hundreds of beautiful birds — including unusual doves — can be viewed at this family-run moshav. Better yet, you can take many of the birds out of their cages and hold them. Transparent nesting boxes allow you to observe egg-laying, roosting, hatching, and mothers feeding their young. There's also a large petting farm.

A Day in the Country - Honey Production

Moshav Mishmeret
PHONE: (09) 967-146
HOURS: Call ahead.
ADMISSION: Fee

This fascinating program about honey production includes kid-sized bee-keeper costumes, plus honey-tasting. Plan on several hours. You can picnic and enjoy the petting farm after the demonstration. The owner was an elementary school teacher and her knowledge of children shows.

WHERE TO STAY

Netanya has hotels at all price levels, but most offer simple facilities, expecting visitors to be more interested in the beach than the decor. The beach is a relatively long walk from most hotels.

Apartment Hotel. La Promenade. New and luxurious; each unit has a kitchenette. **PHONE:** (09) 626-450; **U.S.:** (718) 338-6537

The Seasons. A more luxurious hotel (formerly called the Four Seasons). **PHONE:** (09) 618-555; **FAX:** (09) 623-022

Blue Bay. For better or worse, this hotel is north of town. It's quiet and offers a children's program and direct access to a wide, sandy beach, but you need to take a shuttle to get to town. **PHONE:** (09) 603-602; **FAX:** (09) 337-474

Emek Hefer Youth Hostel at Kfar Vitkin. Family rooms, a kitchen for guest use, and a swimming pool at a reasonable price. **PHONE/FAX:** (09) 666-032

Shefayim Kibbutz Guest House. Use of the water park is included in the price. **PHONE:** (09) 595-595; **FAX:** (09) 595-555

HADERA

Sihek Otah Playland

Hadera Industrial Area
PHONE: (06) 323-421
HOURS: Sun.-Thurs. 2-7 p.m.; Sat./holidays: 9 a.m.-sundown; closed Fri.
ADMISSION: Fee

Kiddie cars, trampolines, and ball pools for kids ages 1-13.

Khan Historical Museum

74 Hagiborim Street
PHONE: (06) 322-330
ADMISSION: Fee

A museum built in one of the city's first homes, with "talking" exhibits which tell the story of the town.

Okvim Lohatim Activity Center

Moshav Amikim
PHONE: (06) 388-675, 389-578
HOURS: Open evenings; call ahead.
ADMISSION: Fee

Hiking, donkey rides, trampolines, and biking are featured at this play area off the beaten path. Trail guides are available. On weekends and holidays you can bake your own pita and shop at a Bedouin-style bazaar.

Avi's, an inexpensive grill restauarant, has excellent food and quick service. It's even worth the drive from Caesarea. Hadera Junction, Old Road. **PHONE:** (06) 331-115

CAESAREA

Caesarea was once the largest city in Judea. Herod built a splendid port here, which he dedicated to Augustus Caesar, the Roman Emperor. Later, Rabbi Akiva and other Jewish martyrs were tortured and burned here after the Bar Kochba Revolt. Today, Caesarea is a resort town. Wealthy families have built villas, and it is home to Israel's only golf course. The extensive archeological remains have been restored.

Caesarea National Park

PHONE: (06) 361-358
HOURS: Summer: Sat.-Thurs. 8 a.m.-6 p.m.; Friday until 5 p.m.
Winter: Daily 8 a.m.-4 p.m.
ADMISSION: Fee; you can see the Amphitheater and the Crusader City on the same ticket.

Roman Amphitheater: This 5,000-seat building is now a site for outdoor summer concerts of music, dance, and opera. The acoustics are wonderful. Check a city ticket agency or call directly. **PHONE:** (06) 361-358

Crusader City: Hebrew and English signs enable you to follow the sites, which include a large moat, massive walls, a restored bridge, and a tower.

The **Hippodrome,** a horse-racing arena that could seat 20,000; giant headless statues on **Byzantine Street**; and the **Roman Aqueduct** are also worth seeing.

English-speaking guide Ilana Berner offers family tours around the area. **PHONE:** (06) 363-936

Gal Mor Diving Center
At the site of the ancient harbor
PHONE: (06) 361-787
ADMISSION: Fee

Ten year-old swimmers can dive with a guide, Diving courses, for teens 15 and over, are popular with Israeli kids. The beach has umbrellas and chairs and a shallow area for toddlers. You can see underwater ruins from Roman times.

Herod's Stables. PHONE: (06) 361-181. Horseback tours.

Kibbutz Sdot Yam
Just south of Caesarea
PHONE: (06) 364-444, 364-470
ADMISSION: Fee

The kibbutz offers guided tours and at night, occasional reen-actments of the rescue of clandestine immigrants. The **Hannah Senesh Study Center** has daily audio-visual shows about her life and rescue missions to Hungary during the Holocaust.

Kef Yam, Sdot Yam's vacation village, offers rides on Israel's fastest speed boat, as well as a more leisurely glass-bottom boat ride to view the ancient harbor and watch the fish. There's even a cruise to Cyprus. You can combine a jeep tour with coastal sailing. If your child gets seasick, avoid days when the sea is choppy.

Amat Taninim Park
Beit Hanania
PHONE: (06) 363-903
HOURS: 9 a.m.-sunset
ADMISSION: Fee

Horse and wagons, mountain bikes, donkey rides, and a lake for rafting, boating, and fishing. The family running this new site offers explanations of the area in English or French. Picnic area.

WHERE TO STAY

Kef Yam Guest House. Kibbutz Sdot Yam. PHONE: (06) 364-470

Dan Caesarea. PHONE: (06) 362-266; FAX: 362-392

Ilana Berner's Bed and Breakfast, a one-story villa on Harimon Street in Caesarea, has a huge yard, pool, and suites with kitchen-ettes. Ilana loves kids. PHONE: (06) 363-936; U.S.: (703) 536-4064

Villa Rentals. If you want to use Caesarea as your base, you can rent a villa. In 1995, the cheapest was $3,500/month without a pool. A fancy house with a pool could run as high as $12,000/month. Believe it or not, you must call well in advance; the supply is limited. **PHONE:** (06) 363-936

TO ZICHRON YA'AKOV

There are tours of old **Benyamina**, including the Museum of Early Settlers. **PHONE:** (06) 388-511

Shoni
Jabotinsky Park between Zichron and Benyamina
PHONE: (06) 389-730
ADMISSION: Fee

Children 10 and over may like the museum and audio-visual presentation dealing with the Roman artifacts found here, and with the training of the underground Etzel movement to fight the British in 1948. The park is a good place to picnic.

Baron Winery. For a fee, you can tour this family winery and sample wine, bread, and cheese. **PHONE**: (06) 380-434

Eliaz Winery's tour includes a film about wine-making, a visit to the cellars, exhibits of wine in Jewish ritual, and tasting. There is a fee. Phone ahead to say you're coming. **PHONE:** (06) 386-434

Combine a winery tour with a visit to **Jabotinsky Park** or call ahead and The Milman family will show yours how the bee makes honey. There's a fee. **PHONE:** (06) 380-608

Hama'ayan Fishing Park
Route 4 (The Old Road)
PHONE: (06) 320-001
ADMISSION: Fee

You can rent fishing gear, go fishing, or use the swimming pool at Kibbutz Ma'ayan Tzvi, which runs this park. Picnic area.

Natural History Museum
Kibbutz Ma'ayan Tzvi
PHONE: (06) 395-113
HOURS: The museum opens only for 10 or more guests with reservations.
ADMISSION: Fee

The collection of stuffed animals and the nature films highlight the animal life of the area. You also may request a tour of the kibbutz's high-yield fish ponds.

ZICHRON YA'AKOV

Zichron, one of the country's oldest settlements, is located on a hill high above the coast. Drop in at the Municipality Building and ask for a brochure about the history of the community.

Zichron is the center of wine country. During the grape harvest (August and September) you will see tractors of grapes rolling into town toward the Carmel Winery. The grapes are dumped into a huge bin, and the drivers wait for them to be graded by sweetness.

If you haven't been to Zichron in a long time, you won't recognize the town, which has awakened to its historical importance. Part of downtown has been closed to create an attractive walking area. There are a few small winery tours in addition to Carmel. New hotels have opened, and there are lots of activities in a small area.

Visitor's Center. PHONE: (06) 398-811

Carmel Winery
Wine Street, a short walk from the town center
PHONE: (06) 390-105, 390-108
HOURS: Sunday-Thursday 9 a.m.-3 p.m.; Friday until 1 p.m.
ADMISSION: Fee

Allow an hour to see the winery, taste the wine, and shop. The tour includes a 3-D sight and sound show about the history of Carmel Wine. Visitors get a small bottle of wine.

> Check at the **Visitor's Center** near the bus station to see which of the smaller wineries allow tourists.

Aaronson House
40 Mayesdim Street
PHONE: (06) 390-120
HOURS: Sunday-Thursday 9:30 a.m.-12:30 p.m.
ADMISSION: Fee

Nili was the code name given the Aaronson family — Sarah and her brothers— who farmed at nearby Atlit and worked as spies for the British during World War I. There is a 15-minute film about the Nili group. You can see the trap-door of their secret hiding place. My kids were fascinated by a gun-shaped purse. Later, peek into the large synagogue at the center of town. After the Nili spies were captured by the enemy Turks, the people of Zichron were held here while the Aaronsons were tortured.

At **Pioneer's House** you can meet with the Berkowitz family, authentic Zichron old-timers, and hear the stories of the early settlement. The building used to be the threshing floor for agricultural produce. There is a fee. Call ahead. PHONE: (06) 399-308

Rothschild Memorial Gardens
Ramat Hanadiv
PHONE: (06) 399-117
HOURS: Daily 10 a.m.-3 p.m.
ADMISSION: Free

Can your kids tell time on the sundial? If it's summer, you will have to add an hour for Daylight Savings Time. The snack bar of this lovely park is a nice place for lunch.

Ask at the tourist office whether any of the local potters are at work and would enjoy showing you their craft.

Sportan Country Club
PHONE: (06) 397-788
ADMISSION: Fee

Sports club with swimming pool and tennis courts.

Tut Niyar Paper Mill
39 Mayesdim
PHONE: (06) 397-631
ADMISSION: Fee

The mill produces hand-made paper from local plants. You can buy stationery and greeting cards. Call ahead to arrange a family or group paper-making workshop. It takes about two hours and is recommended for children ages 5 and over.

Active Farming
PHONE: (06) 398-248
HOURS: Shabbat and holidays
ADMISSION: Fee

Old-fashioned farming activities include making cheese and butter, grinding wheat, baking pita, and milking goats.

Sky Free Fall Club at Tzomet Habonim is for teens over 13.
PHONE: (06) 391-068

Michura Stables at Kerem Maharal has everything from pony rides and riding lessons to day trips. Teens can take overnight trips, camp out, and enjoy the beautiful view.

> The **Kerem Maharal JNF Forest** is a lovely picnic stop.
> Nearby **Ofer Lookout** has a wonderful view.

Birdwatching: SPNI Field School, Kibbutz Ma'agan Michael.
PHONE: (06) 399-655

Dor Beach
Kibbutz Nahsholim
PHONE: (06) 387-180
HOURS: Daily during swimming season.
ADMISSION: Fee

Because it is a bay, Dor Beach is terrific for family swimming.
The water is shallow and gentle, and even toddlers can venture in
with supervision. A separate stretch, to the right of the main
beach, has enough waves to interest older children. There are
children's activities and air-conditioned igloos right on the beach.

Dor Glass Museum
Near Dor Beach Guest House
PHONE: (06) 390-950
HOURS: Weekdays 8:30 a.m. -2 p.m.; Shabbat 10:30 a.m.-3 p.m.
ADMISSION: Fee

The Dor Museum has been moved into the old glass factory, set
up by Baron Rothschild in 1891. There's an audio-visual. show
and display of early glass. Unfortunately, the nearby beach sand,
wonderful for playing, wasn't good for glass-making.

Open Air Restoration Museum and Kibbutz Adventures
Kibbutz Ein Shemer
PHONE : (06) 374-327
HOURS: Weekdays 8 a.m.-4 p.m.; Fri. until 1 p.m.; Shabbat 9 a.m.-4 p.m.
ADMISSION: Fee

The museum will open only for groups. It is an excellent
restoration of an early kibbutz, with an amusing and interesting
film about kibbutz life. You also can take a kibbutz tour, ride on
a tractor or restored Turkish railroad car, work the old-fashioned
plows (they're hooked up to electricity), and go for a guided hike.
Call ahead to request an English-speaking guide.

Cave Reserve
8 miles north of Faredis Junction on the old Haifa-Tel Aviv Road
PHONE: (04) 984-1750
HOURS: Saturday-Thursday 8 a.m.-4 p.m.; Friday 8 a.m.-1 p.m.
ADMISSION: Fee

Climb up and see the only caves in Israel where skeletons of

Neanderthal and Cro-Magnin man were found. The audio-visual show is right in the cave.

Horseback Riding at Beit Oren includes riding lessons and day trips on horseback. **PHONE:** (04) 307-242

> If your family can manage a 3-hour hike, you can walk from Kibbutz Beit Oren along the path the Palmach took to liberate the Jews held in the Atlit Detention camp in 1945.

Atlit Detention Camp
PHONE: (04) 984-1980
ADMISSION: Fee

You'll remember this illegal immigration camp, set up by the British in 1938, from the movie *Exodus*. Guided tours include an audio-visual presentation (Hebrew, English, Spanish, or Russian). Educational programs include exciting reenactments of landings of illegal immigrants. Call to find out if you can take part in one.

Neveh Yam Water Park
Atlit
PHONE: (04) 984-4870
HOURS: May-September 9 a.m.-5 p.m.; night swimming in summer.
ADMISSION: Fee

The park includes slides for small children ages 2-10 and very exciting slides for older kids. There is a large swimming pool and access to the beach.

WHERE TO STAY

Havat Habaron Suite Hotel in Zichron Ya'akov has a swimming pool and on-site supermarket. **PHONE:** (06) 300-333

Eden Inn, also in Zichron, has a family atmosphere and nice grass to play on. **PHONE:** (06) 390-070; **FAX:** 391-271

Beit Maimon is a small hotel in Zichron with a lovely view, pleasant breeze, and family atmosphere. Some rooms have kitchenettes. **PHONE:** (06) 396-547; **FAX:** 396-547

Beit Oren Kibbutz Guest House. Country atmosphere in a pretty setting. Good place to hike. Swimming pool. **PHONE** (04) 222-111; **FAX:** 231-443

Neveh Yam Vacation Village. Holiday apartments, children's activities, and a water park. **PHONE:** (04) 842-542; **FAX :** 843-344

Nahsholim Kibbutz Holiday Village. Holiday apartments and a family-style restaurant in this kibbutz on the beach. Playground and tennis courts. Children's activities on weekends and holidays. **PHONE:** (06) 399-533; **FAX:** 397-614

Nir Etzion Kibbutz Hotel. A more traditional place, this kibbutz guest house set in the country, has Shabbat activities, playground, swimming pool, horseback riding, and transportation to nearby Dor Beach. **PHONE:** (04) 842-542; **FAX:** 843-344

Moshav Dor. Also on the beach, this moshav has a guest house with air-conditioned bungalows for up to six persons, as well as camping facilities, including cabins. Fishing is allowed. **PHONE:** (06) 399-018; **FAX:** 397-180

See Separate Section for Haifa

ACRE

Acre (*Akko* in Hebrew), 14 miles north of Haifa, is a promontory on the northern end of Haifa Bay. But driving takes longer than you think, because of the traffic jams of Haifa's suburbs.

The city is almost 4,000 years old. Because of its geographical location, every army waging campaigns in Syria and Israel sought to occupy it. Caesar landed there in 48 BCE, and nine years later Herod made it the base for conquering his kingdom. In 1775, Ahmed Al Jazzar rebuilt and fortified the town.

There's a lot to see in the Old City, but with children you'll want to choose one or two sites, including the sunken children's playground near the entrance. Later you may want to swim at the free public beach or stroll the colorful market streets. During Sukkot there is an Alternative Theater Festival with street performances.

Tourist Office
Across from Mosque
PHONE: (04) 991-1764
HOURS: Sun.-Thurs. 8:30 a.m.-4 p.m.; closes earlier on Friday.

Subterranean Crusader City
PHONE: (04) 991-0251; Mosque 911-0078
HOURS: Daily 9 a.m.-4:45 p.m.; Fri. until 1:45 p.m.
    Mosque: Daily 9:30 a.m.-5 p.m.; Friday 9 a.m.-noon
ADMISSION: Ticket is also good at the Municipal Museum.
    Separate ticket for Mosque.

This underground site is cool and spooky. See where the Crusaders lived and worked. There are gates, towers, tunnels, and

long, dark, secret passageways. In the **Knights' Hall**, ask to see the 20-minute film on the city's history. There are kids' activities and theater performances on holidays.

At the **Municipal Museum** in Ahmet Zessar Pasha's Turkish Bath House, you can see the ornate steam rooms and a folklore exhibit. Then walk the ramparts for a magnificent sea view. The **Mosque of Jazzar**, one of the most beautiful examples of Ottoman architecture, is still used by Acre's Muslim community.

Museum of Underground Prisoners
PHONE: (04) 991-8264
HOURS: Weekdays 9 a.m.-5 p.m.; closed Shabbat. Call ahead.
Because of excavations, parts of the museum may be closed.
ADMISSION: Fee

The museum is a tribute to the underground fighters and leaders of Israel's independence movement. The entrance is a rather long walk from the Old City. Drive or take a cab to save energy to walk inside the museum. The building was used as a Turkish and British prison. Pictures of the eight Irgun members executed here by the British are displayed not far from the gallows. You also can see a model of the mass escape by 200 Jewish prisoners in May 1947, made famous by the movie *Exodus*.

Neve Afek Reserve, west of Kibbutz Afek, is a lovely nature reserve with an audio-visual show, crusader fort, and flour mill.
PHONE: (04) 779-992

Look for a **Miniature Golf Course** off the Acre-Nahariya highway. PHONE: (04) 985-7859

Beaches:

Acre Beach and Marina. PHONE: (04) 991-9287
Argamon Beach. PHONE: (04) 991-1672
Rami's Diving. Courses/equipment rental. PHONE: (04) 991-8990

WHERE TO STAY

Palm Beach Hotel. Children 2-12 in parents' room pay half price. Children in a separate room pay 80%. Guests have free use of the country club. PHONE: (04) 910-888, 912-891

Acre Youth Hostel. Family rooms and shared guest kitchen in a magnificent building in the old city. PHONE: (04) 991-1982

Kibbutz Shomrat Rustic Accommodations between Acre and Nahariya. PHONE: (04) 985-4897; FAX: 985-4828

TO NAHARIYA

Children's Holocaust Museum
Kibbutz Lohame Hagetaot
PHONE: (04) 995-8080
HOURS: Currently 9 a.m.-1 p.m., but call ahead. Hours change.
ADMISSION: Free

This remarkable new memorial/museum designed by Ram Caspi (who also designed the new Jerusalem Supreme Court), is a wing of a larger museum in a kibbutz founded by survivors of the Warsaw Ghetto. As children walk through the 3-dimensional display, they experience what it is like being removed from home, moving into the ghetto, and being transported to a concentration camp. An excellent hand-held recorder coded for each section of the museum broadcasts English-speaking children telling personal stories about the Holocaust.

One section of the museum is dedicated to **Yanosh Korczak**, a teacher and writer who organized an orphanage in Poland during the Nazi period and chose to perish along with the orphans. The exhibits are geared to children 8-15. Use your discretion with younger children.

The larger museum has a section on Sephardic Jewry, an exhibition on youth movements before the war, horrifying artifacts from the Holocaust, and a model of the Warsaw ghetto.

NAHARIYA

Nahariya is among the most charming cities in Israel. A mountain stream runs through the center of town (*nahar* means river), and horse-drawn carriages share the streets with bicycles. A favorite honeymoon spot for Israelis, it is a lovely place for tourists.

Tourist Information Office
Ha-Ga'aton Street
PHONE: (04) 987-9800
HOURS: Sunday-Thursday 9 a.m.-1 p.m. and 4-7 p.m.; Friday until 4 p.m.

Rent a Bike. Young and old bike everywhere in Nahariya. Special bike lanes have been created on the outskirts of town. You can even pedal to **Achziv Beach** (2½ miles). Currently there are two bike rental stores on Herzl Street. The Hebrew word for bike is *ofnayim*. To rent a bike is *l'haskir ofnayim*.

Galei-Galil Beach
PHONE: (04) 924-424
ADMISSION: Fee

This beach curves to form a bay, making it a perfect place for toddlers. In addition, there is an olympic-size swimming pool, a children's pool with an elephant-shaped slide, and a playground. Call for information about sailing and diving.

Boat Rides. During the summer, you can rent a small paddle boat in the seaside lake called Agam Hashashuim.

Nahariya Glass Factory. Call ahead to arrange a short tour to see artistic glassware being made. PHONE: (04) 992-0066

> Make sure you visit the **Memorial Statue to Illegal Immigration** at the end of Ha-Ga'aton Street. It's made from pieces of the *Aliyah*, one of the ships which brought Jewish refugees to Palestine in spite of the British quotas.
>
> Just beyond the statue is a lovely playground with climbing toys. Look for an ice cream peddler — on a bicycle!

Tennis courts on Henrietta Szold Street are open every morning except Saturday. PHONE: (04) 982-6181

Family Dancing sponsored by the city is held at the Amphitheater on Ha-Ga'aton Street twice weekly in July and August. Younger children like the beginners sessions from 7-8 p.m.

WHERE TO STAY

Carlton Hotel. Family suites, a pool, children's play area, and children's program. PHONE: (04) 992-2211; FAX: 982-3771

Shlomi Youth Hostel in the Hanita Forest is one of the newest and nicest hostels in Israel. Family rooms are available. PHONE: (04) 980-8975; FAX: (04) 980-9163

Kalman Youth Hostel on Jabotinsky Street, a short walk from the beach and the Nahariya Bus Station, has air-conditioned family rooms. PHONE : (04) 920-355; FAX: 992-6539

> Nahariya has many modest hotels. The public pool is lovely, so you can consider a hotel without one.

NORTH TO THE BORDER

Achziv National Park
North of Nahariya
PHONE: (04) 982-3263
HOURS: Daily 8 a.m.-7 p.m. Lifeguard on beach 8 a.m.-5 p.m.
ADMISSION: Fee or National Parks Ticket

This park was created on the ruins of the old Canaanite and

Byzantine settlement of Achziv, mentioned in the conquests of Joshua in the Bible. It's a lovely spot for a picnic. The five nearby islands are bird sanctuaries.

At **Achziv Diving School,** acoss the highway from the beach, you can learn diving with experienced instructors. They also have fast boat rides. PHONE: (04) 982-3671

Eilon Mosaics
Kibbutz Eilon; Northern Road toward Bir Am
PHONE: (04) 858-125
HOURS: Daily 6 a.m.-2 p.m.; Saturday 10 a..m.-2 p.m.
ADMISSION: Free

Watch the kibbutz craftsmen make beautiful mosaics from local stones. Products are for sale. You can even order a mural for your home. If you phone ahead, you may arrange for a kibbutznik to give you a tour and recount the history of the settlement.

Look for the **Aqueduct** and **Double Aqueduct** near Kibbutz Gesher Haziv. The Turkish ruler who rebuilt Acre added to the Roman structure.

Another **Memorial to Illegal Immigration** sits on the coast below Rosh Hanikra. The black statue is constructed from the wrecks of ships which tried to reach safe shores. Kids can take off ther shoes and walk along the shallow beach and pools formed by the rocks. A refreshment stand is nearby.

Cable Car at Rosh Hanikra
6 miles north of Nahariya
PHONE: 177-022-9484 (Toll-free)
HOURS: Opens daily at 8:30 a.m. Closes before sundown.
ADMISSION: Fee

The view from the cliffs is breathtaking. On a clear day you can see all the way to Haifa. A short ride in large, new cable cars takes you down to the white grottoes carved by the waves lapping at the rocks. You can see a 3-D audio-visual display. There is a restaurant here and a public phone used mostly by soldiers guarding this border. The cars going south are arriving from Lebanon!

Betzet Beach and **Rosh Hanikra Reserve** are nice for walking and exploring, but the surf is difficult for children. The **JNF Park** at the Shlomi Junction is good for picnics and play.

INLAND

Kibbutz Hanita
Northern Road, near Shlomit Junction
HOURS: Sun.-Thurs. 8:30-11:30 a.m. and 12-2; Fri. until 1; Sat. 9:30-noon.
ADMISSION: Fee

History buffs can learn about the "wall and tower" method used to settle Palestine. View the exhibits, see a movie, hear a talk, and tour the kibbutz which was established in 1938.

> **The Shayara,** south of Kabri Junction, commemorates the War of Independence battle for the road to beseiged Kibbutz Yehiam. A relief map sketches the battle in which a Haganah convoy of 46 was killed in ambush.

Yehiam Castle
Kibbutz Yehiam, east of Nahariya
HOURS: Sun.-Thurs. 8 a.m.-5 p.m.; Fri., Sat. until noon
Closes earlier October-March
ADMISSION: Fee or National Parks Ticket

The Turkish fortress was built in the 18th century on the site of a Crusader castle. The kibbutz is named for Yehiam Weitz who fell in the Night of Bridges action June 16, 1944. There are music festivals during school vacations.

WHERE TO STAY

Yad le Yad Youth Hostel. Family-style rooms and kitchen facilities. Discounts at Achziv National Park. PHONE: (04) 982-3345

Achziv Club Med. An all-inclusive resort with activities for the whole family. PHONE: (04) 982-1459

Achziv Holiday Village. PHONE: (04) 982-6302

Gesher Haziv Rustic Accommodations. Swimming pool. Discount at seaside diving center. PHONE: (04) 995-8568

SPNI Achziv Field School. This facility is a good base for visiting the area's nature reserves. PHONE: (04) 982-3762

THE NORTH

If you line up a ruler through the cities of Beit Shean, Afula, and Haifa, you will mark off the area called the Galilee (*Galil*), from the Hebrew word "to roll." This northern area, in contrast to the south, is characterized by lush green fields and hillsides, clear mountain streams and in spring, beds of colorful wildflowers. The **Kinneret (Sea of Galilee),** Israel's major water source and popular tourist spot, is located here.

The Galilee can be divided into two main regions: a southern one of moderate elevation called **Lower Galilee,** and a northern one with the highest mountains in the area called **Upper Galilee.** A strip of land, **Etzbah Hagalil,** the "finger" or panhandle of the Galilee, protrudes into Lebanon just below Mt. Hermon. The **Golan Heights** forms the border with Syria.

GOING NORTH

If you are driving from Jerusalem, the quickest route is to bypass Jericho and continue north along the Jordanian border. Because of unstable relations with Palestinians, and because the road is winding and isolated, you may not wish to drive it at night. An alternative route is through Afula.

LOWER GALILEE

Pezael (called Fezael!) Crocodile Farm
Jordan Valley — about an hour from Jerusalem
PHONE: (02) 994-1207
HOURS: Daily 8 a.m.-4 p.m.
ADMISSION: Nominal fee

More than 4000 Nile crocodiles flourish here. The biggest are 12 feet long. Children can hold the babies and feed the adults Look for the famous jawless crocodiles. A short film is shown. This is a good place for cold drinks and restrooms.

BEIT SHEAN VALLEY

Beit Shean National Park Visitors' Center
HOURS: Sat.-Thurs. 8 a.m.-5 p.m.; Fri. until 3 p.m.
PHONE: (06) 587-189
ADMISSION: Fee

Beit Shean's incredible archeological treasures have been restored. There are several layers of cities from different ages. The ruins include Israel's best preserved Roman Theater, restored with the help of the Los Angeles Jewish Federation. There are frequent outdoor concerts and operas, and a Performing Arts Festival in May which features international stars. A playground and picnic area are located near the entrance.

The city of Beit Shean is famous for **felafel** and **shwarma.** Try the **Rosco Center** near the Bus Station, or **Etzel Rachel,** a Moroccan restaurant across from Bank Leumi.

The Beit Shean Valley is very hot. Keep touring hours short in the summer. For cooling off, stop at the swimming pool at **Ma'ayan Harod.** PHONE: (06) 532-211 or at **Huga Park.**

Huga Park
Entrance near Roman Bridge
PHONE: (06) 581-874
HOURS: Daily 9 a.m.-5 p.m.
ADMISSION: Fee

This park, across from Beit Shean's archeological sites, has a natural swimming hole fed by fresh springs. It is deep only in the middle and therefore good for small children.

TEENS

Gan Hashlosha (Sachne)
Near Kibbutz Beit Alpha, off Route 90 before Beit Shean
PHONE: (06) 586-219
HOURS: Daily 8 a.m.-5 p.m.; open later in summer; closes earlier in winter.
ADMISSION: Fee or National Parks Ticket

Here is an absolutely beautiful park, with shaded lawns and refreshing pools boasting a year-round temperature in the 80's. There are long, natural water slides in addition to shallow pools with small waterfalls where young children can swim if supervised. Older children love to swim under the larger waterfalls. There also is a tower and stockade exhibit and an old mill where children can try their hand at making bread.

The park is a wonderful place to relax and picnic. There are changing facilities and a restaurant. The only drawback is overcrowding in summer, particularly on Fridays and Saturdays. If you are in Israel on a sunny day during the spring, fall, or winter, you can have this paradise almost to yourselves. Plan at least an hour to swim here, though you can certainly spend a whole day if you have the time. We have trouble getting our children to leave.

Beit Alpha Synagogue
Kibbutz Heftzibah
PHONE: (06) 531-400
HOURS: April-September: Daily except Friday 8 a.m.-5 p.m.
ADMISSION: Fee or National Parks Ticket

When kibbutzniks were installing water pipes, they uncovered a magnificent mosaic full of scenes from the Bible and a large zodiac wheel. Your children may enjoy finding their birthday signs.

Belvoir Crusader Fortress (Kochav Hayarden)
4 miles north of Beit Shean
PHONE: (06) 587-000
HOURS: April -September 8 a.m.-5 p.m.; October-March 8 a.m.-4 p.m.
ADMISSION: Fee or National Parks Ticket

A good place to stretch your legs and your horizons is Belvoir, a 12th century fortress perched on a promontory overlooking the Jordan Valley. You'll understand its name (Belvoir means beautiful view) when you reach the top and see the magnificent vista below. The walk is just enough to wake up the kids for the rest of the trip. A snack bar, fresh drinking water, and clean bathrooms are located on the site. If your child has a bee allergy, however, skip this excursion. Apiaries are located nearby.

There are good hiking trails on **Mt. Gilboa.** Check with SPNI.

Beit Sturman Museum and Institute for Harod Valley Studies
Kibbutz Ein Harod
PHONE: (06) 531-605
HOURS: Sun.-Thurs. 8 a.m.-3 p.m.; closed Fri.; Sat. 10 a.m.-2 p.m.
ADMISSION: Fee

Exhibits and a film tell the story of early settlement in the area.

Kibbutz Ma'aleh Gilboa's dining room is a good place for a kosher lunch and a great view. **PHONE:** (06) 539-500

Yifat Pioneering Museum
Kibbutz Yifat
PHONE (06) 548-974
HOURS: Sat.-Thurs. 8 a.m.-2:30 p.m.; Fri. until 1 p.m.
ADMISSION: Fee

A hands-on museum with original work tools and artifacts of the settlement period.

Old Gesher
Kibbutz Gesher
PHONE: (06) 758-783
HOURS: Daily 10 a.m.-4 p.m.; Friday until 1 p.m.

Inside a War of Independence bunker you can see an audio-visual show that documents the difficult battle for this kibbutz.

WHERE TO STAY

Ma'ayan Harod Youth Hostel. Plain, reasonably-priced accommodations in a good location for touring the Mt. Gilboa area.
PHONE/FAX: (06) 531-660

Call the **Gidona Valley Council Tourist Association** for a list of bed and breakfasts in the area. **PHONE:** (06) 532-047, 532-048

NORTH VIA AFULA

Yokneam Fishing Area
PHONE: (04) 989-4095
HOURS: Daily 8 a.m.-6 p.m.
ADMISSION: Fee

You can fish, then clean and grill your catch here. On weekends and holidays there are arts and crafts activities related to fishing.

Tefen Industrial Park and Open Museum
Near Ma'alot
PHONE: (04) 987-2977
HOURS: Sun.-Thurs. 9 a.m.-4 p.m.; Sat. 10 a.m.-5 p.m.; closed Fri.
ADMISSION: Fee

This plush green park with a sculpture garden and art exhibit was created by industrialist Stef Wertheimer as a way of attracting business to the north. A film shown in the public relations office explains the concept of the park. The site includes a cafeteria, pottery studio, and a variety of factory stores, as well as an exhibit of the accomplishments of German Jews in Israel.

NAZARETH

Nazareth, in the hills overlooking the Jezreel Valley, is the center of Christianity in Israel, with over 40 churches, convents, monasteries, and schools. The city has the largest Arab community outside Jerusalem, about equally divided between Christian and Moslem Arabs. On the hillside above Nazareth is the new Jewish suburb, Nazareth Ilit.

New hotels and a monorail connecting tourist sites are planned for the year 2,000 to celebrate the 2,000th birthday of Jesus.

Tourist Information Office. Casa Nova St. **PHONE:** (06) 573-003

Christian Travel Center. **PHONE:** (06) 570-555

Christian Sites:

Basilica of the Annunciation. This church on Casa Nova Street, the largest in the Middle East, is built over the cave where Gabriel is said to have appeared before Mary.

Church of St. Joseph, next door, is where Joseph's carpentry shop is said to have been located.

Women still come to draw water at **Mary's Well** on Paul VI Street at the **Church of St. Gabriel.**

> The crowded **Arab Market** off Casa Nova St. sells everything from food to household items and antiques. Bargain hard for Arab headdresses, coins, water pipes, and trinkets.

Ein Kamomin Restaurant on Route 85 specializes in homemade goat cheese, freshly baked bread, and garden vegetables. Kids pay half. **PHONE:** (06) 989-894

NEAR NAZARETH

Kibbutz Hannaton
PHONE/FAX: (04) 986-4414
ADMISSION: Fee for tours

Israel's only Conservative kibbutz offers tours of the kibbutz as well as Tzippori Archeological Park, and Kfar Kedem. The kibbutz also will arrange home visits with kibbutz members or neighboring Israeli Arabs. They welcome guests for Shabbat and for programs related to Judaism and Israel. The facilities of the Simon and Betty Greenberg Educational Center as well as 2-3 bedroom cottages are for rent. Breakfast, lunch, and dinner are available.

Kfar Kedem
PHONE: (04) 565-511
HOURS: 8 a.m.-nightfall. Call ahead for the day's schedule
ADMISSION: Fee; ask for discount tickets to Tzippori

The village has donkey rides, pita-baking, and olive oil-pressing.

Monkey Forest
Kibbutz Yotvat
PHONE: (04) 980-1265
ADMISSION: Fee

Squirrel monkeys literally eat out of your hand and perch on your shoulder at this animal petting farm. **Sock Stop:** The kibbutz makes novelty socks and has a warehouse store with a fun selection of kids' socks.

Tzippori (Sepphoris)
Road 79, 7 miles before Nazareth
PHONE: (06) 568-272
HOURS: 8 a.m.-5 p.m; Friday until 4 p.m.
ADMISSION: Fee

Life in this ancient city, capital of the Roman province of Galilee, is reenacted here on holidays and vacations. The programs feature street games and musicians as they were in the year 210. There also are interactive computer games and an audio-visual show. Mosaics include the newly discovered **Mona Lisa of the Galilee**.

At **Misgav** there are musical events and guided tours during Pesach. **PHONE:** (04) 990-2361

Kibbutz Ein Dor Archeological Museum
PHONE: (06) 768-333
HOURS: Sun.-Thurs. 8 a.m.-3 p.m.; Fri. until 2 p.m. Call ahead.
ADMISSION: Entrance fee plus fee for activities.

Children's programs offered during vacations and holidays include pottery and clay work, olive oil production (around Hanukkah), and harvesting with ancient tools (before Shavuot). Call for current program listing.

Combine a visit to **Ein Dor** with a hike on **Mt. Tavor** and a visit to **Kfar Tavor Za'atar Factory and Museums.**

Kfar Tavor Za'atar Factory
PHONE: (06) 760-702
ADMISSION: Free

Za'atar, the Biblical spice hyssop (sometimes called white thyme) is popular with Palestinians. When the supply of wild za'atar began to dwindle, the factory owner's father began commercial production. You can get hot pita bread with za'atar and cheese and hear the story of the factory.

Kfar Tavor Settlement and Farmhouse Museums
PHONE: (06) 765-844
ADMISSION: Fee

Children will enjoy learning how farmers, blacksmiths, and others work the farm and care for the animals. Look for the audio-visual show in the cowshed. There's a vegetarian restaurant.

Bedouin Folklore Museum
Kfar Shibli
PHONE : (06) 767-875
HOURS: Daily except Friday 9 a.m.-4 p.m.
ADMISSION: Nominal fee

You can sit in a tent, sip Bedouin coffee or tea and listen to a sheik tell stories.

Balfour Forest, just south of Nazareth, is a lovely pine forest with places to play. A JNF tree-planting center is open mornings.

Tivon Park also has places to climb and play, picnic benches, and walking paths.

Beit Shearim Catacombs
8 miles west of Nazareth
PHONE: (04) 983-1643
HOURS: April-Sept. Daily 8 a.m.-5 p.m.; Oct.-Mar. closes at 4 p.m.
Closes earlier on Fridays
ADMISSION: Fee or National Parks Ticket

The Sanhedrin (tribunal) met here 1700 years ago, and Rabbi Judah Hanasi and his colleagues edited the *Mishnah* in 200 CE. They and hundreds of Jewish scholars, businessmen, and government officials were brought here for burial. Children will find these eerie chambers and caverns fascinating. There are restrooms and a snack bar at the site.

Palmach Cave
Kibbutz Mishmar Ha'emek; Haifa-Afula Road via Yokneam
PHONE: (04) 989-6847
HOURS: Daily 8 a.m.-4 p.m.
ADMISSION: Fee

An audio-visual show inside the cave shows you the history of this underground hiding place for the Palmach before 1948. Believe it or not, you can arrange to have a Bar/Bat Mitzvah here!

WHERE TO STAY

Kibbutz Hannaton Guest House. Family facilities at a modest price. **PHONE:** (04) 986-4414; **FAX:** 986-4410

THE KINNERET

The Kinneret, otherwise known as the Sea of Galilee or Lake Tiberias, has attracted civilization from prehistoric times. Its name in Hebrew means violin because of its shape. Some of the earliest artifacts in Israel have been found in this region. The abundant water, fertile land, bountiful fish supply, and nice weather account for its rich history and present popularity.

Israelis have strong, romantic feelings about the Kinneret. Few bodies of water have been celebrated by poets as often as this deep blue lake.

Don't be surprised to hear a news report about the level of the lake. Israelis love to hear that it is full, and are urged to conserve water when it is low. Fresh water is pumped from the Kinneret to as far away as the Negev.

As unlikely as it sounds, Israel's number one fresh water source is also the country's top water vacation site. In the summer, thousands of families cluster around the lake. As a result, many family vacation options have developed. Visits to Safed, the Upper Galilee, and the Golan Heights are easily combined with swimming and water sports in the lake. Accommodations range from modest campsites to lovely 5-star hotels. You will compete with Israelis for rooms and use of facilities, especially during Passover and the first three weeks of August. Book well in advance.

Weather in the area is mild even in winter, and you can swim here much of the year. Try to visit in fall or spring when accommodations are cheaper and more available.

Around the Kinneret are many Jewish and Christian religious sites. In Tiberias, you will find the **tombs of Rabbi Akiva, Rabbi Meir Baal Haness, and Maimonides,** the great 12th Century scholar/rabbi/physician. Christian sites include the **Pilgrim's Baptism** site near Kibbutz Degania (where you might see a Baptism ceremony being performed); **Capernaum,** the village Jesus lived in for three years; the **Church of the Multiplication of the Loaves and Fishes** at Tabgha; and the **Mount of the Beatitudes.**

Use your discretion about the number of religious sites you wish to include when touring with children. Ours, for example, are generally not too keen on visiting graves, but they were fascinated by Maimonides' tomb, because they know a lot about this towering scholar.

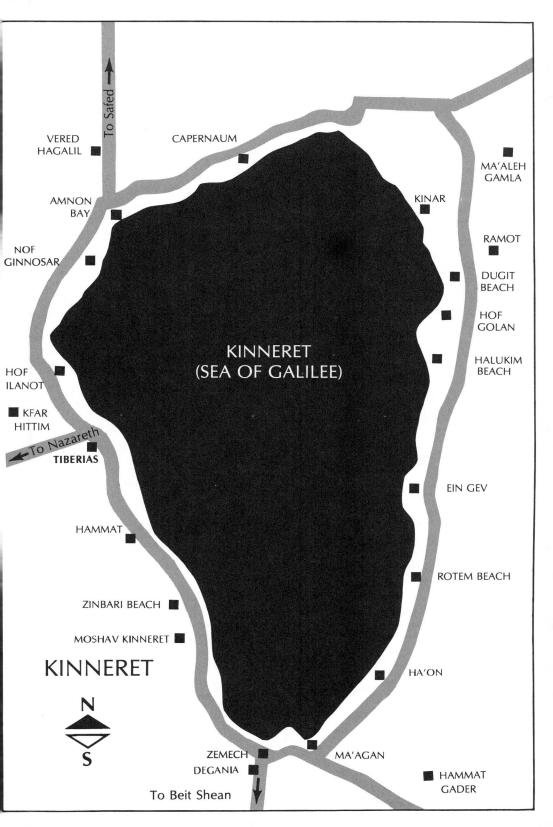

If you approach Tiberias from Tel Aviv or Haifa on Route 77, you will come to the **Golani Junction,** one of the main crossing points for Israeli soldiers going north. In addition to the **Tourist Information Center,** PHONE: (06) 733-846, there is the **Golani Brigade Museum and Tank Park,** PHONE: (06) 726-215, a **JNF Tree Planting Center,** and an enormous **McDonalds Restaurant** (non-kosher).

Golani Brigade Museum
HOURS: Sun-Thurs. 9 a.m.-4 p.m.; Fri.until 1 p.m.; Sat. until 5 p.m.
PHONE: (06) 767-215
ADMISSION: Fee

While your kids climb on the tanks in the park outdoors, you may wish to see the museum and watch a film (in Hebrew and English) honoring one of Israel's most famous military brigades.

TIBERIAS

Tiberias became the center of Jewish life after Jerusalem was destroyed in 70 C.E. The Jerusalem Talmud was compiled here around 400. Once the capital of the Galilee, this 2,000-year-old town has gone through ups and downs. Recently, Tiberias has experienced dramatic growth as the Kinneret has become a more important tourist center. The population today is 35,000. There is frequent bus service from Jerusalem, Tel Aviv, and Haifa.

The city is an excellent base for exploring the north, but take into consideration the traffic jams which make for a slow return to the city in the late afternoons on holiday weekends. For kids there are lots of fast-food and all-you-can-eat fried fish restaurants.

CITY NOTES

Area code: (06). If you are calling from out of town, you must dial these numbers first.

Tourist Information Office. 23 Habanim Street. The Mall, 2nd floor. PHONE: (06) 720-992, 720-089

Central Bus Station and Egged Tour Information. Hayarden St. PHONE: (06) 791-080

Galilee Tours. 10 Jordan St. PHONE: (06) 720-330

Both Galilee and Egged have day-long guided tours of the Golan Heights.

Yad Shitrit Library is open Sunday-Thursday mornings and afternoons with a lunch break.

Walking tours leave from the Plaza Hotel every Saturday morning. Check for times.

War of Independence Museum
Hagedud Haivri Street
PHONE: (06) 739-580
HOURS: Sunday-Thursday 4-9 p.m.
ADMISSION: Nominal fee

Exhibits and an audio-visual show (Hebrew only) focus on the War of Independence in the Galilee.

Caprice Center
PHONE: (06) 792-615
ADMISSION: Free, including a boat ride to the factory.

A film, multi-media presentation, and short demonstration of diamond cutting.

The Galilee Experience
On the Promenade
PHONE: (06) 723-620
ADMISSION: Fee

Christian tourists will enjoy this inspiring, multi-projector audio-visual show about Old and New Testament roots of the Galilee.

Hiking: Fill your canteen, and hike to the top of **Mt. Berenice** (*Berniki)* to see the ruins of a Byzantine Church. It is said to have been the site of the palace of Herod's great granddaughter who fell in love with Emperor Titus and followed him to Rome.

Biking: Israeli teens love biking around the Kinneret. You can rent bikes at the Aviv Hotel and join them. Watch for traffic. PHONE : (06) 720-007

Water Sports: The **Tiberias Municipal Beach,** open daily from 9 a.m.-7 p.m., has shower facilities and life guards. PHONE: (06) 720-254. A **Water Sports Center** on Kaplan Blvd. rents kayaks, rowboats, and sailing equipment. PHONE: (06) 723-977

Tiberias Hot Springs has a heated outdoor pool that may appeal to kids, but your best bet is to involve them in a children's activity while you have a soak and a massage. PHONE: (06) 791-967

Boating: Ferries make frequent trips across the Kinneret. Caprice

Jewelry Factory offers a free ride which includes a factory tour. I prefer the shorter, 45-minute ride with kids. Ask your hotel for discount tickets. There are also dinner cruises.

WHERE TO STAY

Moriah Plaza's family plan features children's programming on holiday weekends. This is a popular place during Passover, when religious services are held right in the hotel. **PHONE:** (06) 792-233; **U.S.:** (800) 221-0203 (Toll-free)

Carmel Jordan River. Take a ride in the glass elevator even if you don't stay here. Children up to age 12 in their parents' rooms are half price. **PHONE:** (06) 721-111

Caesar. The rooms are plain, but the Middle Eastern food is particularly good. Indoor and outdoor pools. **PHONE:** (06) 723-333

Hof Gai. Guests can use the lovely beach and water park. **PHONE:** (06) 790-790; **FAX:** 792-776

Holiday Inn charges by the room, making it a bargain for families. Children receive a modest, but thoughtful gift of holiday toys. Guests can use the hot springs spa with its indoor and outdoor pools at no charge. **PHONE:** (06) 792-890; 177-022-8900 (Toll-free)

Be sure to request a **Guest Card** from your hotel desk, for discounts at stores, restaurants, beach entry and tourist attractions.

Peniel-by-the-Galilee YMCA Lodge off Rte. 90 has family rooms and kitchenettes. Food is not kosher. **PHONE :** (06) 720-685

Quiet Beach Hotel on Gdud Barak Road has undergone a renovation and is no longer the bargain of the past. It offers a full program of sports and beach activities, making its name something of a misnomer. There is a large heated pool, and rooms are large enough for five persons. **PHONE:** (06) 790-125; **FAX:** 790-261

Kibbutz Lavi Guest House, 15 minutes from Tiberias, offers family activities with a religious flavor. It is a popular place for Bar Mitzvahs. **PHONE:** (06) 799-450; **FAX:** 779-399

Tired of fish? **Pagoda** is a good Chinese restaurant in Tiberias!

Kibbutz Degania Aleph
PHONE: (06) 758-410 (Founder's Farmyard); 750-040 (Beit Gordon)

One stop will bring you to a cool, natural history museum and a preserved, original house on Israel's first kibbutz.

Moshav Kinneret
PHONE: (06) 751-172 (Museum); 751-170 (Founder's Farmyard)
HOURS: Daily 9 a.m.-2 p.m.
ADMISSION: Free

Visit an early settlement and hear the founders' stories.

Jordan Mini-Crossover and Old Electric Plant
8 kilometers south of Kinneret
PHONE: (06) 709-143
HOURS: 9 a.m.-5 p.m.
ADMISSION: Fee

At the now defunct Naharayim hydro-electric complex, you can take a very short novelty trip into the Jordan by crossing through the old mandatory customs station. You are admitted by a friendly Jordanian soldier and can fish by the stream and tour the old electric company.

Ostrich Farm at Ha-On
Southeast part of lake. Turn east at Zemach Junction.
PHONE: (06) 751-039
HOURS: Daily 8 a.m.-4 p.m.
ADMISSION: Fee

Here you can observe ostriches from the egg stage through full size and view a film about them. Ostriches are the biggest birds in the world. Once in danger of extinction because of feather hunters, they are protected today on ostrich farms such as this one. Combine your visit with a meal at the **Ha-On Restaurant.**

Gavriel House
PHONE: (06) 751-175
ADMISSION: Entrance free; fee for performances

This is a pretty place to stop, with nice gardens, children's movies, occasional musical performances, and an Italian restaurant.

A refreshing Kinneret hike is to the **Zaki** where the Jordan tributaries merge in the northern park of the lake. You'll be walking mostly in water, so take appropriate shoes and clothing. Adults should be able to swim; take water wings for young children. To get there, turn off Highway 87 on the road from the Arik Bridge to Katzrin and follow signs.

Hammat Gader Spa and Recreation Area

Turn east at southern end of Kinneret
PHONE: (06) 751-039 (Hebrew recording)
HOURS: Monday-Saturday 7 a.m.-11 p.m.; Sunday until 4:30 p.m.
ADMISSION: Fee

This is a spa and recreation area on the Jordanian border. In fact, Arab families on both sides sometimes gather at the fence to chat. The 5-mile ride along the border to the Yarmuch Valley is scenic. Hammat Gader's hot water baths are open to children, but you may have to coax the kids to try them. They'll prefer the lawn toys, water slides, and alligators.

The hot, mineral springs (80-125°F) were used by the Romans, and one of the most beautiful and luxurious bath house complexes in the whole Roman Empire has been reconstructed here. The Romans used to put on alligator spectacles in their theaters. You can see dozens of alligators from birth to full size in the Hammat Gader park, and sometimes there are shows. There are several restaurants.

Kibbutz Ein Gev

PHONE: (06) 758-035; 758-888 (Anchor Museum)
ADMISSION: Separate fees for train ride and museum.
  Discount on train ride if you eat at the Ein Gev restaurant.

A train takes you around the kibbutz. The museum exhibits reflect the history of fishing in the area. There's a fish restaurant, beach, and lakeside promenade.

Yigal Allon Center and the Old Boat

Kibbutz Ginossar on the northwest side of the Kinneret
PHONE: (06) 721-495
HOURS: Sunday-Friday: 8 a.m.-5 p.m.; Saturday: 9 a.m.-5 p.m.
ADMISSION: Museum free; fee to see the boat.

A 2000-year old boat, related to the time of Jesus and remarkably preserved is displayed in a special, cooled room. In the museum, an audio-visual presentation in English and Hebrew about the Galilee may interest older children, although the text is difficult to follow.

BEACHES

There are beaches all around the lake. Many have kiddie pools. Ask for a list at the Tiberias Tourist Information Office. Some beaches charge for parking and/or admission. Watch out! Many beaches are rocky. If you have rubber sandals or old sneakers, this is the place to use them. Hof Ginossar has a sandy beach.

WATER PARKS

The water parks around the Kinneret are popular with children. They are expensive, but many hotels offer discount tickets.

Luna Gai Water Park
In Tiberias, just south of the Town Center
PHONE: (06) 720-257
ADMISSION: Fee for everyone over age 3

The selection of slides is modest but good. You can enjoy both swimming in the Kinneret and in the wave pool, which is set on a well-kept, attractive grassy beach front. This is an excellent choice for tourists staying in Tiberias who don't have cars.

 TEENS

Zemech Water Park
First beach driving north from Beit Shean to Tiberias
PHONE: (06) 752-440
HOURS: Daily in summer 9a.m.-9p.m.; later on Friday night
ADMISSION: Fee for everyone over age 3; covers all attractions and rides

In addition to the beach and water slides, the park has **Zemechland,** an amusement park with slides, pirate ships, a dophin show, and acrobats. Teens will enjoy the evening concerts. Your ticket enables you to come and go during the day. Snack bar.

TEENS

Luna Gal Water Park
Golan Beach on the northeast side of the Kinneret
PHONE: (06) 763-750
HOURS: Daily April-Oct. 9:30a.m.-6p.m; until midnight in July and Aug.
    The park may be closed for a private activity, so phone ahead to make
    sure it's open the day you plan to go.
ADMISSION: Fee; lower if you come in the afternoon

In the summer you'll want to stay the day and even into the night, because admission to Israel's largest water park is steep (about $15), and lines are long. Your ticket will permit you to leave for a swim at Hof Golan Beach and return for more fun. The park has a variety of water slides, bumper boats, and wild rapids that you descend in an inner tube. There is also a large swimming pool.

WATER SPORTS

Golan Beach (Hof Golan)
ADMISSION: Discount with Luna Gal Water Park ticket. Otherwise,
    you have to pay to park your car in the shared lot.

TEENS

You can enjoy waterskiing, paddle boats, para-sailing, and night swimming. Kayak tours of the Kinneret are available here. Your boat is pulled by motor boat to the Jordan Park, where you can experience the flowing Jordan River. A restaurant, snack bar, and good bathroom facilities adjoin the beach. Bring your passport as a security deposit for renting boats. You can borrow life jackets free at the boat rental stand.

Air Boats

B'Derech Hateva at the Jordan Park Junction
PHONE: (06) 339-863
ADMISSON: Fee

Ride a swamp boat through the northern section of the Kinneret with its more tropical fauna and flora. You are much closer to the water than in a regular boat and can see turtles, birds, and nests.

Lavnoon Beach

PHONE: (06) 732-044
ADMISSION: Fee

Swimmers age 7 and up can be pulled on waterskis behind a motor boat, covered inner tube, or banana boat. You also can rent pedal boats, kayaks, or motor boats.

There is **canoeing at Rob Roy** near Kibbutz Degania, daily from 9a.m.-5p.m. **PHONE:** (06) 733-999. **Zinbari Berniki Beach** has showers, a snack bar, and boats for hire. **PHONE:** (06) 751-079

OTHER SPORTS

Tractor Rides

Hovevei Teva; just over the Arik Bridge from Tiberias
PHONE: (06) 961-511

Ride a mini-tractor up the hills and through the streams. Israeli teenagers are very keen on this ride.

Horseback Riding;

Kfar Hittim. Open on weekends, holidays, and in summer. **PHONE:** (06) 795-921

Holiday Inn. Riding for all ages. **PHONE:** (06) 792-890

Ramot (northeast side of lake). Short rides for youngsters and longer excursions for children 12 and up. **PHONE:** (06) 763-363, 763-730

WHERE TO STAY

Ma'agan Holiday Village. This lakeside tent and bungalow village has upgraded to moderately-priced, lovely, air-conditioned bungalow-suites. It has a mini-zoo, water sports, and children's pool. Built-in grills allow you to barbecue in the evening on the grass near your bungalow. **PHONE:** (06) 753-753; **FAX:** 753-707

Nof Ginnosar Kibbutz Hotel. A lakeside vacation resort with good view, pool, and excellent Kinneret swimming. **PHONE:** (06) 792-161; **FAX:** 792-170

Ginnosar Inn. Family bungalows with access to the Ginnosar

Beach. There's an informal restaurant, the **Cock-A-Doodle Galilee**, and a small market nearby. **PHONE:** (06) 798-762; **FAX:** 798-887

Paradise Holiday Village. Amnon Bay, north of the Kinneret. Family suites, some with kitchenettes. Beach access. **PHONE:** (06) 934-431; **FAX:** 934-432

Ein Gev Holiday Village. Rooms for 2-4 with kitchenettes. Beach access and lots of sports. **PHONE:** (06) 752-540; **FAX:** 751-590

Kinar Vacation Village. Northeast of the Kinneret. This religious village offers separate swimming facilities and a children's program. **PHONE:** (06) 732-670

Ramot Vacation Village. One part of this resort is a luxury hotel. The other includes cabins and A-frames. There is a pool, children's program, and horseback riding on the premises. **PHONE:** (06) 732-636; **FAX:** 793-590

YOUTH HOSTELS

Karei Deshe Youth and Family Hostel. North of Tiberias on the lake. This new and lovely hostel offers family rooms, a dining area, and its own beach. **PHONE:** (06) 724-814; **FAX:** 724-818

Kibbutz Hukok Youth Hostel. **PHONE** : (06) 799-940

CAMPING

Camping is permitted in open spaces around the Kinneret. You pay about $12 to park your car, but camping is free. I recommend you make reservations at one of the organized campgrounds:

Hof Hailanot. Migdal, western side. **PHONE:** (06) 722-925

Hof Rotem/Sizaf. Southeast Kinneret

Hof Zinbari. Near Tiberias. **PHONE:** (06) 751-079

Hof Sironit. **PHONE:** (06) 721-449

Campgrounds with more complete facilities, including air-conditioned cabins, playgrounds, restaurants, and grocery stores:

Kfar Hittim. Horseback riding and a swimming pool. **PHONE:** (06) 795-921

Dugit. Northeast. **PHONE:** (06) 732-226

Kibbutz HaOn. Half board is required in summer. **PHONE:** (06) 757-555, 757-556

Ma'agan. Kibbutz Ma'agan. Swimming pool and water sports. **PHONE:** (06) 753-753

SAFED

Safed (*Tzefat*) is a charming city, with cobblestoned streets and winding alleyways. Perched on a mountaintop, its mystic aura reflects its history. Leading kabbalists (Jewish mystics) including Rabbi Isaac Luria (called the "Ari") and his disciples lived here in the 16th Century. So did Rabbi Joseph Karo, the author of the *Shulchan Aruch*, an important codification of Jewish law. Safed is considered among the sacred cities of the Holy Land and is famous for its synagogues. Because of its quaintness and natural beauty, it has become a favorite spot for artists.

Important Phone Numbers:

Tourist Office. 50 Jerusalem Street. Ask about daily walking tours. **PHONE:** (06) 920-961

Bus Information. PHONE: (06) 921-122

SITES

Artists Quarter
Short walk along Jerusalem Avenue from Bus Station
PHONE: (06) 989-085
HOURS: Sun.-Thurs.: 9 a.m.-6 p.m.; Fri.: until 2 p.m.; Sat. 10 a.m.-2 p.m.
ADMISSION: Some artists charge admission.

Sixty artists have studios and exhibit their works in these quaint stone houses. Children may enjoy the papier mache sculpture by Mike Leaf. Many exhibits are open in spring and summer only.

Printing Museum
Artists Quarter
HOURS: Sun.-Thurs. 10 a.m.-noon and 4-6 p.m.; Fri. 10 a.m.-noon
ADMISSION: Free

Safed was the first place in the Holy Land where books were printed. A 16th-century Hebrew printing press is on display along with other fascinating exhibits on printing and the *alef bet* (Hebrew alphabet).

Safed Candles
Rehov Ha'ari
PHONE: (06) 921-093
HOURS: Sunday-Thursday 8:30 a.m.-6:30 p.m.; Friday until 1 p.m.
ADMISSION: Free

Watch candles being made, and stock up on Shabbat, Hanukkah, Havdallah, and decorative candles. If you call ahead, they may be able to arrange a group or family candle-making activity.

Ethiopian Crafts Center
Yosef Caro Alley in Artists Quarter
PHONE: (06) 972-222

ADMISSION: Free

Musical instruments, weaving, embroidery, jewelry, and original crafts made by Ethiopian immigrants are displayed and on sale.

Beit Hameiri
Down the Olei Hagardon staircase from the Crafts Center
HOURS: Sunday-Friday 9 a.m.-2 p.m.; will open Saturday for groups.
ADMISSION: Fee

This lovely museum, housed in a 16th-century building, has displays on Safed of 500 years ago, including paintings and artifacts.

The Synagogues

Safed was the center of the Kabbalistic (mystical) movement in Judaism, and rabbis and scholars gathered in the city to study. The ancient synagogues were named for famous rabbis, many of whom are buried in the cemetery nearby. The most interesting of the synagogues for children are probably the **Abuhav** (it is said that the ancient Torah was written in the 1400s by the rabbi himself), and the Ashkenazi synagogue of the **Ari** (Rabbi Isaac Luria). Admission is free, but a custodian may ask for a donation toward the synagogues' upkeep.

The Cemetery
Across from the Ha-Ari synagogue and ritual bath

There actually are three cemeteries. One contains the tombs of the Kabbalists. A *hassid* will be chanting psalms at the grave of the Ari all day. The underground Stern and Irgun fighters, including those executed by the British in Acre prison, are buried in the second. The third is a military cemetery with the graves of soldiers who fell in Israel's wars. The 22 children killed in the Maalot massacre are buried here.

PARKS AND RECREATION

The Citadel and Park: Children will enjoy climbing to the top of this 12th century Crusader citadel. The view is terrific; on a clear day you can see the Kinneret. It's a great place for a picnic.

Emek Hatechelet (Blue Valley) Pool. This popular site has adult and children's pools, a playground, miniature golf, and a restaurant. It's open daily from 9 a.m.-5 p.m., but some afternoons are reserved for separate swimming. There's a fee. **PHONE:** (06) 920-217

Heated Swimming Pool. Call for separate hours for men and women. **PHONE:** (06) 974-294.

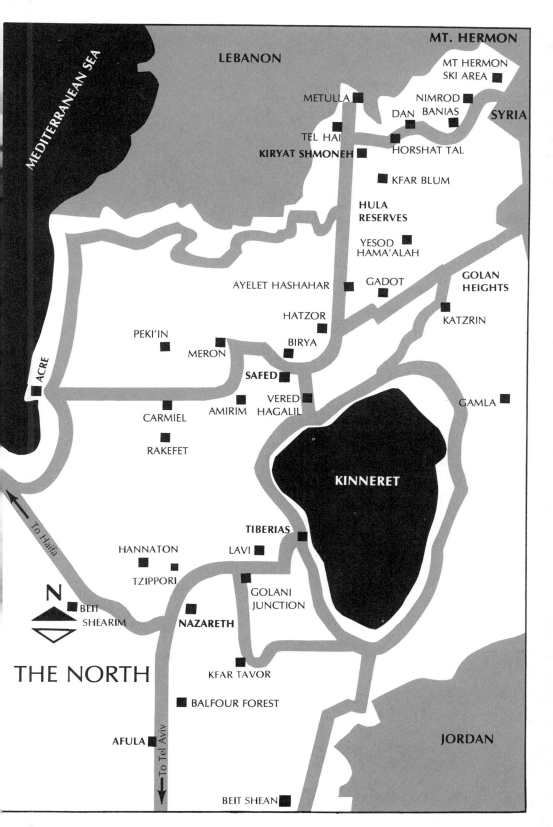

Meron, five miles west of Safed, is the site of the grave of Rabbi Shimon Bar Yochai, a Talmudic scholar who defied the Romans and hid in a cave where he wrote mystical literature. On Lag B'Omer, Orthodox Jews gather at his tomb and rejoice around a bonfire. Three-year old boys are given their first haircuts here. Other sages buried in Meron are Rabbis Hillel and Shammai. There is a large forest and park with picnic tables.

Meron Nature Reserve. Mt. Meron is the second highest mountain in Israel. You can take a 45-minute circular hike around the peak and enjoy the best views of Safed and the Upper Galilee. The reserve is always open and is free.

Carmiel, a successful new town southwest of Safed, is a good place to stock up on food. You may hear a lot of English spoken here, because many of the settlers are from the U.S. and Canada.

Peki'in has had continuous Jewish settlement since the days of the Bible. It is thought to be the site of the cave where Rabbi Shimon Bar Yochai hid from the Romans. Stop for a delicious pita, made before your eyes, by a roadside pita-maker.

Ein Zeitim, on the Acre-Safed road toward Dalton is a nice play area with picnic tables and great climbing toys.

Bat Ya'ar Ranch has horse-back riding, wagon rides, and mountain tours in the **Biriya Forest.** You can rent baby strollers specially designed for wilderness trails, as well as mountain bikes. The forest is a favorite hiking spot for Israeli teens, especially members of B'nei Akiva. A favorite family hike is through **Nahal Amud**. The ranch also will arrange for Land Rover rides and a Friday afternoon walking tour of Safed. **PHONE:** (06) 921-788

Kibbutz Lotam has tours to Arab villages. **PHONE:** (06) 787-293

There's a **Petting Zoo** at Kibbutz Yaron and you also can rent small boats. **PHONE:** (06) 988-304

Rimon Inn in the Safed Artist Colony has a family plan and children's programs during the holidays and summer. **PHONE:** (06) 920-665; **FAX:** 920-456

Manof Recreation Village. Apartments with kitchens. **PHONE:** (04) 914-583

Moshav Amirim. Near Carmiel. This is a one-of-a-kind vegetarian moshav set in shady hills, which makes it a good summer choice. You can rent rooms or a whole house directly from the members. You can arrange for room only, bed and breakfast, or half board. The food is vegetarian. If your kids hate eggplant, let your host know. There are other creative choices. The moshav has a communal swimming pool, and our kids got to milk the goats. **PHONE:** (06) 989-045; **FAX:** (06) 980-772

Moshav Rakefet. The *moshavniks* in this young settlement south of Carmiel have moved into permanent homes and have turned their first lodgings into family-style vacation cottages with 1-3 bedrooms, living room, and equipped kitchen. Up to 8 people may share a cottage. Tours are available. **PHONE:** (04) 800-403; 800-637

UPPER GALILEE

Our favorite way to see the Golan and Upper Galilee is to base ourselves at one of the three northern SPNI Field Schools, and tour from there. See *Where to Stay.*

The SPNI has organized hiking and jeep tours of the area, or you can see the major tourist sites on your own. If you plan to hike in the hills, don't go alone. The area is still full of Syrian ground mines. You can hire your own private SPNI guide if you don't want to take one of the scheduled tours.

You can **Fly Over the North** with Gur Aviation. There are several tours and a small discount for children. **PHONE:** (06) 934-394

The **Sonol Gas Station** between Rosh Pina and Kiryat Shmoneh offers touring information. **PHONE:** (06) 938-712.

Amiad Winery
PHONE: (06) 933-850
ADMISSION: Fee

You can tour this interesting winery, where wines are made from fruit instead of grapes.

Rosh Pina
PHONE: (06) 936-603
ADMISSION: Fee

If you're lucky, you'll find an old-timer at the Old Rosh Pina development office to tell you the story of this charming town, settled in 1892. Ask to look at the old synagogue.

Hatzor Hagalili, a small development town near the ancient site of Hatzor, has a swimming pool and several small parks.

Tel Hatzor
PHONE: (06) 934-855 (tel); 937-313 (museum)
HOURS: Daily 8 a.m.-4 p.m.; closes an hour earlier Oct.-March.
ADMISSION: Fee or Nat'l Parks Ticket admits you to both Park and Museum.

Archeology lovers will enjoy visiting this site where 21 strata, from the Early Bronze Age to the 2nd century BCE, have been excavated. Artifacts collected in the area are displayed at the Hatzor Museum at the entrance to Kibbutz Ayelet Hashahar.

The **Hula Valley** forms part of the northern Jordan Valley, which together with the Dead Sea and the northern Negev desert are part of the **Great Afro-Syrian Rift.** Therefore, the reserve is the northernmost point for growth of certain plants and the southernmost for others. For example, you will find papyrus growing, as well as Jordan tamarisks.

Hula Reserves
North on Route 90, right at Hula-Dobrovin signs
PHONE: (06) 937-069
HOURS: Saturday-Thursday 8 a.m.-4 p.m.; Friday until 1 p.m.
ADMISSION: Fee

This park includes part of the original, undrained Hula swamp. At the entrance is a cool, shaded picnic ground beneath the swamp-draining eucalyptus trees. Pick up a map and follow the self-guided trail. Be sure to wear a hat and insect repellent. Swamps mean mosquitos! Part of the trail is a long, wooden floating bridge, part of which is covered. There are benches for bird-watching. You might see a water buffalo or wild hog, but more likely you'll see fish and turtles. An observation tower offers a panoramic view. There are restrooms, a snack bar, and a souvenir stand.

The Valley is currently being reflooded by the JNF which promises more boating and fishing opportunities.

Dobrovin Farm
Turn at sign for Hula Reserve and again at Yesod Hama'alah.
PHONE: (06) 937-371
HOURS: Daily except Fri. 9 a.m.-6 p.m.; Fri. until 5 p.m.
Call ahead to request an English-speaking guide.
ADMISSION: Fee

On this reconstructed turn-of-the-century farm you can watch a potter work and visit the horses and chickens in their old-fashioned stables. There is an audio-visual show about the pioneers who settled the mosquito-infested area in the 1950's and drained the swamps. This is a good place for a short visit. A restaurant, open 11a.m.-11p.m., provides light meals or popsicles. There are excellent restrooms.

Kiryat Shmoneh

Kiryat Shmoneh — the "town of the eight"— was named in memory of Joseph Trumpledor and seven colleagues killed by Arab marauders in 1920, while defending nearby Kibbutz Tel Hai. Because of its proximity to the northern border, Kiryat Shmoneh has suffered most from enemy fire. Call your children's attention to the "security rooms," reinforced rooms attached to each apartment to protect families from shellings.

Tel Hai
North of Kiryat Shmoneh, near Kfar Giladi
PHONE: (06) 951-333
HOURS: Sun.-Thurs. 8 a.m.-4 p.m.; Fri. until 1p.m.
          Sat./holidays: 8:30 a.m.-2 p.m. Call for an English-speaking guide.
ADMISSION: Fee

Tel Hai was settled in 1918 by a group of workers from the Galilee Farmers Union. It was attacked in 1920, abandoned, and later resettled. Among those wounded in the battle was Joseph Trumpeldor whose words, "It is good to die for our country," have become a motto for the fighting forces. The reconstructed settlement has become a museum commemorating Tel Hai and the valiant stand of the eight fighters. Children's activities include a harvest and bread-making workshop. Stop to see the famous lion statue in the nearby cemetery. Tel Hai is an excellent starting point for picnics and hiking.

If you stop by the Industrial Park, you can see the **Old Car Museum** with dozens of old cars going back to 1927. The same ticket admits you to the Photography Museum.

Photography Museum
Tel Hai
PHONE: (06) 950-769
HOURS: Daily 9 a.m.-4 p.m.; Saturday 10 a.m.-5 p.m.
ADMISSION: Fee

Early photos of Israel and exhibits by Israeli photographers. A hands-on teaching exhibit on the history of photography will open soon.

Beit Hashomer

Kfar Giladi
PHONE: (06) 941-565
HOURS: Sun.-Thurs. 8 a.m.-noon and 4-6 p.m.; Fri. 8:30 a.m.-noon
ADMISSION: Nominal fee

Hashomer were the pioneers who, in 1907, founded a clandestine self-defense organization. The display shows the origins of the movement in Russia. An audio-visual diorama describes the attack on Tel Hai in 1920, and a sound-and-light show describes activities of Hashomer.

Kibbutz Naot Mordechai has an interesting apple-sorting and preparation process which you can ask to see. You may enjoy shopping for sandals at the **Naot Factory Outlet.**

GALILEE PANHANDLE

Metulla, a pretty, 100-year old hilltop town, is the northernmost point in Israel. Just north of the city you can stop to see **The Good Fence**, the crossing point between Israel and Lebanon. Metulla has one of the best sports centers in the country.

Canada Center

PHONE: (06) 950-370
HOURS: Daily 10 a.m.-10 p.m.
ADMISSION: Fee

Ice-skating, swimming, squash — you can do it all in this unusual center, where you can spend most of a day. You may also be able to see the skating instructors, most of them Russian immigrants, perform on the ice. Get there early in the day for the best choice in skate sizes. You can have your hand stamped, go out for lunch at the picnic site nearby, and return.

> At the Center's **Shooting Range,** open 10 a.m.-7 p.m., children 14 and older can rent air guns and even Uzis in a well-supervised shooting range, while their parents practice with rifles and pistols. The owner's motto is "we aim to serve you!" **PHONE:** (06) 951-514

Nahal Iyun

PHONE: (06) 951-519
ADMISSION: Fee

On this particularly beautiful hike, you see four waterfalls, among them the famous **Tanur**, so-named because it's shaped like an oven. The hike takes about two hours.

Tel Dan Nature Reserve

Past Kiryat Shmoneh, right at Metsudot Junction
PHONE: (06) 951-579
HOURS: Daily 8 a.m.-4 p.m.
ADMISSION: Fee

The Dan river flows over stones and foliage in this beautiful nature reserve, dense with towering trees. Our 6 year-old found the 90-minute walk on the stone trails a challenge, but the 3 year-old had to be carried much of the time. The tel covers ruins of Laish, the ancient capital of the tribe of Dan. There is a picnic area.

> You can buy a combination ticket to Tel Dan, Nahal Iyun, Gamla, and Banias. See *Golan Heights*.

Beit Ussishkin Nature Museum

Kibbutz Dan
PHONE: (06) 941-704
HOURS: Sun.-Thurs. 9 a.m.-noon and 1-3 p.m.
Fri. until 12:30 p.m.; Sat. 10 a.m.-2 p.m.
ADMISSION: Fee

An audio-visual program focuses on the animals, insects, and flowers of the Galilee. Flora and fauna of the area are displayed.

Horshat Tal National Park

Route 99, off northern Route 90
PHONE: (06) 940-400, 942-360
HOURS: Daily 8 a.m.-4 p.m.; closes earlier on Fridays.
ADMISSION: Fee or National Parks Ticket

Camping facilities and rental cabins are set in a lovely park in the hills of the Upper Galilee. There are natural pools and waterfalls, but you can swim only in the park's swimming pool.

Regional Museum of Prehistory

Ma'ayan Baruch, across from Horshat Tal
PHONE: (06) 944-570
HOURS: Daily 9 a.m.-noon or by appointment. Call ahead.
ADMISSION: Fee

Ask for a curator tour to see archeology come alive. There are toys for small children.

GOLAN HEIGHTS

Gamla

Route 869, northeast side of Kinneret
PHONE: (06) 760-404
HOURS: Daily 8 a.m.-4 p.m.; Friday until 3 p.m.
ADMISSION: Fee

The ancient city of Gamla was destroyed in the year 67, three

years before the destruction of the Temple in Jerusalem. Gamla's defenders lost their lives to the Roman soldiers. The word "Gamla" comes from the same root as the word for camel, and when you look at the hill from afar, you can see how the city got its name. In l967, 1900 years after its destruction, Gamla was returned to Jewish hands.

It is still being excavated. Eventually a tractor will take you to the site, but for now you have to walk. The trail to the ruins, which is difficult for young children, leads past an ancient burial ground of huge dolomite stones, a lovely natural spring, and a vulture observatory. Near the parking lot is a memorial to Israeli soldiers who fell on the Golan Heights. This site is prettiest in the spring. Don't attempt it during the hottest hours of the day. There are restrooms and cold drinks available.

Yehudiah Reserve. Israeli teens particularly like this hike, which involves leaping into cold water from a cliff and climbing down a ladder. You must know how to swim. A shorter hike along the Zavitan takes you to an easier-to-reach, equally cold water hole. The paths are well-marked.

Day and Night Jeep Safaris. You won't see elephants, but you can spot deer and see an ancient synagogue by moonlight as you ride jeeps through the Golan. PHONE: (06) 983-990

Never allow children to wander unguided in the Golan, which is still full of Syrian ground mines. Stay on marked, well-traveled paths, and note fenced-in areas and the triangular roadside warnings.

Katzrin, a new development town in the Golan, is a good place to fill up your gas tank, pick up some groceries, or have a snack. If you have time, take a dip in the municipal swimming pool or visit some of the interesting museums.

Mei Eden Natural Water Factory
PHONE: (06) 961-050
HOURS: Sunday-Thursday 8 a.m.-4 p.m.
ADMISSION: Fee includes a bottle of water and a handy carrier!

A guided tour and video take you through the process of bottling natural mineral water. You get a cool drink at the end!

Doll Museum at Katzrin

PHONE: (06) 962-982
HOURS: Sun.-Thurs. 9 a.m.-5 p.m.; Fri. until 2 p.m.; Sat. 10 a.m.-6 p.m.
ADMISSION: Fee

Dolls and dioramas are used to tell Bible stories and folktales, explain Jewish historical events, and portray Jewish holidays. It's a wonderful museum for children and fascinating for history buffs.

Golan Museum and Ancient Katzrin Park

PHONE: (06) 962-412 (Park); 969-636 (Museum)
HOURS: Sun.-Thurs. 8 a.m.-5 p.m.; Fri. until 3 p.m.
Sat. and holidays 10 a.m.-4 p.m.
ADMISSION: You can buy a joint ticket to both the Park and Museum.

An audio-visual show tells about the city of Gamla, an excavated village from the time of the Talmud. The synagogue and reconstructed and furnished homes demonstrate the life-style of a Jewish family from that period.

Golan Heights Winery

PHONE : (06) 962-001, 961-646
HOURS: Sun.-Thurs. 8 a.m.-4 p.m.; Fri. until 1 p.m.; closed Saturday.
ADMISSION: Fee

You can tour this successful new winery and its bottling plant, see a video, and taste Yarden, Gamla, and Golan wines.

Golan Fruits

Near Kibbutz Meron Golan
HOURS: From early morning; last tour leaves at 1:30 p.m.
ADMISSION: Donation

The 45-minute tour shows the orchards and packing rooms for apples, pears, and cherries. You can buy hot lunch in the workers' cafeteria.

At **Moshav Sha'al**, you can "pick and pay" your own berries — blueberries, blackberries, currants, and cherries according to the season. **PHONE:** (06) 981-860

Kibbutz Ortal Farms

Northeast of Katzrin
PHONE: (06) 960-808
HOURS: Daily 4:30-7:30 a.m.; 12:45-3:45 p.m.; 6:30-9:30 p.m.
ADMISSION: Fee

You can visit the high-tech dairy farm, the beef division, and/or the vineyard and orchards. Call ahead to request an English-speaking guide.

Druze Hospitality Center
Ein Kinya, Southern Hermon
PHONE: (06) 983-638
ADMISSION: Fee

You can see a slide show and exhibit of Druze life. Refreshments are served: pita, cheese, coffee, and sweets. Call to make sure someone who speaks English is at the site.

Donkey Farm
Neve Eitan
PHONE : (06) 762-151, 762-057, 763-084
ADMISSION: Fee

You'll find a variety of donkey rides, hikes, and combination tours for all ages. Even reluctant riders will enjoy. Special events such as Bar/Bat Mitzvah and birthday celebrations can be arranged. There's good hiking nearby at **Nahal El Al.**

Mitzpe Gadot
Route 91, near Bnot Yaakov Road

From here you can see the bunkers where the Syrians shot at Israeli kibbutzim before the 1967 war. Eli Cohen, Israel's master spy, encouraged the Syrians to plant the shade trees you see. These trees helped Israeli soldiers locate the Syrian bunkers during the Six Day War.

Banias Waterfall
North on Route 90, past Kiryat Shmoneh, east at Metzudot Junction
PHONE: (06) 950-272
HOURS: Daily except Friday 8 a.m.-5 p.m.; Friday until 4 p.m.
ADMISSION: Fee

It is a lovely walk on shaded paths down to the large, powerful waterfalls that descend from Mt. Hermon. Banias is one of the principal sources of the Jordan River, and you can swim in the river and wander through ruins of a Herodian city. The trek is manageable for children who can walk, but difficult terrain for a stroller. There is no picnic area, but there is a small restaurant, or you can picnic in the nearby Banias Reserves.

Nimrod Fortress
2 miles east of Banias
PHONE: (06) 942-360
HOURS: April-Sept. 8 a.m.-5 p.m.; Oct.-Mar. until 4p.m.; closes early Fri.
ADMISSION: Fee or National Parks Ticket

The largest complete fortress in the Middle East, the Nimrod Castle was built by Moslems (not Crusaders as originally thought) in the 12th century. The fortress stood above the principal trade route from Damascus, the Via Maris, but nonetheless was frequently conquered in ancient times. Our children loved climbing down into the dungeon and through the tunnels.

Mt. Hermon Ski Resort
Follow signs to Druze Village of Mijdal Sharms; buses run from Kiryat Shmoneh
PHONE: (06) 981-337
HOURS: Daily 8:30 a.m.-3:30 p.m. weather permitting

This is Israel's only ski resort, with gentle slopes for beginners, steep slopes for good skiers, and even a lift for non-skiers. There is a rental shop and ski school. In season the hotels, the parking lot, and the lifts fill up quickly. Plan to arrive early. In addition to renting ski equipment, you can rent sleds for young children. It's cold! Bring a jacket, even in spring. Guided hikes include a ride on the chair lift.

Rubber Rafting. Riding down the Jordan on an inner tube has become a very popular sport. New concessions are always springing up along the banks, but the more organized rental spots are at Ma'ayan Baruch for ages 18 and over and at Kibbutz Sde Nehemiah for ages 10 and up. Be careful. Although rubber rafting looks as if it's the easiest of the river rides, it is the most hazardous. **Ma'ayan Baruch.** PHONE: (06) 951-350; **Kibbutz Sde Nehemiah.** PHONE: (06) 946-010

Whitewater Rafting. Gadot Junction. The two former Navy commandos who run this firm are very experienced. They offer everything from gentle family raft rides to two-hour wild, whitewater adventures that teens will love. PHONE: (06) 934-622

Catarafting. Kibbutz Kfar Hanassi. These ingenious watercraft were suggested by Russian immigrants to the folks at the kibbutz. You can take a gentle, pleasant family ride with a few rapids at the end (ages 3 and up), or a more exciting adventure down the river. Children under age 12 must be accompanied by an adult for all rafting. Teens will love the white water trip by cataraft. You can book a package that includes cliff rappeling, mountain bike and jeep trips, plus bed-and-breakfast. PHONE: (06) 932-992

Kayaking. Kibbutz Kfar Blum, southeast of Kiryat Shmoneh, is the launching pad for kayak rides down the Jordan. There's also a park with rides for children. PHONE: (06) 948-755

Abukayak uses rubber kayaks with paddles. PHONE: (06) 921-078

TEENS

Shooting Range. Ayelet Hashahar. Children ages 13 and up can shoot air guns in a closed range. If you're over 18, you can operate pistols in an open range. **PHONE:** (06) 932-628

HORSEBACK RIDING

Vered Hagalil
12 miles north of Tiberias
PHONE: (06) 935-785

This ranch specializes in horseback riding tours around the Kinneret and Jordan River Delta. You can ride for an hour, half a day, or a week. Tours are open to visitors, but ranch guests get a discount. See also *Where to Stay*. There are pony rides for children.

The following also have horseback riding tours through the Galil:

Katzrin Horse Farm. PHONE: (06) 962-515

Ayelet Hashahar. PHONE: (06) 932-628

Rodeo Ramot. PHONE: (06) 731-112. Also has rodeo shows.

Baba Yona Ranch. PHONE: (06) 938-773. There are jeep and guided horseback tours, as well as pony rides and a playground for young children. Restaurant on premises.

WHERE TO STAY

Hermon Field School. The newest of the field schools is at the foot of Mt. Herman between Kibbutz Dan and the Banias, on property donated by Kibbutz Snir. The rooms have attractive pine bunkbeds and a private bath. A full Israeli breakfast and filling supper are included. Lunch is generally not served because visitors are out hiking. At breakfast you are given rolls, sandwich spreads, and plastic bags to prepare your own picnic. You can reserve by calling direct or through the SPNI main office. Book well in advance for the limited number of rooms. **PHONE:** (06) 944-449, 941-091

The other field schools in the area provide similar, but less luxurious accommodations:

Golan-Katzrin Field School. PHONE: (06 961-947.

Camping. PHONE: (06) 961-234

Keshet Yehonatan. Moshav Keshet. **PHONE:** (06) 961-636

Vered Hagalil. If you enjoy horseback riding in a country setting, this is a perfect vacation spot. The guest house has cottage apartments with kitchenettes that sleep up to six. (The food is not kosher.) Cabins and rooms sleep 4-5, or you can put the kids in the bunkhouse. Children enjoy spending time with the horses and playing ping-pong, billards, or games in the lobby, while the adults relish the relaxed, country atmosphere. **PHONE:** (06) 935-785

GUEST HOUSES

Kibbutz Ayelet Hashahar. Swimming pool and horseback riding, jeep tours and children's activities are available, along with guided tours of the kibbutz and lectures on kibbutz life. There are family plan rates. **PHONE:** (06) 932-628

Hagoshrim Kibbutz Guest House. This pleasant kibbutz hotel has a swimming pool, tennis courts, and a picturesque location. A touring and hiking center will arrange tractor-wagon rides and hikes. Teens will like the hike to the Disappearing Valley. **PHONE:** (06) 956-231

Kibbutz Dafna. A particularly nice rural accommodation with a pool, tennis courts, a movie theater, and petting farm in a great location. Book well in advance. **PHONE:** (06) 945-011; **FAX:** 945-795

Kibbutz Gonen. Rustic accommodations in a friendly, old-fashioned kibbutz with family rooms and apartments. There is a pool, and a tour of the kibbutz is offered. **PHONE/FAX:** (06) 955-247

Moshav Neve Ativ Holiday Village. Vacation cottages with an upstairs for kids. The central building has a heated swimming pool. There are also accommodations with private bath and meals at members homes. PHONE: (06) 746-479

Other guest houses and accommodations with family facilities:

Hotel Arazim. Metulla. PHONE: (06) 944-143

Kibbutz Kfar Blum. Tennis, sauna, olympic pool, and fishing. PHONE: (06) 943-666

Kfar Giladi. Special Bar/Bat Mitzvah program, children's program, swimming pool. PHONE: (06) 941-414

Shaar Hayishuv. PHONE: (06) 741-768

Holiday Apartments. 9 Halevanon, Metulla. PHONE: (06) 949-393

RUSTIC LIVING

Throughout the north there are dozens of bed-and-breakfast and rustic accommodations in kibbutzim, moshavim, and private homes. You can make reservations through a central booking agency, **Mevo'ot Hagalil Reservation Service.** PHONE: (06) 951-806, 935-016; FAX: 959-861

Golanit will send you a brochure of Rustic Accommodations (currently only in Hebrew). Write c/o Commercial Area, Katzrin, Golan Heights. PHONE: (06) 962-885

Lapid Rustic Accommodations. Katzrin. PHONE: (06) 961-403

Alonei Habashan. North of Katzrin. PHONE: (06) 960-009; FAX: 962-503

Rustic Rooms and Apartments. Metulla. PHONE: (06) 902-265; FAX: 997-347

For information on **camping** in the Golan. PHONE: (06 961-657; FAX: 959-861

THE SOUTH

You simply cannot understand the drama of Israel without a visit to the Negev, the desert that makes up 4,600 square miles, or about half the country. The ability of Israelis to cope with the desert is legendary.

I love the desert. I am fascinated by the broad expanses of brown, rocky terrain, the silent cliffs, and the trees and flowers that defy a lack of water, and bloom. An early morning nature hike in Sde Boker, Ein Gedi, Mitzpeh Ramon, or the Ye'elim area should be part of your desert itinerary. Even if your trip does not allow you time to go all the way to Eilat, make sure you devote some time to desert-based activities.

Distances between sites in the Negev are relatively long. This is a good time to take out your kids' walkman. But keep their eyes focused out the window. The scenery is breathtaking!

Climate

The Negev lies within the subtropical desert belt of the northern hemisphere. Its climate is what meteorologists call "continental"— hot days, cold nights (except for summer), and little rainfall. In the 1960s, the National Water Carrier pipeline was built to transport water from the north. The Negev also gets water from underground springs and an occasional flash flood.

I am an advocate of seeing the Negev in an adventurous way. Check out tour companies who will show you the sites from a jeep or a camel, or provide other creative desert experiences.

DEAD SEA

Visitor Information. PHONE: (07) 584-153.
Ambulance service: PHONE: (07) 584-348; night 584-211

Qumran National Park
PHONE: (02) 994-2533
HOURS: Daily 8:30 a.m.-6 p.m.
ADMISSION: Fee or National Parks Ticket

This is where the Dead Sea Scrolls were found. The antiquities are maintained by the National Parks Authority. A restaurant serves cold drinks and light meals and has convenient bathrooms.

Beit Hasofer

Kibbutz Almog
PHONE: (02) 994-5201
HOURS: 9 a.m.-5 p.m.
ADMISSION: Fee

Come in out of the hot sun and see an audio-visual show about the first 9,000 years of Dead Sea history, with emphasis on the Dead Sea Scrolls.

Ein Fashka Natural Reserves (Einot Zukim)

PHONE: (02) 994-2355
ADMISSION: Fee includes shower and storage for clothing

The easiest way to try the waters of the Dead Sea is to take a bus (or drive) from Jerusalem to Ein Fashka, the northernmost point on the sea. The ride takes about an hour. You can take a dip in the water and cover yourself in Dead Sea mud. You can also take advantage of fresh water springs which are warm (about 80°) all year. There are changing facilities and a snack bar.

A word on the **Dead Sea**, that salty body of water that will hold you afloat no matter how hard you try to sink. **Children do not like it,** unless they are old enough and stoical enough to endure the pain that ensues from exposing scratches and bites to the salty water. If they insist on trying, be prepared for them to come out complaining and uncomfortable. Take special care to prevent water from getting in their eyes, and make sure they rinse off well in the showers on the beach. The rocky beach can be very hot. **Wear old sneakers or plastic sandals.**

Metsokei Dragot Cliff Rappeling

Kibbutz Mitzpe Shalem Guest House
PHONE: (02) 996-4501

I went down these cliffs by rope to prove that mom can do cliff rappeling, too. Adults and children over 16 can take one of the courses offered, or you can tour the desert in a safari vehicle. If you hire your own guide for the day, even younger children (and grandparents) can climb the lower cliffs.

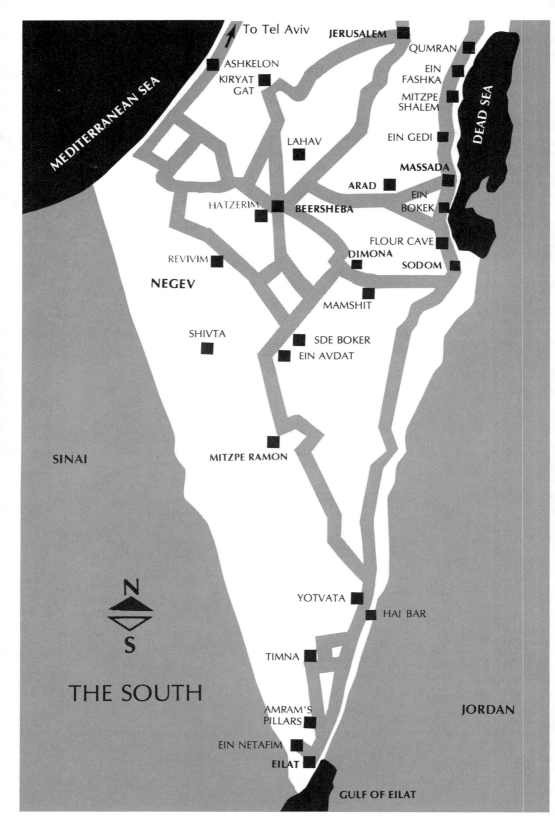

Ein Gedi Nature Reserve
PHONE: (07) 584-285
HOURS: Winter: Saturday-Thursday 8 a.m.-4 p.m.; Friday until 3 p.m.
   Stays open an hour later in summer.
ADMISSION: Fee

Ein Gedi is a picturesque oasis, suitable for a lovely hike and a swim in cool mountain pools. Even a small child can climb the paths to the waterfalls. Follow the trail through trees and flowers, past tiny waterfalls and pools, to David's Spring, a 100-foot falls cascading down the cliffs. It's a magic sight. Across from the highway is another popular beach for swimming in the Dead Sea.

> Further south along the Dead Sea are more luxurious spas and beaches. There is a solarium for special skin problems at **Ein Bokek**. **Ein Gedi, Hamei Zohar,** and **Ein Bokek** have mineral baths and spa facilities.

Attractzia Water Park
Kalya Beach
PHONE: (02) 994-2393
HOURS: March-Oct.: Daily 9 a.m.-5 p.m.; closes earlier in fall.
ADMISSION: Fee

Even when it's cool in Jerusalem, it's warm here. There is a fresh water pool, access to the Dead Sea beach, and shows during vacations.

Karting 2000
Near Attractzia Water Park
HOURS: Open Shabbat and vacations
PHONE: (02) 942-681

Kids of all ages will enjoy racing these small cars along the track.

Dead Sea Works
Sodom
HOURS: Open to the public Passover week and Israel Independence Day.

This is one of Israel's most successful companies. The plant occupies an area as large as Tel Aviv. You can view a film about harvesting chemicals from the Dead Sea and see the saltwater ponds and pipeline. Since the Dead Sea is the lowest point in the world, the synagogue on the premises calls itself "the lowest synagogue in the world!"

MASSADA

You will not want to miss visiting Massada. This site marks the heroic resistance of 900 Jewish settlers after the destruction of the Temple in Jerusalem in 70 C.E. Rather than surrender to the 10,000 Roman soldiers, they took their own lives. On top is an extensive excavation of the city, once King Herod's summer palace. Below you can see the outlines of the Roman encampments.

To appreciate the full drama of this important historic monument, take a book on Massada with you, tour the site with a guide, or rent a talking phone that will tell the story and explain the ruins as you climb. The excavated synagogue here, one of the oldest in history, is a popular place for Bar/Bat Mitzvah ceremonies.

PHONE: (07) 584-207, 584-208
HOURS: Open every day except Yom Kippur. The site opens officially at 7:30 a.m., although the gates to the foot paths open before sunrise. If you arrive before, you will be asked to pay when you leave. The **Cable Car** runs daily 8 a.m.-4 p.m. except Friday and holiday eves when it closes earlier.
ADMISSION: You can use your National Parks Ticket or pay a small fee to enter. The Cable Car is additional, and there are one-way and round-trip tickets.

If you climb, plan to begin before sunrise, because of the intense heat. It makes sense to sleep at a nearby youth hostel (you can rent sleeping bags) or hotel the night before. The easiest path is **The Battery** on the mountain side. But the more popular is the **Snake Path** which winds its way up on the Dead Sea side. Wear a hat and carry a canteen!

There is a **Sound and Light Show** on Tuesday and Thursday evenings on the Arad side of the mountain. But call ahead, because the schedule changes frequently. **PHONE:** (07) 955-052

Flour Cave
Har Sdom area
ADMISSION: Free

Kids love this cave because you come out all white from the limestone dust. A touring map is available from the SPNI.

Salt Cave

Ask your guide to point this out. The walls are...salty!

ARAD

This small, successful desert town, 25 miles from Massada, has a dry climate good for folks with asthma. The Hebrew Rock Music Festival in July attracts thousands of teens and students.

Arad Visitor's Center

28 Ben Yair Street
PHONE: (07) 954-409
HOURS: Daily 9 a.m.-5 p.m.; Friday until 2:30 p.m.

An audio-visual show tells the history and geography of the area. There is also an archeological exhibit.

Susiya

New Road from Arad Valley
PHONE: (02) 996-3012
ADMISSION: Fee; discount on family ticket.

Jews had a thriving community here from the 3rd-9th centuries, and much of the old city has been excavated. It's a less well-known site, but an enthusiastic team of guides will show you the active olive press and pottery barn and take you donkey riding and climbing through the caves. There's also an audio-visual show. You can sleep over in the field school.

TEENS ▷

Nokdim Village

Between Arad and Massada
PHONE: (07) 957-326
ADMISSION: Fee

90-minute trips (but who's counting?) on camels (for ages 12+) and donkeys. You can eat and drink in the Bedouin tent, and sometimes there are evening lectures on area zoology.

Half a dozen private operators run **jeep tours** through this area. Pick up a list at one of the Tourist Centers. You can also take **camel tours**. **PHONE:** (07) 553-259

WHERE TO STAY

There are several hotel clusters on the Dead Sea.

Guest House at Metsokei Dragot. Not fancy, but if you're interested in rappeling and Dead Sea hiking, it's a good place to stay. **PHONE:** (02) 996-4501

Ein Gedi Field School. Contact SPNI for information about lodging and tours. **PHONE:** (07) 584-350

Beit Sara Ein Gedi Youth Hostel. Basic accommodations in a great location at the entrance to Nahal David. **PHONE:** (07) 584-165; **FAX:** 584-445

Ein Gedi Guesthouse. Swimming pool. **PHONE:** (07) 594-222; **FAX:** 584-328

Ein Gedi Camping Village Kibbutz Hotel. Less expensive than the guest house, this facility has caravans and rooms with kitchenettes. **PHONE:** (07) 584-342; **FAX:** 584-328

Nirvana. I know this is a family book, but I can't help recommending this terrific spa on the Dead Sea, with its wide range of wonderful health soaks, wraps, and massages. Perfect for mom and dad who have been good sports after a camel or jeep ride. The rooms are nice and there's a pool. **PHONE:** (07) 584-614

Isaac Taylor Youth Hostel at Massada. If you plan to climb Massada this is the closest place to stay. There are air-conditioned family rooms. Book well ahead for summer. **PHONE:** (07) 584-349; **FAX:** 584-650

Blau-Weiss Youth Hostel in Arad. Modern hostel with family rooms, a kitchen, and TV room. **PHONE:** (07) 957-150; **FAX:** 955-078

Susiya Field School. Simple family accommodations. **PHONE:** (02) 996-3424

Kibbutz Almog. Family rooms. **PHONE:** (07) 565-134; **FAX:** 565-145

TO BEERSHEVA

As of this printing, going south via Hebron is inadvisable because of political unrest. The other route is via Kiryat Gat. Driving takes less than 2 hours. Leave early before the Negev heats up.

Buses: From **Jerusalem** #470 (non-stop — 1½ hours) or #447 (2 hours) leave every half hour. **PHONE:** (02) 304-555. Buses also leave frequently from the Central Bus Station in **Tel Aviv.**

The **Tourist Information Center** at the Beit Kama Intersection is a good place to stop before you get to Beersheva for Negev maps, tour information, restrooms, and cold drinks. **PHONE:** (07) 919-888; **FAX:** 919-401

WHAT TO SEE

Bedouin Heritage Center in Rahat
PHONE: (07) 918-263
HOURS: Daily 8 a.m.-5 p.m.; closed Friday but may open for a group.
　　Bedouin Market: Saturday 6-11 a.m.

Rahat was the first, and is the largest Bedouin city in the world, with over 30,000 residents. Here you can get a taste of Bedouin culture, take a short camel or donkey ride, bake pita bread, learn how to weave a rug, or shop for handicrafts. You can also spend the night in a tent if you bring a sleeping bag, and arrange for camel or donkey hikes in the area. There's even a kosher Bedouin restaurant with incredible pita.

The staff loves to chat and will tell you about Bedouin life today. If they have time, they may even take you around Rahat. On Saturdays there is a major outdoor animal market. The gift shop sells Bedouin embroidery, saddle bags, drums, and clothing.

Keifofun Play Center
Kibbutz Dvir
HOURS: 9 a.m.-sunset
ADMISSION: Fee

This air-conditioned play center has games and construction toys for small children. Outside is a large grassy area and a go-cart track even teens will like. Call ahead and book a guided 2-hour jeep ride to the Lahav Forest to see the caves and the archeological site of Ramon. In summer, when there's a full moon, there's an all night jeep tour for which you have to book ahead.

Horbat Za'ak
North of Lahav Forest
ADMISSION: Free

You'll need flashlights to go through the cave that may have been a hideout in Bar Kochba's time. Wear comfortable clothes; you have to crawl through the tunnels!

Museum of Bedouin Culture
Joe Alon Center, near Kibbutz Lahav
PHONE: (07) 918-597
HOURS: Saturday-Thursday 9 a.m.-3 p.m.; Friday until noon.
ADMISSION: Fee

Displays include the inside of a Bedouin family tent, a woman weaving goat hair into carpet, fishing gear, tools, jewelry, and musical instruments. Your visit includes a rest in Salaam's tent, where you can sample strong, sweet Bedouin coffee. Ask to see the audio-visual show (if it's not being routinely operated). Items similar to those on sale in the Bedouin market are attractively displayed and sold. There's also a small restaurant on the premises, or if you make arrangements, you can lunch in the Kibbutz Lahav dining room (not kosher) or picnic in the nearby Lahav Forest.

BEERSHEVA

Beersheva, the capital of the Negev, is a growing center with a large university and many new Russian immigrants. Despite the modernity, you still might see a donkey or camel on the road.

CITY NOTES

Area Code: (07). If you're calling from out of town, dial these numbers first.

Telanegev (for Negev Info in Tel Aviv). **PHONE:** (03) 572-2444

Tourist InformationCenters:

Shocket Intersection. PHONE: (07) 469-421;
Beersheva. Jewish Agency Bldg. 1 Szold St. **PHONE:** (07) 295-539

The Negev Mall next door to the Central Bus Station is air-conditioned with lots of stores, a busy food court, and a children's play area. It's a good place to take a travel break, have a snack, and stock up on supplies.

WHAT TO SEE

Negev Brigade Memorial
Route 60, just before Beersheva
ADMISSION: Free

The difficult battles for the Negev in the 1948 War of Independence are commemorated here. Explore the memorial site with its bunker, trenches, pipeline, and concrete wall.

Bedouin Market
Tet Neighborhood
HOURS: Thursday only from 7 a.m.-mid-afternoon

Once you could pick up a camel or a donkey here, but today few animals are sold or bartered. Clothing, dry goods, household items, candy, nuts, and spices are available at good prices. Many merchants are Bedouins from nearby settlements, dressed in full garb. Items of particular interest are Bedouin jewelry and art work. Most of the jewelry is new, but if you look hard, you can find older, more interesting pieces. Even the new pieces are fun to buy. You can't go wrong on a necklace or earrings for a dollar. The "rule" on bargaining is not to pay more than half of the initial asking price. Don't be rude, just firm.

Negev Museum
Downtown, corner Ha'atzmaut and Hahaganah Streets
PHONE: (07) 282-056/7
HOURS: Sun.-Thurs. 11 a.m.-5 p.m.; Fri. 10 a.m.-1 p.m.; Sat. 7-9 p.m.
ADMISSION: Nominal fee

The museum was founded in 1953, in a mosque built at the turn of

the century. The archeological room is small but interesting. You can see how cave dwellings were built. Ask the guard to open the tower so you can climb up. Children especially like the **Comparative Art Wing.** The first exhibit compares Israeli and Japanese children's drawings, and asks visitors about the pictures. Worksheets are in Hebrew, but the staff will help translate. The museum also runs summer art workshops for children, in co-operation with the city's Art Center. Call for the schedule.

Ethiopian Arts Center
Taubel Community Center
PHONE: (07) 277-576
HOURS: Mon., Tues., Thurs. 8:30 a.m.-12:30 p.m.; Mon., Tues. 4-7 p.m.

Watch Ethiopian craftspersons making pottery, embroidery, and gourd decorations. There's also an exhibit and shop. You may want to stop by the traditional **Ethiopian Synagogue** on Shaul Hamelech Street.

City Library
12 Hamishachririm St.
PHONE: (07) 277-899
CHILDREN'S HOURS: Sunday-Friday 1-6 p.m.

A cool center for an afternoon break, with some books in English.

Beersheva Arts Center
21 Anilevech St.
PHONE: (07) 239-565

Art classes for children, as well as full-day activities on school holidays. If you're in the area, call ahead and ask to visit the children's art gallery, opened on request.

Beersheva Theater
PHONE: (07) 238-278

The city's regional theater performs mostly in Hebrew, but there's a local company that performs in English. Check the schedule.

The Zoo
Hatzerim neighborhood
PHONE: (07) 414-777
HOURS: Sun.-Thurs. 9 a.m.-6 p.m.; Fri. until 1 p.m.; Sat. 10 a.m.-4 p.m.
ADMISSION: Fee

This pleasant, modest zoo has 150 kinds of animals. There are zoo clubs which meet during the year and day camps on holidays and during vacations. Before registering make sure your child's counselor speaks English!

SPORTS

Ice Skating
Kiryat Yehudit Industrial Area
PHONE: (07) 450-465
HOURS: 10 a.m.-midnight; open later on weekends.
ADMISSION: Fee covers entrance and skate-rental.

Believe it or not, ice-skating in the capital of the Negev!

Tennis Center. PHONE: (07) 436-444

Luna Negev Amusement Park and Pool
1 Yehudah Halevy St. (across from Comprehensive High School Dalid)
PHONE: (07) 436-129
HOURS: Call ahead

Rides and a swimming pool

Rata Shooting Range
Beersheva Mall
PHONE: (07) 233-577
HOURS: Daily 9:30 a.m.-1 p.m. and 4:30-6:30 p.m. (except Mon./Tues.)

No license necessary if you are over 18.

Beersheva Sports and Country Club
Western exit; special buses run from the city in summer
PHONE: (07) 419-292, 434-629

Swiming pool, kiddie pool, and water slides

WHERE TO EAT

The local **Beersheva Ice Cream** is available in the Negev Mall. **Montana Ice Cream,** at the Neveh Noy Intersection, sells soft ice cream.

Burger-a-gesher. Haye'elim Blvd. **PHONE:** (07) 238-278. There also is good pizza and felafel in this same "Hey" neighborhood.

El Rancho 100 Tuviha Road. Don't be concerned that this restaurant is in a gas station. Many eating places are. This Argentinian-style grill has good food, reasonable prices, and children's portions. It's open for lunch and dinner. **PHONE:** (07) 434-825

Pinat HaGrill. 65 Hapalmach St. Moroccan specialties and good grilled food are served at this downtown restaurant. The house specialty is grilled chicken breast. Children's portions available. **PHONE:** (07) 232-689

WHERE TO STAY

Desert Inn. This has been Beersheva's main hotel for decades. The air-conditioned rooms can hold up to four persons. Children staying in their parents' room get a 30% discount. There is a nice swimming pool and separate children's pool. **PHONE:** (07) 424-922; **FAX:** 412-772

Beit Yatziv Youth Hostel and Guest House. 79 Ha'atzmaut St. The 4-story guest house has 76 rooms, and the smaller, renovated youth hostel is also good for families. All rooms have private baths, are heated in winter and cooled in summer. There is an adult and two toddler swimming pools. Book well in advance and request the new rooms. **PHONE:** (07) 277-444

Tzabar Reservation Service for Rural Accommodations. Call for Bed-and-Breakfast availability in the area. **PHONE:** (07) 279-707

Bedouin Tents at Rahat Bedouin Village. **PHONE:** (07) 918-267

OUTSIDE BEERSHEVA

Moshav Nevatim and Cochin Synagogue
PHONE: (07) 277-277
HOURS: 7 a.m.-4 p.m. by appointment
ADMISSION: Fee

Jews from Cochin, India, settled this moshav after two other groups failed. They are famous flower producers, and you can ask to tour the hothouses. Jewish families still living in India asked to recreate their traditional synagogue on the moshav and sent furniture and Torah scrolls. The Torah is read from a balcony in front of the women's section. Children who attend synagogue will find this visit interesting. A Heritage Center with a kosher restaurant is planned.

Air Force Museum
Kibbutz Hatzerim
PHONE: (07) 906-855
HOURS: Sun.-Thurs. 8 a.m.-5 p.m.; Fri. until 1 p.m.; closed Sat.
ADMISSION: Fee

When you ask for an English-speaking guide as you enter, you'll get a young woman soldier who will tell you everything you ever wanted to know about airplanes and the famed Israeli Air Force. Why does a pilot wear two uniforms? What's in that box under his seat?

This is a must for plane lovers. There are hundreds of airplanes — Israeli planes, enemy planes, gliders, helicopters, anti-aircraft vehicles. You can climb some, go inside others. Supervise your children, who may get over-enthusiastic. This is a metal playground that heats up in summer.

Try to come on a cool day or early in the morning. There are several films shown inside the very Boeing 707 used in the 1976 rescue of Entebbe. During Pesach and Sukkot weeks, spitfires are flown to the delight of the large crowds of visitors.

Mitzpeh Revivim
Kibbutz Revivim, Highway 222
PHONE: (07) 562-570
HOURS: 9 a.m.-3 p.m.
ADMISSION: Fee

In this excellent recreation of an early kibbutz you can visit the underground bunkers and hidden field hospital from the War of Independence. Ask for an English-speaking guide to learn the richness of the history.

Yerucham, one of the Negev's development towns, has a branch of the University of the Negev and a hostel if you want to spend the night. **Yerucham Park** nearby has a sweet water fish pond and is a nice place to picnic.

Golda Park on Route 222, is a JNF park with a fishing lake and good view.

Tel Sheva
PHONE: (07) 467-286, 469-981
HOURS: Saturday-Thursday 8 a.m.-4 p.m.; Friday until 3 p.m.
ADMISSION: Fee for camel and horseback rides.

A national park with 6000 year-old ruins, a reconstructed fort, and buildings from the early period of kings. A well, perhaps Abraham's, was found! Restaurant on premises.

Kashvan Horseback Riding Center
Tel Sheva Intersection
PHONE: (07) 467-162
ADMISSION: Fee

A horse-breeding project has been converted to a riding school for children only. Lessons for children 8 years and older, weighing less than 165 lbs. Restaurant on premises.

SDE BOKER

Sde Boker refers to both the kibbutz and to the desert campus of Ben Gurion University of the Negev. The name means "cowboy's fields," because the original settlers thought they would raise cattle. You'll need most of a day to explore this area. If you decide to take a hike, consider spending the night. There are terrific hiking sites here. Check with the local SPNI or tour company. Remember to bring lots of water for all Negev hikes.

Ben Gurion's Hut

PHONE: (07) 558-444, 560-320
HOURS: Sunday-Thursday 8:30 a.m.-3:30 p.m.; Fridays, holidays,
   holiday eves until 2 p.m.; Saturday 9 a.m.-2:30 p.m.
ADMISSION: Free

Israel's first Prime Minister, David Ben Gurion, loved the desert and set a personal example as a pioneer by settling at Sde Boker with his wife Paula. Until his death in 1973, he could be seen walking along the kibbutz paths and eating in the dining hall. The hut he lived in contains many of his belongings and memorabilia about the founding of the state. Ask for the children's worksheets (in English and Hebrew) with games, puzzles, and stories that help explain the history. Call to arrange an English-speaking guide.

Ben Gurion's Grave

PHONE: (07) 565-717
HOURS: Call
ADMISSION: Fee

The grave, an easy walk from the hut, is on the rim of the Zin Canyon. The view is beautiful. There's also a 45-minute sound-and-light show which creatively traces Ben Gurion's life and his role in the founding of the state.

Snake Center

Sde Boker Field School
PHONE: (07) 565-828, 565-016
HOURS: Call for hours.
ADMISSION: Fee

The center is usually opened only for groups, but it's so interesting (you can touch the snakes!), call ahead to see if you can join an existing group or form one of your own.

Solar Research Center

Midreshet Sde Boker
PHONE: (07) 555-059, 555-057
HOURS: Sun.-Thurs. 8 a.m.-4 p.m., but call ahead to say you're coming.
   Call for appointment on Fridays and Saturdays
ADMISSION: Nominal fee

If your children are studying energy conservation, they'll enjoy a visit to Israel's solar laboratory, recommended for first graders and up. Plan an hour to tour the giant solar collectors, watch the demonstrations, and ride on the solar play cars. The audio-visual presentation is not suited for small children. You can eat at the Midresha Cafeteria.

> For a particularly nice desert hike through rugged hills, begin at Sde Boker and walk to **Ein Avdat Spring**, a lovely waterfall. You may see an ibex or vulture.

Camel Adventure at Mamshit
2½ miles east of Dimona
PHONE: (07) 551-054
ADMISSION: Fee

You need a group of 20 or more for this unusual adventure! Arieh and Galit Ullman run an experimental camel farm right in the desert, at the site of the ancient city of Mamshit. You can ride camels for two hours, or spend a day or a week riding and exploring the desert, nature, and historical sites. The reconstructed village has a Nabatean marketplace with costumed guides.

MITZPEH RAMON

At 24 miles long, 5½ miles wide, and over 1,000 feet deep, the **Ramon Crater (*Machtesh Ramon*)** is the largest natural crater in the world. If your family loves hiking and geology, don't miss this site. In addition to interesting and colorful geological phenomena, you may see ibex, gazelles, wolves, hyenas, and birds of prey. You can take a 2-hour hike or spend days in the canyon.

The town on the rim of the crater, an hour south of Beersheva, is so high that evenings are cool, even in summer. Its superb location and unusual attractions make it wonderful for families. The town itself is old-fashioned, but there are lots of parks and a **Municipal Swimming Pool** with a waterslide. This is a good base for touring the crater and the surrounding desert.

Tourist Information. PHONE: (07) 557-314

TOURS

Tzel Midbar "Desert Shade" Center for Desert Tours
PHONE: (03) 575-6885 (Tel Aviv); (07) 586-229 (Negev)

This company has a wide range of programs for exploring the Negev — from day to week-long adventures. Call to arrange a trip that will suit your family. You can sleep in a large, comfortable tent near the Ramon Crater, with bathrooms and restaurants nearby. The company rents mountain bikes, and runs tours on foot, camel, land rover, and mini-bus. Some tours will pick you up in Tel Aviv or Jerusalem. Two tours especially are exciting for teens:

Nabatean Spice Route Tour: Two days of walking and camel-riding.

Desert Survival Course: Six days of geology, desert life, and solo-navigation.

Avi Desert Safari
PHONE: (02) 991-217; FAX: 991-7854

This desert tour company takes you south in a four-wheel drive vehicle, air-conditioned or open. They will tailor the tour to your family — with as much hiking, swimming, and adventure as you want. You can camp out or stay at modest accommodations.

SPNI gives guided tours of the crater. PHONE: (07) 581-516

Avi Haklai Tours. Specializes in tours from Mitzpeh Ramon.
PHONE: (07) 588-205.

WHAT TO SEE

National Geological Park Machtesh Ramon Visitor's Center
PHONE: (07) 588-961
HOURS: Daily except Friday 9 a.m.-4:30 p.m.; Friday until 3 p.m.
ADMISSION: You can buy a joint ticket to the Visitor's Center and Bio-Ramon Animal Center

See a film about the geology and geography of the area and pick up maps. You can reserve tours of the canyon here.

Bio-Ramon Animal Center
PHONE: (07) 588-755
HOURS: 9 a.m.-3:30 p.m.
ADMISSION: Fee

A small, but fascinating assortment of desert flora and fauna — snakes and scorpions, lively lizards and hedgehogs. You can see a black widow spider close up, as well as a web of the spider's victims. Guide sheets are available in English and Hebrew. During holidays there are arts and crafts activities and sometimes evening programs with slide shows. It's worth calling for the schedule if you're planning to be in town.

Alpaca Farm
4 minutes out of town
PHONE: (07) 588-047
HOURS: 8:30 a.m.-6:30 p.m.
ADMISSION: Fee

Llamas and alpacas frolic here, at the only alpaca farm outside South America. The Israelis who own it imported the animals by plane. You can feed and touch them, and children under 65 pounds can ride the llamas. There are hands-on art projects with wool from the animals and stone from the nearby crater. You can also buy local wool and wool products. In good weather, the

center sponsors llama hikes, some with overnights around a camp-fire. Each family gets a llama to carry packs and small children. Older children and adults can ride a camel or walk. During Pesach you can watch the animals being sheared.

TEENS

Desert Archery Fun
On the road to the Alpaca Farm
PHONE: (07) 587-274
HOURS: Call ahead for hours and weather conditions.
ADMISSION: Fee

Children ages 9 and up as well as adults can play this golf-like game with bows and arrows. Arrows are shot along a "course" on the stony, Negev hills. No previous experience is necessary. It's best to play in late afternoon or early morning.

Cliff Rappeling in the crater. **PHONE:** (07) 587-170

> **Machtesh Restaurant** 10/2 Nahal Tzihor St. has reasonably-priced, home-cooked food. The menu always includes grill dishes and french fries, a specialty of the day, and sometimes Yemenite fare. **PHONE:** (07) 588-490

WHERE TO STAY

Ramon Inn. 1 Ein Akev Street, Mitzpeh Ramon. Rooms, suites, and two-bedroom family apartments with kitchenettes are available in this wonderful Isrotel property. The hotel will organize and book a day of family activities for you, including hiking, jeep tours, cliff rappeling, and a visit to the Alpaca Farm. You can use the municipal swimming pool. **PHONE:** (07) 588-255; **FAX:** 588-151; 177-022-3636 (Toll-free)

Beit Noam Youth Hostel. Located on the edge of the crater opposite the Visitor's Center, this hostel is one of the nicest in the country, with pleasant family rooms. Ask the staff to pack you lunch if you're going hiking. **PHONE:** (07) 588-443; **FAX:** 588-074

SPNI Field School at Mitzpeh Ramon. Simple family rooms with desert view. You can book guided bus tours and nature hikes to the crater. **PHONE:** (07) 588-615

Drahim Youth Hostel. 1 Hanasi Blvd., Dimona. This new air-conditioned hostel has family rooms, a pool, health club, restaurant, and snack bar. **PHONE:** (07) 556-811

Hanion Beirot Camping Site. Open day and night with bathroom and cooking facilities. There's a Bedouin who will rent you his tent, but you may want to bring your own. There also are desert huts like the sukkot of old. PHONE: (07) 588-620

Negev Hostel at Kibbutz Tallilim. A rustic hostel. You can take part in 4-wheel drive and camel tours as well as cliff rappeling. PHONE: (03) 613-1780 (Har V'Gai Office)

Sde Boker Field School. Family rooms for those on SPNI tours and others. PHONE: (07) 565-016

Sde Boker Desert Research Institute Guest House. Large air-conditioned family rooms with refrigerators, and a communal kitchen and laundry. You can use the swimming pool on campus. PHONE: (07) 565-933

Yerucham Beyahad Hostel. Simple accommodations that cater more to teens. PHONE: (07) 565-134

Mashabim Inn. Kibbutz Mashabei Sadeh. Nicely renovated family rooms at a reasonable price. Breakfast in the kibbutz dining room is included. There's a petting zoo and swimming pool. PHONE: (07) 565-134; FAX: 565-145

Many of these sites are included in organized bus or jeep tours originating in Eilat, which is less than an hour away.

TO EILAT

Shadmot Ranch
60 miles north of Eilat
PHONE: (07) 581-343

You can ride for an hour or a day at this family ranch. Call ahead.

If you're driving south on the Dead Sea road, stop at **Pundak 101** to stretch your legs. You'll see peacocks, ducks, tigers, and the humorous sculpture of Udi Dayan, son of General Moshe Dayan.

Kibbutz Yotvata Visitor's Center
PHONE: (07) 376-018
ADMISSION: Fee; the film is free with a ticket to Hai Bar.

Kibbutz Yotvata is known for its extraordinary dairy cows and chocolate milk. We have never passed this way without stopping for a cold drink. (My favorite flavor is mocha!) Remember to check the water in your car and canteens.

The air-conditioned **Visitor's Center** has both an audio-visual presentation and an exhibit on Negev ecology. If you plan to hike in the area, you can get information and maps here. There are excellent restrooms.

If you're hungry for a meal, stop next door at the **Ye'elim Holiday Village** where lunch includes a welcome dip in the pool. There's even a small water slide.

Hai Bar Wildlife Reserve and Visitor's Center
PHONE: (07) 373-057
HOURS: Visitor's Center: 8 a.m.-3 p.m.
       Guided Tours: 9 a.m., 10:30   a.m., noon, 1:30 p.m.
       Predators' Center: 8:30 a.m.-3 p.m.
       Call ahead to confirm; hours change.
ADMISSION: Fee

The Hai Bar Nature Reserve Authority attempts to save rare and endangered desert animals— herbivores and carnivores. You can tour the reserve only by car or bus and see the animals at close range. The Visitor's Center has an audio-visual show illustrating the history, flora, and fauna of the desert.

WHERE TO STAY

Ye'elim Desert Resort Village. Near Yotvata. Cottages, camp-grounds, and a swimming pool. **PHONE:** (07) 374-362; **FAX:** 357-734

Camel Riders Tent. Ma'aleh Shahrut. The owners will pick you up at Uvda airport in Eilat, 45 miles south. Your camel ride begins with tea in the Desert Exploration Center. There are trips lasting 2-15 days. Sleeping bags are provided and you can camp out even if you're not taking a camel tour. You can even have a Bar/Bat Mitzvah celebration here! **PHONE:** (07) 373-218; **FAX:** 371-944

EILAT

Remember that Sleeping Beauty at the southern tip of Israel's desert? Well, Eilat has come alive! The city has become a resort town frequented by natives and tourists, especially sun-seeking Europeans who arrive daily on direct charter flights.

Eilat is a free port, and shoppers can take advantage of duty-free items. There is no VAT or other tax on goods and services, so you pay lower prices for food, entertainment, sports and diving, rental equipment, and taxis.

The city is very hot, but if you follow the rule of never being far from water — both drinking water and swimming water — the dry heat can be more pleasant than humid conditions elsewhere. Tap water in Eilat is drinkable thanks to desalinization.

There are two major sections of town: **North Beach,** with hotels, shops, and swimming; and **Coral Beach,** with the underwater observatory, coral beaches, and more hotels. Be aware that Eilat's beaches are popular with topless sunbathers!

GETTING THERE

Bus: You can take an air-conditioned bus from either Jerusalem or Tel Aviv. The ride takes 4-5 hours, so you may want to stop overnight in Mamshit, Beersheva, Sde Boker, or Mitzpeh Ramon, and continue the trip the next day.

Plane: Arkia flies from Jerusalem, Tel Aviv, or Haifa in less than an hour. The airline offers package deals with hotels. Children fly for half fare. Check with your travel agent. You may want to go one way by plane and one way by ground transportation. Contact Arkia in Tel Aviv at Dov Airport. PHONE: (03) 690-3333 or in Jerusalem at Klal Center, 97 Jaffa Road. PHONE: (02) 225-888.

Car: You can drive to Eilat via Beersheva and Mitzpe Ramon, or via the Dead Sea and Massada (a shorter route from Jerusalem). Carry a supply of water for both your car engine and for you.

CITY NOTES

Area Code: (07) If you are calling from out of town, dial these numbers first.

Municipal Tourist Information Office
1 Hatemarim Boulevard opposite Bus Station
HOURS: Sunday-Thursday 8 a.m.-6 p.m.; Friday until 1 p.m.
PHONE: (07) 374-233

To meet an Eilat family, apply here at least two days in advance.

Eilat Marina Tourist Information. PHONE: (07) 334-353

Tourist Information Center. Yotam-Ha'aravah Corner. There are maps, brochures, coupons, and an info-tour computer. PHONE: (07) 372-111

Egged Information. PHONE: (07) 375-161

International Airport. PHONE: (07) 363-838

Uvda Airport. This airport is open from September-May and handles mostly charters from Europe. PHONE: (07) 375-880

TOURS

Most touring companies offer half-day tours from Eilat to nearby sites such as Timna Park, Hai Bar, Yotvata, and the Red Canyon. It is also possible to visit Egypt, the Sinai Peninsula, and Jordan. Teenagers often make their way to the Sinai for adventure vacations. The ancient city of Petra in Jordan also is a popular attraction.

United Tours offers a one-day tour to Massada and Ein Gedi, a one-day tour to the Santa Katarina Monastery on Mt. Sinai, or a two-day tour through the Sinai Desert. PHONE: (07) 371-720

Johnny Tours gives half and full-day camel tours and jeep safaris in the Eilat mountains. They also have trips to Petra, Sinai and Egypt. PHONE: (07) 376-777

Currently, you can get visas for the Sinai at border crossings, and for Egypt as a whole at the Cairo Airport. You can get a Jordanian visa in your home country or at the American Embassy in Jerusalem. However, as joint tourist ventures increase, the visa requirements may change. Call the appropriate Embassy for updated information.

SPNI gives nature tours of the Eilat area. You can also arrange a private guide. Contact their area Field School. PHONE: (07) 372-021

Neot Hakikar-Geographical Tours is an experienced company that will take you around Eilat and through the Sinai Peninsula on any combination of jeep, camel, and foot. PHONE: (07) 330-426

Polaris Jeep Tours has professionally-guided tours (from half-day to several days) in jeeps or self-driven small tractors. Cliff-rappeling is also available. PHONE: (07) 375-190

Desert Shade adventures include cliff-rappeling and mountain bike and jeep tours. **PHONE:** (07) 335-277

Lucky Divers Boat Trips runs 7-14 day cruises on a 78-ft. yacht with full board and unlimited diving for about $125/person/day. **PHONE:** (07) 335-967; **FAX:** 371-057

Tour Eilat offers 2-6 day diving safaris and a 4-day camping/jeep safari. **PHONE:** (07) 378-108

Nature's Way has special family hikes in the nature reserve around Eilat with an emphasis on ecology. **PHONE:** (07) 370-648

Travelis runs regular and budget camping tours with a sleep-over in Petra, as well as tours of Mt. Sinai. **PHONE:** (07) 336-111, 371-820

Arkia Airlines' two-day bus tour can be purchased together with a flight package to Eilat. **PHONE:** (07) 373-388

Mazada Tours. PHONE: (02) 255-454

Galilee Tours. PHONE: (07) 335-131

Avi Desert Safari. PHONE: (07) 378-871 (see *Mitzpeh Ramon*).

PLANNING YOUR DAY

The only time that Eilat is somewhat cool in summer is early in the morning. Plan your day accordingly. We like to start with a dip in the Red Sea. The public beach near the Moriah Hotel has slides built into the water. Or we swim at Coral Beach where snorkeling is ideal. Bring sneakers or plastic sandals; the beaches are rocky.

In the middle of the day we do a cool, indoor activity, take part in poolside sports, watch in-house movies, or rest. Kids stay up late in Eilat. They enjoy the North Beach boardwalk where they can race toy motor cars, ride the merry-go-round, and eat lots of felafel and ice cream.

WHAT TO SEE

Coral Beach Nature Reserve
3 miles south of City Center; Bus 15 leaves every half hour
  from the Central Bus Station and city stops.
PHONE: (07) 376-829
HOURS: Daily 9 a.m.-5 p.m.; summer until 6 p.m.
ADMISSION: Fee to use the beach; separate fee to rent equipment.

The reefs begin only a few yards from shore, and even young children can borrow a pair of goggles and look down into the shallow water at the colorful array of fish and plant life. If you are a good swimmer, you can rent snorkels, masks, and fins and see

the wonderful world of this tropical reef, which extends for more than half a mile. Coral can be dangerous. Protective shoes are a must, and warn your children not to touch the corals to preserve the delicate eco-system.

Dolphin Reef
PHONE: (07) 373-417
HOURS: Daily 9a.m.-5p.m.
ADMISSION: Fee; free after 5 p.m.

Watch the dolphin show, join a group and swim with the dolphins off the sandy beach, or take a beautiful underwater dive to see the magnificent coral. Children dive one-on-one with an instructor. Snorkels are for rent. Evenings, there's live music and dancing.

Coral World Underwater Observatory and Aquarium
PHONE: (07) 376-666
HOURS: Daily 8 a.m.-4:30 p.m.
ADMISSION: Fee

This is a must for children visiting Eilat. There are fascinating exhibits of Red Sea coral and fish in their natural habitat. To reach the observatory, which has been placed 300 feet out in the sea, you must walk onto a pier and descend a winding staircase. The colorful fish, some of which glow in the dark, swim by all around you. There also are tanks of turtles and sharks, a Maritime Museum, and a cafeteria.

Jules Verne Explorer
PHONE: (07) 377-702; **Laser Show:** 334-668
ADMISSION: Fee

Look through the windows under this boat for a view of the Coral Reefs and Japanese Garden. Sometimes there's a singer on board.

Several evenings a week the boat goes on a **20,000 Leagues Under the Sea Deep Water Laser Show** adventure. Based on Jules Verne's book, Captain Nemo is attacked by a giant squid in the depths of the sea.

Yellow Submarine
PHONE: (07) 376-666
ADMISSION: Fee

A two-hour underwater close-up of the corals and sponges. Decide whether your child can sit still that long.

International Birdwatching Center
City Center
PHONE: (07) 374-276
HOURS: Tours Tuesday and Thursday at 8:30 a.m., but call to confirm.

About 4 million migrating birds of prey fly past here each year! The center organizes birdwatching hikes from February to May and hosts an International Birdwatchers Festival in March. If birdwatching is among your hobbies, you also will be interested in the birdwatching and banding station at Kibbutz Eilot.

Malkit Eilat Stone Factory
Schunat Hadekel
PHONE: (07) 373-372

See the blue-green Eilat stones being turned into jewelry. You can also shop in the factory store and order custom-designed items. If you call the factory, they will pick you up from your hotel.

Cadurite Eilat Stone Factory
PHONE: (07) 378-551

Take a cab to the factory, and they will refund your fare.

Municipal Library
Opposite City Hall
PHONE: (07) 376-121
HOURS: Sun., Mon., Tues., Thurs. noon-6:45 p.m.; Friday 9-11:45 a.m.

A cool place to read at midday, though you can't take out books. Sometimes there's a Hebrew story hour for children.

IN THE AREA

Timna Valley National Park — Solomon's Pillars
18 miles north of Eilat
TRANSPORTATION: Timna Express. PHONE: (07) 374-741
  ETI. PHONE: (07) 370-380
  Egged Tours (Friday only). **PHONE:** (07) 373-148
PHONE: (07) 356-215
HOURS: Daily 8 a.m.-5 p.m.
ADMISSION: Fee

There are many things to see including the ancient copper mines; "The Mushroom," a natural sandstone sculpture; and pre-historic rock carvings. Start with the video show at the entrance, and then spend a lovely day hiking and climbing. Solomon's Pillars and remains of an ancient Egyptian Temple are about a 30-minute walk from the parking area. You can also visit the Copper Center, where there's a talk on the history of copper mining and a demonstration of mining techniques.

Pillars of Amram
8 miles north of Eilat along Arava Road

These red sandstone pillars, which look like a magnificent cathedral, were carved by erosion. It's a 10-minute walk from the parking lot to the site.

Red Canyon
18 miles north of Eilat in Shani Valley
ADMISSION: Free

This dramatic canyon is formed from layers of red sandstone and large limestone boulders washed down by floods.

Ein Netafim
6 miles west of Eilat off Yatom Road
ADMISSION: Free

You can reach the spring only by foot or 4-wheel drive. The scenery is spectacular, but the climb is too hard for small children.

SPORTS AND RECREATION

The Country Club
North Beach near the Sport Hotel
PHONE: (07) 333-333
ADMISSION: Fee

If you are in Eilat for the weekend or longer, you can take part in country club activities which include squash, aerobics, tennis, basketball, raquetball, croquet, archery, and mini-football.

Red Sea Sports Club
King's Wharf, North Beach at Caravan Swim Club Hotel.
PHONE: (07) 379-685
ADMISSION: Fee

This sports facility offers paddleboats, canoes, mini-speed boats, speedboats, deep-water fishing, diving, sailing, water-skiing, para-sailing, and windsurfing. Children 12 and up can take a 3-hour introductory diving course. You can rent a bike and pedal out to Coral Beach or up to the Boardwalk.

The club offers a half-day yacht cruise with lunch and snorkeling off the side of the boat. Or you can rent a sailboat and captain for a family voyage down to the Egyptian border. Night camel rides are geared for adults and teens. Horseback and jeep tours also can be arranged.

The **Amusement Park** at the Eilat Marina is open evenings and has a variety of rides. **PHONE:** (07) 376-095

Snuba Diving

BUS: 15 to just north of the Princess Hotel
PHONE: (07) 372-722
ADMISSION: Fee includes 75 minutes of diving and use of a mask
    to paddle around the area.

Children 8 and up can have a different diving experience! In snuba-diving, the diver is hooked up to an air tank that is attached to a boat, freeing the diver from carrying the tank.

TEENS >

Siam Diving

PHONE: (07) 360-360
ADMISSION: Fee (Intro dive: $40; course $280)

Siam offers a two-part course — you can train in Jerusalem and dive in the Red Sea. They also offer introductory dives, sail and dive options, and snorkel tours of the coral reefs.

TEENS >

Airodium — Fly Like A Bird

Behind the Riviera Hotel
PHONE: (07) 332-386
ADMISSION: Fee

Put on a bright-colored suit, jump into the air, and fly like a bird. No experience necessary.

Donkey Ride

Ostrich Show Farm
PHONE: (07) 373-213
ADMISSION: Fee

There are only a handful of ostriches at this unusual restaurant-pub, but you can ride in a donkey cart up the hills.

TEENS >

Desert Quad Runners

PHONE: (07) 377-774
ADMISSON: Fee

You need to be 17½ to drive these small tractors on adventures up the hillsides.

Texas Camel Ranch

PHONE: (07) 376-663
ADMISSION: Fee

A western-style city with a saloon and a riding school, camel and horse tours.

Pequod Charter Fishing Boats

PHONE: (07) 78558
ADMISSION: Fee

Sailfish, dorado, and tuna fishing.

Folklore Show on Kibbutz Eilot

PHONE: (07) 375-468
HOURS: Evenings October-April
ADMISSION: Fee

This 3-hour evening program, which takes place in the kibbutz dining hall/entertainment center, includes a kosher dinner and folklore performance. The kibbutz provides transportation from Eilat. The same company also runs Bedouin evenings.

Holiday Charters

PHONE: (07) 331-717
HOURS: 10 a.m.-4 p.m.
ADMISSION: Kids up to age 2 are free, except for an insurance payment; children 2-12 get a 20% discount.

Boat trips with swimming, snorkeling, and lunch, as well as jeep tours, para-sailing, water-skiing, jet-skiing, banana boat rides, and diving. If you're 15 or over, you can drive an electric waterbike under an instructor's supervision.

Glass-Bottomed Boat Rides

PHONE: (07) 375-528, 332-325
ADMISSION: Fee

A wonderful view of the coral and fish. Evening cruises with disco music can be arranged for groups.

Municipal Tennis Courts

Yotam Road behind High School
HOURS: 7 a.m.-3 p.m.
ADMISSION: Nominal fee

Bike Rentals:

Red Sea Sports Club. PHONE: (07) 379-685

ATI. PHONE: (07) 375-190

Midbar Trackteronim. PHONE: (07) 377-774

WHERE TO STAY

There are several dozen hotels and youth hostels in the city. The better ones are well-organized with children's programs and movies for hot, mid-afternoon hours. Some offer these programs only during the busy season, so check to see if they are available when you plan to come.

Before you call a hotel yourself, ask a travel agent about special Eilat package deals. Some are only marketed abroad. If you don't have reservations when you get to Israel, contact an Israeli agent whose specialty is in-country tourism.

HOTELS

Isrotel Chain. British businessman David Lewis has nudged Eilat into becoming the resort it is today by establishing a chain which features the concept of total vacation. There are family suites and programs for children and adults throughout the day. Dinner is served family style in a variety of restaurants. If you stay in any Isrotel, you can use facilities in the others until 10 p.m. You can book Isrotels in the U.S. **PHONE:** (800) 552-0140 (Toll-free) Canada: (800) 526-5343 (Toll-free)

Isrotel— King's Solomon's Palace. An attractive, well-run hotel with plentiful, excellent food and a good kids' program. Synagogue on the premises. **PHONE:** (07) 334-111; **FAX:** 334-189

Isrotel—New Lagoona. A scaled-down version of King Solomon's Palace right next door. **PHONE:** (07) 366-666; **FAX:** 366-699

Isrotel— Sport. A smaller and somewhat less expensive hotel next door to a good sports club. There are family rooms and two outdoor pools. **PHONE:** (07) 333-333; **FAX:** 332-776

Isrotel—Riviera Apartment Hotel. The chain's all-suite hotel. **PHONE:** (07) 333-944; **FAX:** 333-939

Eilat Princess. 15 minutes from town near the Taba border. One of the newest, fanciest hotels, the Princess has several swimming pools and a kids' club for ages 4 and up. The suites don't have kitchenettes. Ask your travel agent for the best deal. **PHONE:** (07) 365-555; **FAX:** 376-333

Club In at Coral Beach. At this great family hotel you get good kids' activities, a children's menu, and a whole apartment with a kitchenette. Its only disadvantage is being away from the center of town. There are excellent package deals marketed abroad. **PHONE:** (07) 334-555; **FAX:** 334-519

The New Caesar. Recently renovated, this hotel features a children's program and good food. **PHONE:** (07) 333-111

Sun Suites. Small, medium, and large suites for up to five persons. The kids' program includes activities run by a pre-school teacher. **PHONE:** (07) 376-222; **FAX:** 375-888

Marina Club. An all-suite hotel with a children's club and pool. Special rates Sunday through Thursday. **PHONE:** (07) 354-191; **FAX:** 334-206

The Orchid at Coral Beach. Each of the 135 units in this interesting new resort has its own balcony. The village has a swimming pool and a children's club. **PHONE:** (07) 360-360; **FAX:** 375-323

Moriah Plaza. Renovated and reopened as part of the Best Western chain, this hotel has rooms and suites. There are three swimming pools. **PHONE:** (07) 361-111; **FAX:** 334-158

Paradise Eilat. On North Beach near the Isrotel chain. The hotel has a particularly good children's club. **PHONE:** (07) 335-050; **FAX:** 332-348

Holiday Inn. Kids up to age 19 stay free in their parents' room. Freckles Kids Club includes age-appropriate gifts. **PHONE:** (07) 367-777; **U.S.:** (800) HOLIDAY (Toll-free)

Neptune. Synagogue on the premises. **PHONE:** (07) 334-333; **FAX:** 334-389

Club Med. A full program of Club Med-style activities for all ages. Children ages 3 and over have their own Mini-Club activities. You must join Club Med to stay here. There's a kosher restaurant on the premises. **PHONE:** (800) CLUBMED (Toll-free)

HOSTEL

Eilat Youth Hostel. Book well ahead for the family rooms in this very popular, air-conditioned hostel. Bring your own towels. **PHONE:** (07) 370-088; **FAX:** 375-835

CAMPING

Mamshit Camping. Air-conditioned wooden bungalows are for rent on this beautiful beach. You can also camp out with your own tent **PHONE:** (07) 374-411; **FAX:** 375-206

Caroline Camping. A new camping facility is opening with bungalows and outdoor sites. **PHONE:** (07) 371-911; **FAX:** 371-115

APPENDIX

SAY IT IN HEBREW

First Things First!

Money	Kesef
Bank	Bank
Telephone	Telephone
Telephone token	Asimon
Bathroom	Sherutim, Beit shimush
Map	Mapa
I don't speak Hebrew	Ani lo m'daber Ivrit (m.) Ani lo m'daberet Ivrit (f.)
Yes	Ken
No	Lo

Polite Words

Please/You're welcome	B'vakasha
Thank you	Todah
Hello/Goodbye	Shalom
Until we meet again	L'hitraot
Excuse me	S'licha
Good morning	Boker tov
Good evening	Erev tov
Good night	Laila tov
How are you?	Mah shlomcha (m), Mah shlomech (f)

Numbers

1	Achat
2	Shtayim
3	Shalosh
4	Arba
5	Chamesh
6	Shesh
7	Sheva
8	Shmoneh
9	Tesha
10	Eser
20	Esrim
50	Chamishim
100	Meya

People

Man	Ish
Women	Isha
Boy	Yeled
Girl	Yaldah
Tour Guide	Madrich (m), Madricha (f)
Tourists	Tayarim
Soldier	Chayal (m), Chayelet (f)
Police	Shoter (m), Shoteret (f)

Questions

Where is...?	Ayfo...?
How many?	Kama?
How much does this cost?	Kama zeh oleh?
Who?	Mi?
Why?	Lama?
What's this?	Mah zeh?
When?	Matai?
Do you have...?	Yesh l'cha (m)...? Yesh lach (f) ...?

Clothing

Hat	Kova
Shoes	Na'alayim
Shirt	Chultzah
Dress	Simla
Skirt	Chatza'it
Socks	Garbayim
Tights	Garbiyonim
Underpants	Tachtonim
Undershirt	Gufiya
Sweatshirt	Sweshir
Bathing Suit	Beged-yam

Pronunciation: The accent on most Hebrew words is on the last syllable. The gutteral "Ch" is pronounced as in Bach.

Transliteration: The English spelling of Hebrew is arbitrary. You may need to use some imagination to figure out that Safed, Tsefat, and Zefat are all the same city!

Food

To eat	Le'echol
Restaurant	Misada
Table	Shulchan
Waiter	Meltzar
Menu	Tafrit
Check	Cheshbon
Water	Mayim
Ice	Kerach
Breakfast	Aruchat boker
Lunch	Aruchat tzaharayim
Supper	Aruchat erev
Meat	Basar
Tomato	Agvaniah
Ice cream	Glidah
Cookie	Oogiah
Candy	Sukariah
Chocolate	Shokolat
Pretzel	Bagelah
Soup	Marak
Fruit	Perot
Apple	Tapuach
Orange	Tapooz
Cheese	Gevinah
Chicken	Oaf
Egg	Beitzah

Play Words

Park, playground	Gan
Swings	Nadnedot
See-saw	Nadnedah
Sandbox	Argaz chol
Swimming	S'chiyah
Daycamp	Kaitanah
Counselor	Madrich (m), madricha (f)

Pronouns

I	Ani
You (singular)	At (f), Atah (m)
You (plural)	Aten (f), Atem (m)
He	Hu
She	He
We	Anachnu
They	Hem (m), Hen (f)

Places

House	Bayit
Apartment	Dirah
Floor/story	Komah
Museum	Muzayon
Theater	Tayatron
Movie	Kolno'a
Synagogue	Beit knesset
Church	K'nisiyah
Mosque	Misgad
Store	Chanut
Market	Shuk
Grocery	Makolet
Hotel	Malon
Room	Cheder
Youth hostel	Achsaniat noar
Post Office	Doar
Bank	Bank
Laundry	Machbesa

Baby Words

Diapers	Chitulim
Bottle	Bakbuk
Stroller	Agalah
Pacifier	Motzets
Crib	Mitat-tinok
Playpen	Lul
Toys	Tza'atzu'im
Nursery school	Gan
Childcare giver	Mitapelet
High chair	Kisay-tinok
Babysitter	Shmar-tof or babysitter

Time

What time is it?	Ma ha'sha'ah?
The time is...	Hasha'ah...
Minute	Rega
Hour	Sha'ah
Day	Yom
Week	Shavua
Year	Shanah
Today	Hayom
Yesterday	Etmol
Tomorrow	Machar

Travel Words

Airport	S'day t'ufa
Airplane	Matos
Ticket	Kartis
Suitcase	Mizvada
Passport	Darkon
Bus	Autobus
Taxi	Taxi, monit
Group Taxi	Sherut
Bus stop	Tachanah
Central Bus Station	Tachanah Merkazit
Train	Rakevet
Driver	Nahag
Right	Y'mina
Left	S'mola
Straight ahead	Yashar
Tell me where to get off	Tagid li ayfo laredet
Wait a minute!	Rega!

Miscellaneous

Gift	Matanah
Stamp	Bul
Receipt	Kabalah
Letter	Michtav
Birthday	Yom huledet

Health Words

Doctor	Rofeh
Dentist	Rofeh-shinayim
Nurse	Achot
Hospital	Beit cholim
Sick	Choleh
Examination	B'dikah
Diarrhea	Shilshul
Help	Ezra
Medicine	T'rufah
Pill	Kadur
Pharmacy	Beit-mirkachat

Around You

Sky	Shamayim
Sea	Yam
Sand	Chol
Beach	Chof
Desert	Midbar
Village	Kfar
City	Ir
Mountain	Har
Collective settlement	Kibbutz/Moshav

SOME ARABIC

Please	Min Fadlach	Shoes	Kundara
Thank you	Shukran	Shirt	Kamis
You're Welcome	Afwad	Dress	Forstan
Hello/goodbye	Ahalan	Bathroom	Merhad
Excuse me	Smahli	Water	Maya
Yes	Aywa	1	Wahad
No	La	2	Tnin
Where is?	Wayne	3	Tlata
How much does it cost?	Adesh biswa?	4	Arba
What's this?	Shoo hada?	5	Hamsah
What time is it?	Akam sha'ah?	6	Sita
Bread	Hubis	7	Saba
Drink	Shurbeh	8	Temanya
Ice Cream	Busa	9	Tisa
Hat	Taieh	10	Ashara
		100	Mia

METRIC CONVERSION

Temperature

Body Temperature			Air Temperature	
C	F		C	F
37	98.6		0	32
38	100		5	41
39	102		10	50
40	104		20	68
			25	77
			30	86

To change Celsius to Farenheit: $(9/5 \times C) + 32 = F$
For a quick approximation, double the C and add 32.
To change Farenheit to Celsius: $(F - 32) \times 5/9 = C$
For a quick approximation subtract 32 from the F and halve.

Liquid		**Dry**	
1 tsp.	5 milliliters (ml)	1 kg	2.2 lbs.
1 TBSP.	15 ml	450 grams	1 lb.
1 cup	250 ml		
1 qt.	1 liter		

Grams to pounds: For easy conversion subtract 1/10 and halve
Pounds to grams: For easy conversion add 1/10 and double

Miles

1 km	.6 miles
1 mile	1.6 km

Km to miles: For quick approximation, multiply by .6, or multiply by 5 and divide by 8.

Length

1 cm.	.4 inches
1 meter	4.0 inches
1 inch	2.5 cm.
1 ft.	30.5 cm.
1 yd.	91.5 cm.

TELEPHONE AREA CODES

02	Jerusalem, Bethlehem, Judea and Samaria
03	Tel Aviv area including Ramat Gan, Ramat Aviv, Givatayim, Petach Tikvah, Lod, Ben Gurion Airport
04	Haifa, Acre, Nahariya, Carmiel
06	Galilee
07	Beersheva, Mitzpe Ramon, Arad, Sde Boker, Eilat
08	Ashkelon
09	Herziliya, Netanya
177	Toll-Free

AVERAGE DAILY TEMPERATURES
(Fahrenheit)

	January	August
Jerusalem	37-46	64-82
Tel Aviv	52-68	72-86
Beersheva	46-68	68-86
Eilat	42-73	68-92
Upper Gailee	46-70	64-93

ROAD DISTANCES — IN MILES

	Jerusalem	Tel Aviv	Haifa	Tiberias	Beersheva
Jerusalem		39	99	97	52
Tel Aviv	39		59	82	70
Haifa	99	56		43	130
Tiberias	97	82	43		147
Beersheva	52	70	130	147	
Beit Shean	75	73	42	23	123
Eilat	194	220	280	250	150

ISRAEL GOVERNMENT TOURIST OFFICES ABROAD

Britain
18 Gt. Marlborough St., London W1V 1AF. **PHONE:** (171) 434-3651; **FAX:** 437-0527

Canada
180 Bloor St., West, #700, Toronto, Ont. M5S 2V6. **PHONE:** (416) 964-3784; **FAX:** 964-2420

South Africa
5th Floor, Nedbank Gardens, 33 Bath Avenue, Rosebank, POB 52560, Saxonwold 2132
   Johannesburg. **PHONE:** (711) 78881703; **FAX:** 447-3104

Australia
6th Floor, 37 York St., Sydney NSW 2000. **PHONE:** (612) 264-7933; **FAX:** 290-2259

395 New South Head Road, Double Bay NSW 2028. **PHONE:** (612) 326-1700; **FAX:** 326-1676

United States
19th Floor, 350 Fifth Ave., NY, NY 10118. **PHONE:** (212) 499-5600; **FAX:** 499-5645

5 South Wabash, Chicago, IL 60603. **PHONE:** (312) 782-4306; **FAX:** 782-1243.

12700 Park Central Dr., Dallas, TX 75251. **PHONE:** (214) 991-9097; **FAX:** 392-3521

6380 Wilshire Blvd. #1700, Los Angeles, CA 90048. **PHONE:** (213) 658-7462. ext. 03

ORGANIZATIONS WITH TOURS TO ISRAEL

Many local federations, JCCs, and synagogues sponsor family, teen, and Bar/Bat Mitzvah tours. Check with your local agencies and these national organizations.

American Jewish Congress. 15 E. 84 St., New York, New York 10022. (212) 879-4588

American Zionist Youth Foundation. 110 E. 59 St., New York, NY 10022. (800) 27-ISRAEL

B'nai Akiva. 25 W. 26 St., 4th Fl., New York, NY 10010. (212) 889-5260

B'nai B'rith Center for Jewish Family Life. 1640 Rhode Island Ave., NW
   Washington, DC 20036. (800) 500-6533

Council of Jewish Federations. 730 Broadway, New York, NY 10003. (212) 475-5000

Emunah Women Tours. 7 Penn Plaza, New York, NY 10001. (212) 947-5454

Hadassah Tour Dept. 50 W. 58 St., New York, NY 10019. (212) 303-8031

Jewish Community Centers Assn. 15 E. 26 St., New York, NY 10010. (212) 532-4949

Jewish National Fund. 42 E. 69 St., New York, NY 10021. (212) 879-9300; (800) 223-7787

Jewish Women Int'l. 1828 L St., NW, #250, Washington D.C. 20036. (202) 857-1300

National Council of Young Israel. 3 W. 16 St., New York, NY 10011. (800) 727-8567

Pioneer Women-Na'amat. 200 Madison Ave., New York, NY 10016. (212) 725-8010

Ramah Programs in Israel. 3080 Broadway, New York, NY 10027. (212) 678-8881

UAHC Tour Committee. 838 Fifth Ave. New York, NY 10021. (212) 249-0100

United Jewish Appeal. 99 Park Avenue, New York, NY 10016. (212) 818-9100

United Synagogue. 155 Fifth Ave., New York, NY 10010. (212) 533-7800; (800) 237-1517

Zionist Organization of America. 4 East 34 St., New York, NY 10016. (212) 481-1500

FOREIGN EMBASSIES IN ISRAEL

United States	71 Hayarkon, Tel Aviv. (03) 517-4338
Canada	220 Hayarkon, Tel Aviv. (03) 527-2929
Australia/ **New Zealand**	37 Shaul Hamelech, Tel Aviv. (03) 695-0451
Britain	192 Hayarkon St., Tel Aviv. (03) 524-9171
South Africa	50 Dizengoff, Tel Aviv. (03) 525-2566
Egypt	54 Basel St., Tel Aviv. (03) 546-4151

CONSULATES

Britain	Sheik Jarrah, Jerusalem. (02) 828-281
United States	18 Agron St., Jerusalem. (02) 253-288
	27 Nablus Rd., Jerusalem. (02) 253-288
	12 Jerusalem St., Haifa. (04) 670-616

RELIGIOUS ORGANIZATIONS

All addresses and phone numbers are in Jerusalem: Area Code (02)

Orthodox

Young Israel	30 Hillel St. 231-361
Union of Orthodox Jewish Congs.	20 Strauss St. 384-206
Chief Rabbinate - Great Synagogue	58 King George St. 247-112

Conservative

Mesorati Movement	25 Keren Hayesod St. 782-433
United Synagogue Center	4 Agron St. 253-539
Jewish Theol. Seminary Student Ctr.	Neve Schechter. 790-755

Reform/Progressive

Hebrew Union College	13 King David St. 203-448

Independent

M'vakshei Derech	Shai Agnon St. 792-501
Kol Haneshama	47 Harakevet St. 724-878

FIVE YEAR CALENDAR OF JEWISH HOLIDAYS

	1996	1997	1998	1999	2000
PURIM [1]	March 5	March 23	March 12	March 2	March 21
PESACH [2] (Passover)	April 4-10	April 22-28	April 11-17	April 1-7	April 20-26
YOM HASHOAH (Holocaust Day)	April 16	May 4	April 23	April 13	May 2
YOM HA'ATZMAUT (Independence Day)	April 24	May 12	April 30	April 21	May 10
LAG BA'OMER	May 7	May 25	May 14	May 4	May 23
SHAVUOT	May 24	June 11	May 31	May 21	June 9
TISHA B'AV	July 25	August 12	August 2	July 22	August 10
ROSH HASHANAH	Sept.14-15	October 2-3	Sept.21-22	Sept.11-12	Sept.30-Oct.1
YOM KIPPUR	Sept. 23	October 11	Sept. 30	Sept. 20	October 9
SUKKOT [3]	Sept.28-Oct.4	Oct.16-22	Oct. 5-11	Sept.25-Oct.1	Oct.14-20
SHEMINI ATZERET/ SIMCHAT TORAH [4]	October 5	October 23	October 12	October 2	October 21
HANUKKAH	Dec. 6-13	Dec. 24-31	Dec. 14-21	Dec. 4-11	Dec. 22-29

Jewish holidays begin at sundown the evening before.

[1] Purim: The Megillah is read on Purim eve and Purim day. Shushan Purim is celebrated the day after in walled cities such as Jerusalem and Safed.

[2] Pesach: Seder takes place Pesach eve. The first and last days are holidays — no work is done; public transportation does not function.

[3] Sukkot: The first day is a holiday.

[4] Shemini Atzeret/Simchat Torah: Festive Torah parades are held in synagogues throughout the country on the eve of the holiday.

Some Conservative and Orthodox Jews who live outside of Israel celebrate Sukkot, Passover, and Shavuot for an extra day.

BIBLIOGRAPHY

Travel Guides

Baedeker's Israel, 3rd Edition. 1995. Macmillan Travel
Bazak Guide to Israel by Avraham Levi
Berlitz Discover Israel by Carlton Reid. 1995
Carta's Jogger's Guide to Jerusalem by Joel Ruskin. Available from SPNI
Culture Shock: Israel by Dick Winter. Macmillan Travel, 1992
Fodor's Israel, 1995
Footlose in Jerusalem by Sara Fox Kaminker
Frommer's Israel on $45 A Day. Macmillan Travel
Guide to Hiking in Israel Guide to Israel by Zev Vilnay. JPS. Reissued 1995
Hikes in the Jerusalem Hills and Judean Desert. Available from SPNI
Holy Land Archeological Guide by J. O'Connor. Oxford University Press, 1992
Insight Guide: Israel. Houghton Mifflin
Insight Guide: Jerusalem. Houghton Mifflin
Jerusalemwalks by Nitza Rosovsky. Henry Holt. Revised 1992
Lonely Planet Travel Survival Kit: Israel, 1992
Let's Go: The Budget Guide to Israel and Egypt (Including Jordan and the West Bank). Harvard Student Agencies. St. Martin's Press
Marty's Walking Tours of Biblical Jerusalem by Marty Isaacs
Off the Beaten Track in Israel: A Guide to Beautiful Places by Ori Devir.
The Best Jewish Travel Guide to Israel by Asher Israelowitz
The Jerusalem Anthology by Reuven Hammer. JPS, 1995

Children's Books

A Child's Picture Hebrew Dictionary by Ita Meshi. Adama. Ages 5+
A Kid's Catalog of Israel by Chaya Burstein. History, geography, song, and folklore of the state. JPS, 1988. Ages 8+
A Young Person's History of Israel, 2nd Ed. by David Bamberger. Behrman House. The Jewish people and their homeland from the Bible to the present. Ages 10-14
Alef Is One: A Hebrew Counting Book by Katherine Janus Kahn. Kar-Ben, 1988. Count the colorful animals. Ages 3-7.
Alef to Tav by Yaffa Ganz. A story about each letter. Ages 4-7
Alina: A Russian Girl Comes to Israel by Mira Meir. JPS. Nine-year old Alina adjusts to her new home in Israel. Ages 7-10
And Shira Imagined by Giora Carmi. A fantasy trip to Israel. JPS, 1993. Ages 3-7
A Spy for Freedom: The Story of Sarah Aaronson by Ida Cowen and Irene Gunther. The NILI spies who helped the British free Palestine from Turkish rule. Ages 10+
Aviva's Piano by Miriam Chaikin. Clarion. Life on kibbutz in difficult times. Ages 6-9
Becoming Gershona by Nava Semel. Puffin Books, 1992. A young girl comes of age in Tel Aviv in the 50's. Ages 10-14
Ben Gurion: Builder of Israel by Robert St. John. Biography of Israel's first Prime Minister. Ages 12+
Benjy's Bible Trails by Chaya Burstein. Kar-Ben. Follow Benjy as he travels to the places where Biblical stories took place. An activity book. Ages 6-10

Chicken Man by Michelle Edwards. Chicken man makes each kibbutz job fun. Ages 6-9

Eliezer Ben Yehuda: The Father of Modern Hebrew by Malka Drucker. Dutton. A biography of the man who fought for Hebrew as the national language. Ages 10-14

Falasha No More: An Ethiopian Child Comes Home by Arlene Kushner. Steimatzky. An Ethiopian boy adjusts to living in Israel. Ages 7-10

First Thousand Words in Hebrew by H. Amery. Amusing and colorfully illustrated, the words are grouped by categories.

Golden Windows and Other Stories of Jerusalem by Adele Geras. HarperCollins, 1993. Five stories about a family who helps found and defend Israel. Ages 10-14

Hannah Szenes: A Song of Light by Maxine Schur. JPS. The story of the heroine of Jewish resistance. Ages 8-12

Hebrew Alphabet Coloring Book by Chaya Burstein. Beginning vocabulary. Ages 4-8

I Live in Israel by Max Frankel and Judy Hoffman. Behrman House. Information, games, maps, and puzzles. Ages 7-10

Imagine Exploring Israel by Marji Gold-Vukson. Kar-Ben, 1993. "Un-coloring " activities about people and places in Israel. Ages 5-10

In Kindling Flame: The Story of Hannah Senesh by Linda Atkinson. Lothrop Lee and Shepard. A biography based on her diaries. Ages 10+

Israel: Covenant People, Covenant Land by Seymour Rossel. Behrman House. A History of Israel and Judaism. Ages 12+

Israel Fun for Little Hands by Sally Springer. Kar-Ben, 1994. Mazes, puzzles, colorful postcards. Ages 3-7.

Israel Is by Susan Remick Topek. A toddler's first board book. Scenes of the country. Kar-Ben, 1988. Ages 1-4

Jerusalem Mosaic: Young Voices from the Holy City by I.E. Mozeson and Lois Stavsky. Four Winds Press. Interviews with Jerusalem teenagers. Ages 12+

Joshua's Dream: A Journey to the Land of Israel by Sheila F. Segal. UAHC. Joshua plans for the day when he can plant in the soil of Israel. Ages 6-10

Let's Explore Israel by Sarah Feldman. Two activity books about people and places. Berhman House, 1995. Ages 6-8

Letters to My Israel Sons by Lynne Reed Banks. W.H.Allen. An anecdotal survey of Jewish history and modern Zionism. Ages 12+

Lydia, Queen of Palestine by Uri Orlev. Houghton Mifflin, 1993. Lydia, sent to Palestine from Roumania during the war, adjusts to life on a kibbutz. Ages 10-14

My Hebrew Dinosaurus by Peter Fernandez. Kar-Ben, 1994. A coloring book of dinos from alef to tav. Ages 4-8

My Name is Rachamim by Jonathan P. Kendall. UAHC. An Ethiopian family's journey to Israel.

My Land of Israel by Elizabeth Zinbarg Nover. Behrman House. An imaginary trip to Israel. Hands-on activity pages. Ages 5-8

Myriam Mendelow: The Mother of Jerusalem by Phyllis and Barry Cytron. The founder of Lifeline for the Elderly in Jerusalem. Lerner, 1992. Ages 10-14

Neve Shalom - Wahat-al-Salam: Oasis of Peace. Scholastic, 1993. An Israeli school brings together Jewish and Arab children. Ages 7-10

Next Year in Jerusalem: 300 Years of Jewish Stories by Howard Schwartz. Viking, 1995. Legends and historical stories. All ages

On Eagle's Wings and Other Things by Connie Colker Steiner. JPS. Four children from different cultures emigrate to the new state. Ages 5-9

One More River by Lynn Reid Banks. Morrow, 1992. An American teenager spends a summer in Israel. Ages 10+

Our Golda by David Adler. Viking. A biography of the early years of the pioneer who became Israel's prime minister. Ages 8-12

Our Jerusalem by Yaffa Ganz. Behrman House. Eight mini-magazines about people and places in the city. Ages 5-8

Our Land of Israel by Chaya Burstein. UAHC, 1995. Explore Israel through the eyes of Sam, Mohammed, Uriah, and Meirav. With games and puzzles. Ages 9-12

Picture Book of Israel by David Adler. Holiday House. A photo-essay about Israel's many faces. Ages 6-10.

Smoke Over Golan by Uriel Ofek. Harper and Row, 1979. A boy's friendship with his Syrian neighbor is interrupted by the Yom Kippur War. Ages 9-12.

Teddy Kollek: Builder of Jerusalem by Abraham Rabinovich. JPS, 1995. The mayor of Jerusalem who shaped the city. Ages 9-13

Tell Me A Mitzvah by Danny Siegel. Kar-Ben Copies, 1993. Mitzvah heroes including several in Israel. Ages 7-12

The Jewish Kids' Hebrew English Wordbook by Chaya Burstein. JPS. 1993. Useful Hebrew words and phrases. Ages 5-8

Theodore Herzl: The Road to Israel by Miriam Gurko. JPS. A biography of the founder of the State of Israel. Ages 8-12

The Return by Sonia Levitin. Harper and Row. A Jewish girl flees Ethiopia. Ages 10+

The Secret Grove by Barbara Cohen. UAHC. Two boys, Israeli and Arab, learn to understand each other. Ages 8-12

The Secret Ship by Ruth Kluger and Peggy Mann. Doubleday. An exciting story of "illegal" immigration to Israel from Roumania during World War II. Ages 10-14

The Wailing Wall by Leonard Everett Fisher. Simon and Schuster, 1989. Judaism's most holy site. Ages 6-10

When Will the Fighting Stop? A Child's View of Jerusalem by Ann Morris. Simon and Schuster. Ages 8-12

Yoni Netanyahu: Commando at Entebbe by Devra Newberger. JPS, 1995. The short life of the soldier who died rescuing hostages. Ages 9-12

Zionism and Israel by Michael Korman. UAHC/JNF/United Synagogue. An activity book for junior and senior high students. Ages 13-15

Videos

Shalom Sesame Videos. *The People of Israel. Chanukah. Sing Around the Seasons. Aleph-Bet Telathon. Kids Sing Israel. Passover.* 30 minutes each. Produced in cooperation with Children's Television Workshop.

INDEX